The

Surprising

Liberation

Books by Duncan Smith

Conquest By Concept
The Tightarse Tuesday Book Club
The Vortex Winder
The Maelstrom Ascendant
Cultown
The Vast and the Spurious
Hammer and Heat

Music Albums by Lighthouse XIII

Vortex Winder
The Maelstrom Ascendant
Cultown
Waves Upon Waves

Website – www.vortexwinder.com

The Surprising Liberation

Duncan Smith

Alfadex Books

Published by Alfadex Books, Sydney, 2025.

A CIP catalogue record for this book is available from the National
Library of Australia.

ISBN 978-0-6450372-5-8

1. Non-Fiction 2. Politics 3. Culture War

Duncan Smith is an Australian author and musician.

He is the guitarist and songwriter with Lighthouse XIII, a rock band whose albums include *Cultown*, *Vortex Winder*, *Waves Upon Waves*, and *The Maelstrom Ascendant*.

He is the author of the books *The Maelstrom Ascendant*, *Cultown*, *Conquest By Concept*, and *The Tightarse Tuesday Book Club*.

For information on his books and music, go to www.vortexwinder.com

Alfadex Books orders and information - email: matthew.alfadex@gmail.com

Part One - The Global Progressive Regime

Part Two - Sacred Cows: Race

Part Three - Sacred Cows: Gender

Part One

The Global

Progressive

Regime

1
Living in the GPR

We are living in a regime. It is not a regime of armies and physical threats, but of ideas, in which we are supposed to think a certain way.

Some regimes are more obvious than others. An obvious one was the former GDR - communist East Germany during the Cold War. Here, wrong-think came under scrutiny from the Stasi, the government's secret police. It could have severe consequences.

We don't live in the GDR, but rather something I call the GPR - the Global Progressive Regime. This is a far milder form of tyranny. Wrong-think won't get you killed or thrown in jail, it will just get you cancelled. While this is not as severe a punishment as being murdered, it's still hard to live a normal life if you lose your job or reputation. That's why most people go along with the sacred causes of the GPR.

In the Global Progressive Regime - the GPR - there are a number of ideas to which moral and educated people are supposed to pledge their allegiance. They include, for example, 'anti-racism,' feminism, diversity, and equality. When you live in the GPR, you are expected to not just believe in all of these, but enthusiastically support them.

In their simplest form, I do support them. I oppose racism and support women's rights. I believe in equal opportunity, and that some 'diversity' is good. The trouble is that almost all of these causes are only superficially moral. The more you look past the social justice veneer, the more you see how much is wrong with them, or at least the way they are practiced in the GPR today.

One purpose of this book is to try to understand why things which seem noble in principle are so rotten in practice, and why so many people have been taken in by them. But why bother writing

1

this book at all? It's not as if I'm a person of much influence, or have many readers. Besides, when it comes to politics, most people are firmly attached to their beliefs and rarely change their minds. They can get very angry if you question them.

Well, whether or not people read the book, writing it helps clarify my own mind. In some ways, the world has become so strange and dysfunctional you have to write a book just to make sense of it. There's also a certain morbid fascination in seeing the decline of Western nations, which are almost all under the grip of the GPR. Most of the wounds have been self inflicted, and at times it is like watching a civilisation slowly committing suicide. It's worth trying to understand how that happened.

Like most educated white people, I was brought up as a leftist (which the Americans call a liberal). A few years ago, I came to believe that some of the key leftist ideas were wrong, or at least had gone badly off track. I also noticed the strange behaviour of leftists, and began to question their conviction that they were right about everything. Having been brought up as one myself, I had to examine why I no longer agreed with these people. As will become clear, the rest of this book is a detailed criticism of both the beliefs and behaviour of leftists.

The book will be organised as follows. Part One is an introduction. Parts Two and Three will deal with the two main areas of conflict: race and gender. These are the GPR 'sacred cows,' for many race and gender topics are seen as beyond criticism. In the area of race: there will be chapters on multiculturalism, Aboriginal issues, and Black Lives Matter. In the section on gender, the focus will be on feminism.

Part Four, 'Captured Institutions,' will discuss how GPR ideas have affected some of our chief cultural areas, notably the arts scene, and the national broadcasters of Britain and Australia.

Part Five, 'Leftist Pathologies,' will look at the strange workings of leftist psychology, the curious habits and traits of the leftist mind living under GPR conditions.

First, I'll say a little about my term, the Global Progressive Regime, taking each of these words in turn.

Global

People may attach various meanings to the word 'global.' In this book, I am using it in three main ways. First, global as opposed to national. Second, as a set of ideas and policies that have not arisen within nations, but been imposed on them from outside. Third, as an attempt to make uniform standards around the world - or at least in Western countries - and to make these countries more or less the same.

As an example of a policy that is global in these three ways, take multiculturalism. First, this policy is global, not national, in character. In effect, it means re-creating the world within each nation. It is many small 'nations' in each country, with no need to assimilate. The identity of each 'host nation' weakens as it gains this global flavour. The GPR dislikes the concept of *the nation* in itself. It seems to want to destroy Western nations as they once were and transform them into something else - miniature versions of the entire world.

Second, the policy was imposed from outside. It's been remarked that multiculturalism began in most Anglo nations at around the same time. It's hard to believe such an idea arose independently in each one. That would be a rather large coincidence. It's more likely the idea was decided by some external group, then imposed on nations with the help of compliant local leaders.

The citizens of America, Australia, and Britain weren't rising up and asking their governments for large numbers of immigrants and the policy of multiculturalism. This was imposed on them by various elite groups.

It's true there were also a small number of activists working from inside each country for the policy, but it's hard to believe they would have succeeded on their own without the support of more powerful people.

One might say the idea of multiculturalism was simply part of the *zeitgeist*, but this idea was pushed. It didn't arise spontaneously on its own. *You can't stop change* is the slogan adopted by some progressives, but a nation can change in many different ways. The current changes in Western nations were not inevitable, and would not have happened without help.

Third, multiculturalism, oddly enough, leads to a sort of sameness among nations. If all Western nations are multicultural, they begin to lose their points of difference and start to resemble each other. They are no longer nations, but merely franchises for Globalism Inc. Britain is no longer what it was, it is now Multi-Culti (MC) Britain. In the end, what meaningful difference will there be between MC Britain, MC Australia, MC New Zealand, or MC USA? In a hundred years time, if the world's population has been redistributed around the globe, these former nations will all be part of one global system.

But what of the indigenous people of these lands? Does the Global Progressive Regime not champion their rights and identities? Yes, apparently it does. The GPR champions the rights of the indigenous people of Australia, of New Zealand, and of Canada and the USA. Yet strangely, not the indigenous people of Britain. That is odd - and therein lies the clue. If you make a Venn diagram of the people which the GPR does and doesn't support, you get a fair idea what it's all about.

Still, multiculturalism is just one policy that makes up the Global Progressive Regime. There are various others. The GPR includes abstract concepts like diversity and equality. It means ways of thinking, such as identity politics. It means specific movements like feminism and 'anti-racism.'

These concepts all make claims to morality, and what most of them have in common is a critical view of white, Western nations. It may be about past sins like empire and slavery, or present day sins like alleged gender and racial inequality. The GPR claims to be making a better world and that its Cultural Revolution is justified. Whether it actually is, is a matter of opinion.

Now, a disclaimer. It has been said that the term 'globalist' is a reference to Jews, and therefore some kind of anti-Semitic slur. In that case, I'll be clear that I'm not referring to Jews or any one ethnic group in particular. By 'globalist' I mean anyone who supports the Global Progressive Regime and its values.

For example, Australian prime minister, Anthony Albanese, is the son of an Irish-Australian mother and an Italian father. He is a white male, and certainly not Jewish. In many ways, he's a textbook globalist leader. In a brief Australia Day message in January, 2024, he mentioned the country's indigenous people and also the immigrants living here under multiculturalism, but not the British settlers who founded the nation in 1788.

In his time as prime minister, it has often seemed that Albanese doesn't really lead Australia. He simply manages a franchise for Globalism Inc. As for who Globalism Inc actually is, I do not know, and don't assume it is any one ethnic group. There are no doubt many ethnic groups who support and participate in the Global Progressive Regime.

Progressive

Progress isn't necessarily good. We're all progressing towards death, for example.

Apparently, our world is progressing towards a better future. But is the world of today better than it was in, say, 1998? Or 2010? Many would say no.

If we have indeed progressed to a better world, in the 2020s it is a world in which men and women are deeply antagonistic to one another, you can't go a single day without hearing about racism, and our national broadcasters seem to be at war with their own nations.

Social progressives believe we are heading towards a Utopia where we're all equal, tolerant, and united in common values. But right now, society has never been more divided and large sections of the population hate each other. We have 'progressed' to reach this point.

At each moment in history, there is the prospect of change. This might be change for better or worse, and often that's in the eye of the beholder. To say a particular idea or cause is 'progressive' might only mean you happen to like it. It implies such an idea is moral or helpful. It also implies alternative ideas are harmful or regressive.

Some progressives think they are on 'the right side of history.' Some other people believe what we've been sold in the name of progress is actually decline. Maybe we've all been conned.

Regime

Why call the GPR a regime? It is because allegiance to the GPR is not freely given by all, it is compelled. Lots of people do go along with it, but many others have come to despise the GPR, or at least parts of it. If they make their thoughts publicly known, these people may be shunned, shamed, or cancelled.

Censorship has increased in the last few years, a sign of the authoritarian nature of the progressive paradise we've been given.

The GPR project has been imposed on nations and on individuals largely against their will, and often without their knowledge or consent. Those who complain are punished, in one way or another.

Of course, it is still a mild regime, and a very long way from the Soviet or Chinese regimes of the 20th century. That should be obvious - but there are some disturbing signs of the way we're going.

The rest of this book will look at a few aspects of this regime and ask if this is really the sort of progress we want. Apparently we're going to get it whether we want it or not. If that's the case, we should at least try to understand it. This may help us to navigate through the strange world of the Global Progressive Regime; a world that is rarely what it seems to be, and almost never what it pretends to be.

2

Becoming the Enemy

We all live in the Global Progressive Regime (the GPR) and a key part of it is *identity politics*.

This is a system in which people are classified by three main features: their gender, race, and sexuality. There are others, but these are the main ones. Based on these features, people are then seen as members of a group.

Some groups are believed to have unfair advantages compared to others. Leftists call this 'privilege' - as in male privilege or white privilege. Let's say we take the three main identity types and give them points for alleged privilege.

Gender - Male (3 points), Female (1 point)
Race - White (3), Black (1)
Sexuality - Straight (3), Gay (1)

In this points system, it adds up as follows:

9 points - Straight white male.
7 points - Straight white female, straight black male, gay white male.
5 points - Straight black female, gay black male.
3 points - Gay black female.

In the GPR, identity politics is a sort of economy. The 'currency' is privilege, or its flipside, oppression.

In this economy, those with the most points are considered the luckiest and most powerful, and those with the least points are the weakest and most oppressed. The aim of identity politics is to point this out and then fix it by making everyone end up equal.

When we achieve that, we will have reached a state of *equity*. This is apparently a key goal of the GPR.

In the points system listed, some categories are seen as 7s and others as 3s. Those who believe in the holy quest for equity might say their aim is to make everyone end up as, say, a 7.5. That would be impossible, but it's not really the aim. What each group wants is to lift their own group up to about an 8 or 9, and drag the top group - the straight white male - down to a 3 or a 4. For what identity politics is really about is the old Marxist game of class warfare. It's about envy and resentment, and the straight white male is the enemy that unites all other groups.

It does make you wonder, though: if the so called top group was eliminated, would the other groups just turn on each other?

There is a flip side to this points system, however, in which the 'losers' get to win. Those with the *least* number of points are seen as the most victimised and hence the most virtuous. This way, the gay black female is the winner. Indeed, there's a term, *intersectionality*, which means you can be oppressed in more than one way. Thus, the gay black female, is the most oppressed and, in a strange way, becomes the most admired and immune to criticism. The straight white male, on the other hand, is able to oppress every other group automatically, without even trying. He is the most hated type in the GPR system.

The straight white male (SWM) may have grown up with the naive belief he was simply one human being among many. If and when he learns about identity politics, he discovers this is not the case. He learns that his own demographic is the enemy of all others, that he is public enemy number one with a target on his back and every other group taking aim.

That it is the SWM against the rest is clear when you consider that almost every other group would see themselves as allies *of each other*, but not a single group would claim an allegiance with the SWM. He is able to unite all other groups by their enmity towards him.

Having said that, some groups may *demand* an allegiance, rather than claiming one. Feminist women sometimes demand that straight white males help empower them. As the help goes strictly one way, this is not a real allegiance.

It may seem I'm exaggerating, but many leftists really do think like this. We live in the Global Progressive Regime in which leftist ideas prevail. Identity politics is a key way in which leftists organise those ideas. They see people in terms of their race, gender, and sexuality, and make assumptions about them on that basis.

For a long time, many straight white males may not realise they are the enemy. They may be apolitical and go on oblivious. But for the conscious SWM, when you eventually realise your own demographic has been marked 'privileged' and the enemy of all others, you stand accused. You can respond in various ways. You can:

1. Ignore it and try to get on with your life.

2. Accept the guilt assigned to you, apologise, and vow to be an ally to all the groups below you, lifting them up to your (alleged) level.

3. Pretend to accept it, but secretly oppose it.

4. Openly oppose it.

My own choice is option four - to openly oppose the system of identity politics. This is partly personal, and partly because it's a terrible system that does a lot of damage.

First, the personal. A turning point for me came a few years ago after reading a feminist article on male privilege. I found out that feminists apparently believe, without ever knowing me, that I'm automatically powerful simply by being a straight white male.

This was the source of some amazement to me. For much of my life I had struggled, as many do, with the normal business of trying to have a career and a personal life in a complex, difficult world.

One thing's for sure - I never felt I had much social power. I did not advance very far in my career. In younger years, I went some time without having a girlfriend. I never had enough money to travel overseas. As an introverted type, I was not well connected socially.

For quite a while, I had tried to work in the fields of writing and music, but did not advance. I spent a lot of time writing books and music, but those fields are hard to break into and I was poor at self promotion. For various reasons, I made little headway.

None of this is very unusual - the world isn't fair - but to say it was frustrating is to put it mildly. Still, you make peace with it as best you can and don't let it drag you down.

For much of my adult life, I had a sense of powerlessness. Again, this is not very unusual, as many people feel the same way.

However, after all the years of feeling like that, to *then* be informed by feminists that I was some kind of powerful, princely being was a matter for incredulity. This was one factor that led me to look closely at the whole left wing belief system, of which feminism is only one part.

Five Reasons to Oppose Identity Politics

Aside from personal irritation, we should oppose the system of identity politics for its wider destructive effects. I will list five reasons, although there could be many more.

1. Driven by Envy

Identity politics is obsessed with the notion of power. It divides people into teams, and persuades each team it has been wronged and worse treated than the others. Then, fuelled by envy, each team tries to bring down the alleged top team - the straight white male. This is supposed to lead to a new era of equality.

This rotten system will never attain its supposed goal. Instead, it will create exactly what we have now: a divided, dysfunctional society in which large sections of the population hate each other.

Perhaps that was the aim all along.

2. Demand Success Then Blame You For It

As mentioned, straight white males are resented because they're thought to have the most social power. One could easily argue this idea's a myth, but for the sake of argument, let's suppose it was true. If so, you have the odd situation in which we demand men succeed and also blame them when they do.

Men are *expected* to strive for success. They are *supposed* to work hard in achieving their goals. Most women, for example, are attracted to successful men, but want nothing to do with unsuccessful men. The man who is a failure - a 'loser' - attracts little sympathy.

Having been told in no uncertain terms they're supposed to strive for success, it is hardly fair to chastise those who achieve it. It's even worse to chastise those who *fail* to achieve it, simply because they belong to the same class as those who do.

It seems men are wrong either way. If they succeed, they have 'male privilege.' If they fail, they apparently still have it, but they're losers as well.

3. It Weakens Society Overall

Let's suppose, again, that straight white males really were the most powerful group, and add 'productive' to that. If the SWMs were the most powerful and productive group, attacking them weakens society overall.

In deciding who gets jobs, key social positions, and so on, there are two clashing principles: competence and social justice. If competence is the main rule, the best person will get the job, whatever their race and gender. If social justice is the rule, you'll see a quota system in which jobs are shared out among 'diverse' demographics.

It would be a happy coincidence if all the successful diverse candidates were also the most competent, but the chances of that are small. That doesn't matter to leftists, who see 'equity' as more important than the smooth running of society.

But what if straight whites males are *not* the most competent or hard working? Perhaps women or non-whites are better. If so, one would hate to deprive them, thereby also harming society overall. Let's put the challenge to leftists: we will accept the premise that women, gays, and non-whites are every bit as competent as straight white men but if so, they don't need quotas and affirmative action.

Leftists would then complain about systemic obstacles, but trying to fix that just creates more problems. One can try for equality of opportunity and give everyone a chance. That's better than equity, which means equality of outcome. Trying to make all groups end up the same is only possible by discriminating against stronger groups.

The best policy would be to abandon the whole notion of identity politics and treat each person as an individual. Any candidate for a job who tried to make race or gender part of their application should be disqualified.

4. Gestalt Thinking

One of the worst aspects of this sort of class thinking is treating the individual as part of a collective. The individual is seen as belonging to a group, automatically sharing in both its power and its sins.

As mentioned, straight white males are seen as the most powerful social group. This is at best a partial truth, but is really an illusion which comes from the 'apex fallacy.' This illusion occurs when women, for example, focus on the top 10% of straight white males, then falsely attribute their power to the whole group, including the other 90%.

In a similar way, they may look at the bottom 10% of men, morally - the rapists, murderers, and so on - and assign their guilt to the other 90% of the male gender. So, as with some recent murders of women by men, rather than the crimes being blamed on individuals, they're seen in class terms. The entire male gender is seen as somehow responsible for the murders, and told to stop doing it.

We end up with the absurd situation where most men, who are in neither category, are resented both for wealth they don't possess and crimes they don't commit.

In racial terms, gestalt thinking is used as a form of manipulation. A lot is made of historical guilt where, for example, modern day white people are supposed to repent for the actions of their ancestors hundreds of years ago, though having played no part in those events.

These topics will be discussed later in the book.

5. The Mess of Equity

The Global Progressive Regime is chaotic because two of its main ideals - diversity and equality - are incompatible. If you want to sort people into identity groups and also achieve equality, you have an impossible task. Trying to make all these groups 'end up in the same place' requires all sorts of artificial interventions, which won't work anyway but cause lots of trouble.

Equality doesn't even exist in the same family. Take a family with several children. Despite the same basic genes and environment, none of those children are going to end up equal. If you can't achieve it in a family, how could you in a whole society whose citizens have far less in common?

At the start of this chapter, I said people were sorted into groups based on race, gender, and sexuality - that is, white-black, male-female, straight-gay. The various combinations make up the 'teams' in the great struggle that is identity politics.

However, there are many more groups than that. For gender, along with males and females, you have trans and non-binary. Aside from the broad racial categories of black and white, there are Asian, Latino, and many more. Then there are miscellaneous other groups which may also claim victim currency, for example Muslim, Indigenous, immigrant, disabled, the homeless, neuro-divergent, and so on. When all these are thrown into the hideous cauldron of identity politics, it makes for a huge, diverse, dysfunctional mess. All these groups want their own identical slice of the equity pie.

We've often been told that 'diversity is our greatest strength.' This globalist platitude is clearly false, no matter how many times it is piously intoned. The only way diversity could really be a strength is if the many 'teams' worked together harmoniously. If their skills complemented each other, and they genuinely wanted the other teams to succeed, it might work. But that is incompatible with the system of identity politics which is based on envy and the unattainable goal of equity. Feminists are taught to resent men for their alleged male privilege and ethnic groups are taught to resent whites for alleged white privilege. This sort of mentality puts the div in diversity, meaning it can never be a strength.

Under normal circumstances, I would have nothing against any of the other main categories: women, gays, or non-whites. I would wish them well. Yet under the poisonous system of identity politics, these groups have something against me, so any goodwill I may have had is... somewhat reduced.

The Paradox of Identity Politics

The paradox of identity politics is there are certain kinds of identity leftists want to erase, or at least weaken. 'Whiteness,' for example is seen as a bad form of identity.

Some leftists also say that race is itself a false concept, made up by Europeans for their own purposes. *There's only one race: the human race.* If so, racial identities must be seen as in some sense illusory. It is odd, then, that they make such a big deal of it.

Gender has been another area in which the categories of male and female have been targeted. Traditional ideas of maleness and femaleness have been seen as either undesirable, limited, or artificial. Serious efforts have been made to change these traditional forms of identity.

Something else that had a clear identity for a long time was the concept of a family. A family was seen as a man, woman, and children. Leftists have, in various ways, tried to undermine this concept or, as they might say, expand it.

While some of these changes may be worthwhile, it's interesting to note that some types of identity are seen as valuable and others are not. The system of identity politics focuses on race, gender, and sexuality, but also sees some forms of identity as wrong and in need of reform.

It is no coincidence that the regime enemy is the straight white male. Each category extends outward. The Global Progressive Regime is an anti-white, anti-Western system. In attacking the straight white male, the GPR is also attacking white, Western society in its normal or traditional form. The GPR is an ongoing form of Cultural Revolution, an attempted takeover of the Western world. Those who support the GPR are collaborators in this.

Rejecting the 'Allegiance'

When you divide everyone into teams by race and gender, it does not make a cohesive society. The one uniting factor in this mess is all the other groups have been taught to see the straight white male as the bad guy. In the GPR system, with its search for the grail of equity, the straight white male is a regime enemy.

What is the SWM to do? He can either collaborate with the regime, thus becoming a subdued enemy. Or he can reject it and be an explicit enemy.

Most of the other categories - white women, people of colour, gays, and so on - believe the GPR is on their side. They may be mistaken in the long run, but if they do believe the GPR is their friend, it is rational for them to pledge allegiance to it.

It is a curious quirk of such people that they expect straight white males to *also* pledge their allegiance. To become a 'male ally' or a 'white ally,' for example. It's hard to fathom why the SWM would support a system where he is the identified enemy. So, in order to persuade him, the tactic is to claim that the goal of equity is really a universal quest for social justice that all moral men should support. It's nothing to do with the SWM as such, it's about justice. This argument has certainly fooled a few straight white men, but thankfully not all.

Leftists are often outraged when straight whites males don't joyfully join their Cultural Revolution. What's more, they've noticed many of them drifting towards so called right wing groups and beliefs, and apparently this is a surprise to them. But having made one group the enemy and attacked it for decades, you can't then expect an allegiance from that same group.

It seems that after having lectured and vilified them, attributed to them amazing powers they don't have, and generally made war on them, they expect white males to knuckle down and join the crusade against themselves - and many have said no.

I am not going to join a crusade against either men or against whites, especially when both crusades are based on envy, spite, poor reasoning, and naked self interest. If that makes me the enemy, so be it. I never intended to become the enemy. However, it turns out I was the enemy all along and didn't know it.

In that case, I will embrace the role and give an enemy's perspective on the true nature of the Global Progressive Regime.

3

Feeble Demons and the Elites

I've sometimes wondered why leftists all seem to think the same on key issues. They may disagree on minor points but agree on all the main ones. There are several reasons for this, and one is that they *have* to. They're compelled by sideways pressure from their peers and downwards pressure from their superiors.

An interesting version of this idea came from Alan James' book *New Britannia*. His theory was that there's an elite class at the top of society whose values filter down from on high and are enforced by many rungs of people lower down the ladder. This will be explained later in the chapter.

The idea of an elite ruling class will for many conjure an image of a group of white men pushing traditional values - patriarchal, pro-white, and so on. This is an illusion, for these ideas no longer rule. It is now the causes of the Global Progressive Regime which are in power. Causes like feminism, 'anti-racism,' multiculturalism, and an overall anti-white, anti-Western stance.

What does it mean to say these ideas are 'in power?' It means they are seen as the correct ones a moral person is expected to hold. It means that any respectable public figure is expected to support these causes, or at least abstain from criticising them. If you're an aspiring artist, journalist, or politician, you had better go along with the program. Criticising any of them means that you would never, for example, be invited to Sydney Writers Week, be given a job at the ABC, or be able to run for office.

Here is a test for deciding whether an idea is 'in power' or not. All you have to do is ask a simple question. For X, just insert whatever idea you want to test. The question is:

Is it more socially acceptable to praise or to criticise X?

I'll again take multiculturalism as an example. Is it more socially acceptable to praise or to criticise multiculturalism? The answer is clear. One can praise multiculturalism without fear of censure, but to criticise it would make you rather suspect. Thus, the idea of multiculturalism is 'in power.'

Now take a negative example like, say, masculinity. Is it more socially acceptable to praise or to blame masculinity? The answer to that is also clear. It is more acceptable to criticise masculinity, and prefacing it with the word 'toxic' is even better. So, while the idea of masculinity was once viewed favourably, it is no longer in a position of cultural power.

We can extend this test to a general set of values. Imagine an aspiring white male politician and ask yourself which set of statements would allow him to pursue a career in public life, and which would end it.

Option One: My government would make gender equality its top priority, along with ending racism. Diversity is the greatest strength of our wonderful multicultural society. The biggest threat is hate speech and white supremacy. We need to keep Our Democracy safe by cracking down on online misinformation.

Option Two: As women are now full participants in society, the feminist movement is redundant and should retire. Multiculturalism was an optimistic idea which hasn't really worked, and has left our nations rather fractured. If it's to succeed, we need to stop the Anglophobic attacks on the majority population. The best way to protect democracy is to allow free speech for all, and if that offends anyone, too bad.

It should be clear that Option One is the correct script for someone running for office, and those are the lies or the inane platitudes he is expected to mouth. These vague notions of racial and gender equality, and the threat of hate speech, are part of the

Global Progressive Regime and he must swear his allegiance. In other words, support for the GPR causes is expected, and failure to do so will lead to your public cancellation. This shows that the GPR is currently in power.

There are many leftists, however, who will never concede that their side is actually in power. The leftist feels the need to be the permanent underdog, to feel like a freedom fighter 'speaking truth to power,' as they sometimes put it. The truth is, they *are* the power.

Still, many leftists do believe they are fighting an imaginary enemy, that patriarchal white supremacist male at the top of the tree. To show that this is false, let's consider what I call the 'feeble demons' that leftists imagine they're up against.

Feeble Demons

To repeat, many leftists think they're in a life and death struggle against patriarchy and white supremacy, along with traditional values and Christianity as well. But in Western nations, these forces are so weak as to be almost non-existent. They are the 'feeble demons' which leftists somehow see (or pretend to see) as powerful enemies.

White supremacy, for example, is something that existed in the imperial era when white Europeans were colonising other nations and ruling them. To suggest it exists now is absurd, for white people don't even rule their *own* nations. If white supremacy does exist, it's a white supremacy so feeble it has abolished itself through immigration and multiculturalism. It allows the teaching of university courses on the evils of whiteness, and the publication of books about 'white fragility.' Thus, if white supremacy is one of the leftist demons, it's an astonishingly weak one.

Then there's patriarchy. To find an actual patriarchal society today, you would have to go to a non-Western country. In Western nations, women now have full education, positions in public life, and all the other rights possessed by men. They are pandered to by governments and our national broadcaster. There may be some individual male bullies or criminals, and some flawed relationships, but there is no systematic way men are controlling women and dictating their choices. What's more, on average, men are doing far worse in many key areas of life, and masculinity itself is often shamed and criticised.

In light of all this, it's fanciful to believe there's a force called patriarchy holding women back. Or if there is such a force, again, it is so astonishingly weak it's been unable to prevent women rising to their current position and doing all the things they do today, or to prevent men falling into weakness from their alleged position of power. Hence, patriarchy is another feeble demon so weak it may as well not exist.

Western societies may once have been 'patriarchal' in certain ways, but if they were patriarchal in the way feminists suppose, the feminist movement could never even have begun. There would have been none of the scholarships, affirmative action, and countless reforms and concessions of the last few decades.

Let's look at another perceived enemy of the left, a broad category we might call 'traditional values.' These values could include the nuclear family and heterosexuality as norms, for example, or patriotism and national pride. If these were once taken for granted, they are no longer. If traditional values comprise another demon, it is again a very weak one.

As for Christianity, another pet hate of the left, it has diminished as a cultural force and now has a significant rival in Islam. Just consider which of these two religions it is more acceptable to criticise. Christianity is regularly attacked, with little fear of a backlash, so it's hardly the powerful force it once was.

To recap, many leftists still think of themselves as revolutionaries fighting the power, in the form of the imaginary demons of patriarchy, white supremacy, traditional values, or Christianity. The truth is, all of these are very weak in Western nations today.

These feeble demons are ineffective and rather pathetic, if they exist at all. It is leftism which has the cultural power today. It is the values and causes of the GPR which now rule.

And what are they? They are social systems like multiculturalism, causes like feminism and Black Lives Matter, and principles like 'anti-racism' and DEI. Some people think all of these are good and we should rejoice in their ascendancy. I think they are only superficially moral and if you look past the façade, there are major problems with all of them.

These ideas are in power now, even if we don't always know how they got there. Once they are accepted, there's the question of how they are maintained. Here we come to the 'theory of the elites' given by Alan James in his 2013 book, *New Britannia*.

James starts by citing a man named Rubinstein who said that most societies have an elite class of roughly a thousand people. Among this group are the top figures in both political parties, CEOs and other business leaders, major media figures, heads of universities, leading scientists and thinkers, and so on, along with the wealthiest people of that society. James believes this elite class largely controls what can and cannot be said.

> Members of this self-serving group talk mostly to other members. They read or watch the same self-proclaimed "quality" media outlets, from which they derive intellectual justification for the suite of views that they already share. They can and do disagree among themselves on certain issues, but any dissident views beyond these minor areas of permitted debate are dismissed by the protégés of this "top elite" as heretical, and reviled by the use of words like "extremist", "odious", "unacceptable", "divisive", "populist', "racist" and "repugnant."

And there are many such protégés. For every media proprietor in the "top elites" for instance, there are thousands of editors, sub-editors, journalists and broadcasters, commentators, cartoonists, photographers, camera operators, marketing staff, layout people, IT exerts, and all the other functionaries necessary to produce successful newspapers, magazines, books, radio stations, TV stations, websites and the like. In short, all the people who depend financially on those in Rubenstein's "top elites."

The views of the very few members of the "top elites" trickle down to all the functionaries in this much broader group, in much the same way as the financial crumbs fall to them from their masters' tables. The employees can think whatever they like, but they know that to *express* dissident opinions is to put at risk further promotion, at least, and perhaps to incur stronger forms of negative sanction. Equally, any ambitious young journalist or broadcaster or academic can anticipate the views s/he is expected to promote, then advance them with sufficient ardour to be deemed worthy of promotion. They obey their master's voice even when he is not speaking. In short, the top elites have immense power over those further down the chain, who modify their behaviour accordingly.

It must be conceded that this power is largely latent. A few academics and journalists *have* been penalised for expressing deviant views, but the need to make an example of dissidents is required only rarely. The fact is that the elites are cohesive to a remarkable extent, sharing in common political aims, values and norms. Thus, the major newspapers or TV shows often employ one or two commentators who apparently dissent from the prevailing political mood - yet they justify their dissent over this or that issue by appealing to the prevailing norms of the elites.

What's interesting is that today's elites are not pushing what we think of as conservative values, but those of the Global Progressive Regime. It is easy to see this in key institutions. Universities are known for their intolerance of those who depart from GPR values. The ABC, our national broadcaster, is another in which it's hard to see a GPR dissenter climbing very far up the ranks. As for the arts and entertainment, aspiring artists know that left wing views are a condition of entry.

Still, if there are groups of privileged elites setting the agenda, why would they support causes which seem to be egalitarian? It is surely contradictory that the most powerful people would support causes which claim to want to redistribute wealth and power more evenly.

There are a few possible reasons. One is that such values are generally 'for thee but not for me.' It is well known, for example, that while trumpeting the value of racial diversity, wealthy Western elites tend to live in the least diverse areas available. It may be in their economic interests to bring in immigrants to supply them with cheap labour, but these are just numbers on a balance sheet. They don't actually live and interact with them.

As well as being cheap labour, such immigrants may provide cheap virtue points in the new moral economy of the GPR. The elites can praise diversity from a distance. Safely sheltered in their multi-million dollar mansions or gated communities, the elites will be the ones least affected if there are unfortunate side effects of the policies they support.

Some wealthy elites do act from good intentions. They may be philanthropists who want to use their wealth for good. Whether this is motivated by love, guilt, a social conscience, or grandiose ideas of their own wisdom isn't clear. In some cases, a sort of God complex may be at work, as will be seen in the chapter on multiculturalism.

There's also a more disturbing aspect to this. Some trends seem to make no sense. Take the incredibly lax border control of recent years in Britain and the US which has allowed the entry of millions of immigrants, both legal and illegal. This seems of no concern to the elites, despite the problems it will surely cause. Are these elites really so aloof to the lives of ordinary people, and callous about the fate of their own countries?

It is here one can speculate that perhaps elites in a given country are beholden to a higher set of elites, 'global' in origin and disposition, who care nothing for that country and may actually want to undermine it. There are reasons to suspect this may be true. First, it would explain why most of the Anglo nations have been committing slow suicide through actions which seem to make little sense. Second, it may explain the low standard of national leaders in recent times. These people have attained power not because they're competent, intelligent, or strong, but because they are not. They're either well meaning midwits who serve as 'useful idiots' for the foreign elites, or sociopathic careerists who do as they're told to stay in power.

If there *are* hostile elites, the best way they could undermine a country is through the slow poison of rotten ideology. To be effective, it can't be an obvious poison. It has to be disguised as a healthy and wholesome treat. The ideological poison has to have a social justice veneer. 'Anti-racism,' multiculturalism, feminism, and the DIE principles all have that shiny moral coating, enough to fool the midwits who are running our countries, and the people who believe such doctrines benefit them. At the same time, these people have to believe in imaginary enemies like patriarchy and white supremacy, and pretend they are the greatest possible threat.

The fact that we do live in the GPR, and leftist beliefs are in power, can again be proven by repeating the test given earlier in the chapter. Is it more acceptable to praise or to criticise a given idea?

If one aspires to enter public life as an artist, broadcaster, or politician, is it a better option to praise or to criticise GPR concepts like diversity, equity, feminism, or multiculturalism? Is it wiser to condemn patriarchy or white supremacy, or to point out that if they still exist in the West, they're so weak as to be irrelevant.

Answering those questions will tell you whether we're living in the fictional world ruled by the feeble demons of the leftist imagination, or the much more appalling real world of the Global Progressive Regime.

A Note Added Later

I wrote most of this book during 2023 and 2024. At the time of its publication in 2025, there are signs the tide may be turning against leftism. In late 2024, for example, Trump won the US election, and within a few months the ultra progressive Justin Trudeau resigned as prime minster of Canada. There's also been a backlash against 'woke entertainment,' with the failure of some high profile leftist films and TV shows.

While these are signs leftism is losing its dominance, it's too early to see them as decisive. This is just another stage of the culture war, which has raged for decades and will continue for a long while yet.

Apart from that, we still have to face the lasting consequences of everything the progressive left has done in recent decades. Multiculturalism, for instance, has permanently changed Western nations. Feminism is still a powerful ideology. Concepts to do with diversity and equality are still part of the daily conversation, in one way and another. These and other social justice causes have made their way deep into our institutions and our lives.

In other words, the Global Progressive Regime is going through some turbulence, but is still deeply embedded in our social systems.

As for Donald Trump, he is a powerful anomaly. I said that a white male politician could not hope to succeed if he offended against GPR values, but he is the exception. Ever since launching his presidential run in 2015, he has driven leftists insane. This is because by normal GPR standards, Trump should have been cancelled a thousand times in the last decade. Yet despite all the rage, protests, impeachments, and even some attempts to have him jailed, Trump somehow survived and became president again. Some of the reasons for this will be discussed in later chapters.

Whatever the temporary ebb and flow of the culture war may be, a fixture now is the obsession with race. That will be the topic of the next part of this book.

Part Two

Sacred Cows:

Race

4

Anti-Racism and Anglophobia

As I said in another book, a decade ago I had little interest in the topics of race and racism. But when you live in the Global Progressive Regime (the GPR), these topics are forced on you in one way and another. It could be through being told about the merits of diversity and multiculturalism. It might be when you see statues of white settlers being torn down after a 'racial incident' in America. It could be from noticing the BBC's bizarre and ongoing campaign to persuade you England is a majority black nation.

In these and hundreds of other ways, race is constantly brought to your attention and - if you are white - usually in a negative way. Therefore, to understand the GPR, you have to look at some of the key racial areas of conflict. This section of the book will do that. The first chapter will be a brief look at 'anti-racism,' followed by one on multiculturalism. Then there will be some chapters about the Australian Aboriginals, and the Black Lives Matter movement.

These topics are controversial. Racial issues are the main sacred cows of our time. The other sacred cows are the gender issues, of which I'll confine myself to discussing feminism rather than trans. All these topics arouse a great deal of emotion - but as race and gender are the two main areas of conflict in the GPR, there is no avoiding these topics if you want to understand the GPR and its hold over us.

A key point to understand is that for the Global Progressive Regime to achieve its aims, it had to make race a core issue and at the same time a taboo topic in the sense that we could only think about it in very limited ways - and that's how the West was won.

Racism

One of the main crusades of our time is the war on racism.

In Western nations, there is a big fuss made over combating racism towards Muslims, Asians, or any other 'people of colour.' In my country, Australia, sometimes a minor incident will happen, such as a racial slur. At a recent football game, for instance, some kid in the crowd called an Indigenous player a 'black dog.' This led to a hyperbolic over-reaction from various parties.

Whenever this happens and there are grave pronouncements about 'zero tolerance to racism' it's tempting to ask 'why don't you do something about the racism towards white people?' To that, some progressive types would answer: 'What racism? There *is* no racism towards white people.'

It's a curious fact that many of these people seem unaware of anti-white racism. The idea comes as a surprise to them. It seems ridiculous, even offensive. There are several reasons for this. First, they may be so immersed in anti-white racism it's become normalised and thus invisible to them. Second, they may be aware of it but not have thought of it in those terms. Third, they may be active in propagating anti-white racism and consider it a noble line of work.

First, what does 'racism' mean? I'll define it as negative or hostile attitudes towards a particular racial group, expressed in words and actions. It may include offensive portrayals of that group, assumptions about its members, and the desire for harm to come to that racial group or its members.

To the comments: 'What racism? There *is* no racism towards white people' I'll answer by outlining various forms of it. For those seeking a fuller answer, a 2023 book called *Anglophobia* gives a detailed list. The authors, Harry Richardson and Frank Salter, present what is almost a taxonomy of anti-white attitudes.

For now, here are some general types.

Literal Attacks - Verbal attacks on individual whites or white people as a group. These can happen in person, in the media, or on social media. Physical attacks, muggings, sexual assaults, or murders, which have a clear racial motivation. This includes well known cases like the South African farm murders, violent murders of white Britons, the sexual assault of British and European women, and many other such attacks.

Media and Entertainment - The above crimes are often underreported or simply ignored by mainstream media. There is clear bias in the reporting of interracial crime. High profile non-white victims like Stephen Lawrence and George Floyd are given maximum coverage, while white victims might not even be mentioned. The sexual assault of hundreds of British girls by ethnic grooming gangs, for example, was for a long time ignored by the media.

In entertainment, we get negative portrayals of whites in film and TV, or in advertising. There's a push to replace white actors with diverse ones, or else we see white men cast only in the role of villains.

Conceptual - The propagation of anti-white ideas. For example, it is widely taught that white nations are uniquely guilty of historical crimes, that its people have 'white privilege,' or - confusingly - that 'whiteness' is made up and doesn't really exist. These concepts are pushed by our key social institutions, most notably in education. Universities teach courses in Critical Race Theory about 'whiteness,' which is always portrayed in a negative light.

Government Policies - Mass immigration and multiculturalism are policies that hurt whites, especially when followed up with the DIE programs - that is, Diversity, Inclusion, and Equity. These are for the benefit of non-whites and, intended or not, have negative effects for whites.

The current chapter will present a brief overview of these ideas, and later chapters will go into more detail.

The War on Whiteness

White people need to understand that many non-whites harbour some kind of hostility towards them. It doesn't matter if they are 'good-whites' who observe all the racial pieties. This will not exonerate them.

This hostility is for various reasons. It's partly due to the natural tribalism we all have. It may also come from being a minority in a majority-white nation, the desire for more power, and from real or imagined grievances. Some of it is because anti-white sentiment has been actively promoted. Many non-whites do hold resentment towards whites. Anti-white tirades have been common on Twitter, for example, although they would not have been allowed against other racial groups.

All this happens in a larger context of the 'war on whiteness.' The idea of such a war may seem paranoid to those immersed in a left wing bubble. However, it's easy to see, if you care to look, that there is a war on white people - their history, their culture, and their status in the present and future.

This is happening in the Western nations that are, for the time being, majority white. That is Britain, America, Canada, Australia, New Zealand, and some of the European nations like France and Germany. Within these nations, there is strong hostility towards the majority ethnic group. This is coming from the steadily growing non-white population and also - absurdly - from white people who have absorbed decades of anti-white programming.

I'll divide this 'war' into three broad categories - past, present, and future.

War on the Past

The main line of attack is to claim white nations are guilty of historical sins against non-whites. The main sins are colonialism, slavery, and the Holocaust, among others. While there is of course some truth to this, the idea is pushed in a distorted and selective way. First, these failings are stressed *ad nauseum*, while the great advances and contributions made by white societies are rarely mentioned. Second, the idea is that these sins are unique to whites, and are so terrible that white societies today have no moral legitimacy and must do as they're told. Third, it is never revealed why, if Western nations are so terrible, so many non-whites seem desperate to live in them.

The idea of historical guilt is pushed repeatedly. It is enacted in many ways: the grovelling of national leaders through apologies, the renaming of streets or buildings, or the hysterical statue smashing of the 2020 race riots after the death of George Floyd.

Another, more sinister, line of attack on the past is in films and TV programs. Non-white actors are given roles playing either white historical figures or just ordinary people from past eras. While this looks odd to anyone familiar with history, the insertion of 'diverse' actors into crowd scenes may be effective against naïve viewers (especially children) who are being sold the lie that Britain, for example, has always been multicultural. This rewriting of history is a disturbing part of the campaign to undermine the Anglo nations.

War on the Present

The main line of attack here is the idea of 'white privilege.' This is the notion that whites have unfair advantages over non-whites in various ways.

To take one example, that there are more white faces on TV is supposedly a sign of racial privilege. There may indeed be more white people on TV, but it's what you would expect in a majority white nation. It has been changing, so that more 'diverse' faces are appearing. Whites are supposed to applaud this triumph of 'inclusion,' perhaps not realising it is a trend towards their eventual exclusion.

This is the real thrust of the aptly named DIE principles - Diversity, Inclusion, and Equity. (DEI is the official term, but DIE is more accurate). These words are a noble façade but the real agenda is the displacement of whites, and the reduction of their demographic and cultural power. Gullible whites need to realise the high level of enmity many non-whites feel towards them, and that their own naive sentiments of goodwill are often not returned now, and will be returned even less once they become a minority.

Some categories of whites are seduced by temporary alliances. White feminists or gays, for example, see DIE principles as in their interests, and may not be aware that others will ultimately see them in racial terms whether they like it or not. Their so called alliance will count for nothing.

The war on whites in the present also takes the form of a sustained campaign of demoralisation. This is a many-pronged attack. It may included chastising whites for their 'privilege,' hectoring them about their alleged racism, or reminding them of their ancestors' sins for which they now have to make amends. This happens in education, the media, films and TV, and so on.

Another attack is the accusation that some pastime is 'too white.' Classical music is too white. Or museums. Or walks in the English countryside. All these activities are told to become more diverse.

Sometimes the demoralisation comes through the media, as in the negative depiction of whites in films and TV, or the disproportionate casting of diverse actors in key roles.

Then there's advertising. There is a revealing video called '43 Anti-white Commercials' which, at the time of writing, was still on YouTube. As the video explains, these anti-white ads have four main themes:

1. Alpha black male humiliates weak white male (this is never done with races reversed, and is often done in front of a white female).

2. Professional black genius does better than lazy white imbecile.

3. Weak, nerdy, ugly, (and occasionally gay) white male humiliates himself while professional black male looks down at him in pity (often done in front of white woman as well, also never done with races reversed).

4. White males victimising black people (even though FBI crime statistics prove that black on white crime is much higher, even without adjusting for population difference. Also never done with races reversed).

War on the Future

Speaking of advertising, TV viewers may have noticed the strangely high number of mixed race couples featured in both TV shows and the ads. In most cases, this is a black man and a white woman, rarely the other way around. For some reason, Asians don't often feature with either black or white partners. Yet the mixed race couple, with one white member, is a common sight.

Some would say this reflects our social evolution as a species, as we move into the post-national, post-racial age. However, social evolution is one thing and biological evolution is another. Charles Darwin's theory acknowledged that some species thrive, some die out, and some evolve into different forms. A key part of his theory was the concept of *natural selection*, which referred to the way species change over time depending on which ones manage to survive and reproduce in the wild.

Darwin also knew about what he called *artificial selection*, that is to say, the conscious direction of evolution through controlled breeding. Darwin saw this in dog breeding, for example. Different types of dogs were bred together to create new forms. More desirable types were encouraged, and less desirable types 'bred out.'

In terms of all the mixed race couples on TV, it does make you wonder. Is someone trying to breed us like dogs? If so, why?

Most people don't have a problem with interracial marriages if they happen naturally, so to speak. In my younger days, I nearly got engaged to an Indian girl. With my light skin and her much darker skin, our children would have looked most interesting. At least it would have been by choice.

If we *are* being deliberately nudged towards interracial breeding by invisible dog breeders, that is rather disturbing. Is someone trying to get rid of us?

This is all the more strange considering that eugenics - the controlled breeding of humans - is considered a cardinal sin. Yet it is rather obvious that there is some kind of push towards interracial relationships.

A species, or a specific racial group within it, only survives if there is a high enough rate of reproduction for it to go on into the future. It may be a coincidence, but the last few decades have seen a convergence of ideas that work against the reproduction of whites. Apart from mixed marriages, we've seen the enthusiastic promotion of gayness and transgenderism, feminism (with its anti-family slant), easy access to abortion, attacks on the nuclear family, climate change alarmism, mass immigration, multiculturalism, and more. As it happens, I personally support some of these in themselves, such as gay rights and women's right to pursue careers.

However, it's curious that one thing they all have in common is a negative effect on reproduction.

Some hardcore leftists seem to have a problem with what they might call 'heteronormative cisgender' societies. That is, the ones where heterosexual families are in the majority and seen as the norm. Well, these societies are the ones that survive. The rest die out.

This chapter has given a brief outline of the anti-white environment in which we live. Some of us have been immersed in it for so long - even from birth - that we aren't aware of it. Others can see an ongoing campaign of racism against white people that may be overt, subtle, or only implied. This racism takes the form of negative and often hostile ideas, speech, or actions towards white people and Western nations.

An Academic Definition of Racism

There is another definition of racism. At some point in the recent past, it became obvious many non-whites felt racial hostility towards whites. This opened them to the charge of hypocrisy. As a way to evade this, a new definition of racism was conjured up.

Racism = prejudice plus power.

The admission is that various racial groups often do hold negative attitudes towards each other. However, as the whites were said to have power and non-whites none, under the new definition only whites could be guilty of racism.

The strategy from non-white racists here is to give themselves a license to be as hostile to whites as possible while letting themselves off the charge of hypocrisy. Let's hope no one is silly enough to fall for this one.

There are all kinds of absurdities flourishing in the current age of race hysteria. For example, in his book *Whiteness: the Original Sin*, Jim Goad points out that we're alleged to live in the logically impossible idea of a society steeped in white supremacy whose cardinal sin is also white supremacy.

Over the next few chapters, I'll look at some more points of confusion around race, starting with the topic of multiculturalism. This system throws many races together, 'different but equal,' which are supposed to form a coherent, harmonious society. Like many racial concepts, it's good in theory but much harder in practice.

Footnote - In this chapter, I mentioned the social media site Twitter. It has since changed its name to X, but throughout this book, I will continue to call it Twitter, rather than X.

5

From God Complex to
Sorcerer's Apprentice

I recently read a book of science fiction stories by the English author, John Wyndham. In one story, first published in 1956, an English man was visited by people from the Britain of the 21st century, one hundred years in the future.

Although it wasn't stated, we can assume he saw these future people as white Britons. The author felt no need to make this explicit, for he had no reason to doubt that almost all future residents of England would be white Britons like himself. It would never have occurred to him to think otherwise.

In the actual future of the mid twenty-first century, the white British may have reached minority status in their own country. More than half the population may be what are now called *people of colour*. The transformation of Britain is already well underway, and will be further gone by then. This would have been inconceivable to a man like John Wyndham in 1956.

Indeed, at the time I began writing this chapter, in 2023, the UK's prime minister was of Indian descent and the mayor of London had roots in Pakistan and was a Muslim. Both were born in Britain, their parents having immigrated in the 1960s. The first minister of Scotland was the son of a Pakistani father and Kenyan mother, and was also a Muslim. These three men - Rishi Sunak, Sadiq Khan, and Humaz Yousaf - were some of the most powerful men in Britain.

At the same time, the leader of Ireland, Leo Varadkar, was Dublin-born but had an Indian father, and within a year Vaughan Gething would become the first black leader of Wales.

What has brought about such a radical change in Britain and other Western nations? First, of course, immigration, and second the policy of multiculturalism. It is this latter policy the current chapter will look at - its pros and cons, and how it began in the first place.

There had always been some immigrants in Western nations, but until the 1970s the normal process was assimilation. Immigrants were expected to adapt to the culture of their new country. Under the new theory of multiculturalism, they were encouraged to keep their own. Western countries no longer needed to have one dominant culture, but could be a mix of subcultures all living together. Our complacent leaders assumed our own culture would simply carry on, unaffected by this.

What was the reason for the new policy of immigration and multiculturalism? There is no one simple answer. Taking Australia as an example, there is a five hundred page book called *The Origins of Multiculturalism in Australian Politics 1945-1975* which explores the issue in great detail, and there were various factors at work. However, a key part of it, without which it couldn't have happened, was the naïve idealism of white leaders. Some seemed to see it as a kind of Utopian racial experiment. In 1971, the prime minster of Australia, John Gorton, said:

> I think that if we build up gradually inside Australia a proportion of people who are not of white skin, then as that is gradually done, so there will be a complete lack of consciousness of difference between the races. And if this can be done, as I think it can, then that may provide the world with the first truly multi-racial society with no tension of any kind possible between any of the races within it. At any rate, this is our ideal.

If that was the aim of the experiment, it has failed. Fifty years later, Australia is a society obsessed with race. You cannot go a single day without hearing about the topic, either in relation to immigrants or the Indigenous. Australia's national broadcaster, the ABC, puts out a drip feed of news stories about race and racism. It never ends.

In terms of achieving the post-racial society - with no consciousness of race, or tension between different groups - multiculturalism has not just failed to achieve the desired result. It has made the problem worse, and created new problems that weren't there in the first place.

Still, even if multiculturalism has failed to produce a society that doesn't see race, perhaps it has other benefits. What are the pros and cons of a multicultural society? Who is it good for? In answering this, we can look at it from the point of view of first, non-white people, and second, that of the white majority.

Who benefits? The immigrants themselves, of course. They get to live in Western nations *and* keep their own cultures. Multiculturalism is great for them.

For the white population, it's a mixed blessing. Multiculturalism *does* have some benefits for whites. There's a much bigger choice of cuisine. There's a potentially wider range of culture to experience. Immigrants include high skilled workers (e.g. doctors and engineers), and also lower paid workers to do the less skilled jobs. Socially, white people get to meet people they otherwise wouldn't. On the ethical side, virtuous whites get the chance to prove they are not racist, by their enthusiastic embrace of multiculturalism.

All this is true, and it's easy for white people to enjoy these short term benefits as long as they remain ignorant of the bigger picture, which is that the end result of multiculturalism is their demographic and cultural replacement.

Whether or not it was intended, that is the long term result. It's not that white people and their culture will disappear. They will become just another minority within a larger whole. Whether this is in the interests of whites is highly doubtful. To be reduced to a minority in countries they once dominated is hardly a benefit. What makes it worse is that due to the amount of animosity directed at whites today, they will probably be a hated minority.

From my own selfish point of view, I do enjoy some aspects of multiculturalism: exotic food, cultural events, and so on. That doesn't mean I can't see the long term consequences.

Even in the here and now, on the rare occasions I head into the centre of Sydney, there's a sense that Anglo-Australians are *already* a racial minority. Is this really the future that was intended by the naïve, do-gooder politicians of the 1970s when they allowed this fledgling theory to grow? Like most politicians, they probably thought barely five years ahead, never mind fifty.

So, what about the present? While multiculturalism does have short term benefits for whites, it also has short term disadvantages.

First, as mentioned, there is the constant focus on race. Not a day goes by without someone complaining about racism. For example, a recent ABC story about 'Harmony Day' was turned into a harangue about the racism of white Australians. Harmony Day was supposed to celebrate multiculturalism, but the name itself was an attempt to rebrand the United Nations 'International Day for the Elimination of Racial Discrimination.' That gives a clue as to how contrived it all is and who is pushing it. The elites, from their Palaces of Wisdom in the sky, have given us multiculturalism, now they're going to punish anyone who doesn't enthusiastically embrace the harmony they have bestowed upon us.

Second, there is squabbling over racial quotas for jobs in the media, politics, and other key roles in public life. If we're going to 'reflect the community,' to use that hackneyed phrase, we have to include all the various racial groups.

We've not yet reached the point of a racial quota system, but the idea isn't very farfetched. Suppose there were ten jobs available with a company and a white person was applying. In either a white society or a multiracial 'colour-blind' society, that person would have a chance of getting any of those ten jobs. Under a racial quota system, the person could only get one out of the ten.

The prospect of this sort of racial squabbling wasn't mentioned when the idea of multiculturalism was first proposed, debated, and voted for by white populations back in the 1970s.

Oh wait - that's right. Multiculturalism was never proposed, debated, or voted for. It was sneakily introduced without consent.

The third problem is the loss of national unity. A common ethnicity and culture binds a country together as a cohesive whole. There are certain common values and traditions. If you introduce a dozen or more cultures into the same country, there's little unity - just a bunch of different cultures in the same geographical space.

Related to this, a fourth problem is the values of one culture may be offensive to another. Some Muslims, for example, might be offended either by a perceived insult to themselves, or by liberal Western practices like homosexuality or women's 'revealing' clothing. Conflicting values add to racial tension and the chance of offence being given or taken.

This in turn leads to the increase of censorship to maintain the illusion of peace and harmony.

A fifth problem for whites is that a significant number of non-whites are hostile to them, either openly or in secret. This can manifest as the petty squabbling over racial quotas, to more serious hostile acts like the sexual grooming gangs of Rotherham, or actual terrorist attacks. One might say it is amazingly foolish to invite into your country people who hate you, but it would be racist to say such a thing.

Ah yes, racism. We were all taught to see it as the gravest moral offence. We learned that the White Australia policy was an embarrassing relic of our past, one from which we evolved to our current state of enlightened decency. With this new mindset in place, we would never dream of questioning multiculturalism.

It is only recently I began to question the idea myself. Having been through the same indoctrination as everyone else, I remember being slightly shocked a few years ago when Bruce Bawer made a negative remark about multiculturalism at the start of his book *The Victims Revolution*. That was before I began to notice the endless carping about race and the steady stream of anti-white messaging that is all around us. My reaction to Bawer's remark shows how much I had been trained to accept multiculturalism as an unquestionable good.

Could Multiculturalism Succeed?

Even if human nature was as leftist Utopians conceive it - good will to all men, racial harmony, and so on - white people and their culture would still be diluted. If all immigrants were grateful and respectful to their new countries, this might be at least tolerable. However, many immigrants have no love for their new white countrymen, and in some cases resent them.

This is especially true for some of the immigrants' children, who are taught by identity politics to resent the white majority. Meanwhile, whites are accused of historical sins and white privilege. Under these conditions, it's hard to see how the multicultural experiment could succeed. If the powers that be wanted it to succeed, you'd think the anti-white campaign would be toned down or abandoned, but there are no signs of that happening. It's tempting to wonder if multiculturalism itself was *part* of that campaign.

It's curious that multiculturalism began in all the Anglo nations at about the same time. Were the local populations clamouring to have their lives enriched by diversity, and the replacement of their Anglo or European-based culture?

Not particularly. It was given to them from on high, and would be imposed whether they liked it or not. This was a social revolution that had to be achieved by a mix of bribery and force. On the one hand, the 'carrot' was all that exotic food and culture and the chance for whites to prove their virtue. The 'stick' was installing racism as the cardinal sin, with any offense to be punished by social shaming.

Guilt was a key tool of manipulation, aimed at entire populations. The main method in America was guilt over slavery. In Britain it was about the empire, and in Germany the Holocaust. In Australia, it was about settlement of the country itself, 'stealing the land' from Aboriginals, and the later mistreatment of them.

This was used to coerce majority white nations into accepting mass immigration and multiculturalism. 'Guilty' white populations were asked to atone for past sins. Anyone who objected might be reminded of those past sins, with the implied question, *who are you to complain?*

There are all sorts of logical problems with this alleged guilt. In Australia, for example, many of the early white Australians were brought here as convicts, against their will. They had no choice in the matter. Yet they are supposed guilty of stealing the Aboriginals' land. Indeed it's not just *they* who stole it, but their descendants, including those alive today. So, you have people who had no choice in being born as descendants of those who had no choice about being brought here in the first place, yet somehow these people have to do penance for their 'theft.'

One of the main forms of penance is the obligation to allow masses of immigrants to move to Australia, and live in harmony with them. This latter group *does* - mostly - come here by choice, yet none of the censure about stealing the Aboriginals' land is aimed at them. They are not thought to be accessories after the fact, benefitting from the profits of crime, and so on. The lash of historical guilt is reserved exclusively for one racial group - the Anglos.

This brainwashing program has been hugely successful. With racism as the main sin and historical guilt hammered home, generations of whites have been eager to prove their virtue by allowing themselves to be displaced in their own countries. Even now, many virtuous white leftists cheer on diversity, oblivious to the long term effects. Or if they are aware of those effects, they naively see them as desirable.

On the other hand, you have the dissident whites who sense what is going on, and push back. These people are slandered as the worst of the worst, labelled the 'far-right,' and so on.

Such is the battle of the 'good-whites' and 'bad-whites.' These terms were introduced by American writers Steve Sailor and John Derbyshire. Simply put, good-whites are leftists who buy into the idea of historical guilt and observe all the racial pieties, and bad-whites are those who do not.

As a result, we now have dysfunctional countries where these two groups of whites hate each other, while both groups are despised by various ethnic subcultures whose numbers are growing. Meanwhile, we have governments doubling down on their silly mantra that diversity is our greatest strength.

This is the state of the great multicultural experiment, begun mostly in the 1970s in majority-white nations. How did this all begin - and why?

Let's return to the quote from Australia's prime minister, John Gorton, in 1971. He thought we could create a multiracial society in which there was no longer any consciousness of race, in which we would all simply blend into one people.

This experiment was probably doomed to fail due to the false assumptions made - for example, that humans are all the same, therefore interchangeable. This was based on the theory that race is simply a 'social construct' with no basis in biology. Another fashionable idea was that all cultures are equal, and can presumably co-exist in one place. In short, the multicultural experiment was based on the notion that thousands of years of evolution and culture could be overcome by a few social policies dreamed up in the idealistic 1960s.

Having said it was doomed to fail, there are perhaps two ways this experiment could have succeeded. The first way would have been to run it without toxic identity politics and its grievances, and the whole anti-white agenda. That way, racial harmony may have had a chance.

The second way would have been to keep a dominant Anglo-European culture, while allowing ethnic subcultures to exist as minorities. For a while, perhaps through to the end of the twentieth century, this was the case in most Western countries, and multiculturalism may have been seen as a qualified success.

Some have said that Australia, for example, is 'the most successful multicultural nation in the world.' This may be true, but it's been partly because Australia is a fairly rich country, peaceful, blessed with a good climate, and has an easygoing, good natured character coming, coincidentally, from its Anglo majority. But if it was a multicultural success for a while, that is questionable now. In the 2020s, Australia is a divided nation with racial tension and a confused identity. There is little unity, or the sense of a national character that we had in, say, the 1980s.

Multiculturalism might succeed if ethnic minorities stayed at a reasonable size. In Britain, however, immigration increased during the Tony Blair era. Similar trends occurred elsewhere. You had much bigger 'minorities' influencing the countries they now called home. At the same time, the white guilt message and grievance politics were run in our social institutions.

Both of those ways multiculturalism may have succeeded are gone. A third way the experiment can 'succeed' is by further weakening the white majority population. This can be done be thinning out its numbers and reducing its influence. It will also require more censorship and an authoritarian government. That is the direction we're taking.

From God Complex to Sorcerer's Apprentice

From our vantage point in the 2020s, let's look back at those who launched this social experiment more than half a century ago.

It took a while for this project to get going. The term 'multiculturalism' did not come into common use until the early to mid 1970s. As described in *The Origins of Multiculturalism in Australian Politics 1945-1975*, there were various factors leading up to this new social policy - but it didn't happen by itself. It took the persistent effort of a small number of lobbyists for this policy, with far reaching consequences, to take hold.

Some Anglo supporters of the idea were 1960s radicals working for social reform and against what they saw as racial inequality. But if colour-blind equality was an ideal held by whites, some of the non-white lobbyists for multiculturalism were explicitly working for their own ethnic groups. As another author put it, it was a familiar combination of 'starry idealism and hard headed ethnic activism.'

As for the 1970s politicians who saw multiculturalism as a bold social experiment, the most charitable thing you can say is it was well intentioned, if remarkably naive. There may have been some real idealism at work.

Less kindly, one might see the experiment as amazingly arrogant. They seemed to have had some kind of God complex. They thought they could bypass centuries of evolution and culture, and simply create a post-racial society through their own exalted wisdom.

These people were some of the 'elites' mentioned in Chapter Three - those who thought they knew best, and could treat the populations of their own countries like cattle. No doubt there were economic incentives too - cheap labour, economic growth, and other short term benefits.

Who were these elites? Some may have been international organisations using their influence. As has been remarked, it's hard to believe it was a coincidence that all the Anglo nations became multicultural at around the same time.

It was also local elites, including politicians on both sides of parliament. Was the theory of multiculturalism ever put to the vote? Was it ever presented to the Australian people, its merits debated, and a case made? No. Neither was large scale immigration itself. According to one report, these reforms were put through without the Australian public's knowledge or consent.

Indeed, a former prime minister, Bob Hawke, admitted there was 'an implicit pact between the major parties to implement broad policies on immigration that they know are not generally endorsed by the electorate' and 'they have done this by keeping the subject off the political agenda.'

It seems odd that a government would hold a referendum on something trivial like, say, a new national anthem, but when it came to a civilisation-changing policy like multiculturalism, that was never put to the public. On the contrary, it was snuck through in secret. This grand scheme with its far reaching effects was never voted for by the Australian people. Once the scheme was introduced, it was supported by both sides of politics. In a review of a book on Australian history, the comments by Bob Hawke are again mentioned.

> 'The major parties had reached an implicit pact to keep immigration off the political agenda... There are no other issues to which the major parties have been prepared to act in this way... to advance the national interest ahead of where they believed the electorate to be.'

The review goes on to mention a journalist who had written a piece defending this strategy.

> (He) approved of deception in the name of 'ethnic diversification.' He said the government was right to 'do good by stealth... Let the magic do its work, but don't talk about it in front of the children. They'll just get cross and spoil it all.'

> This is typical of the contempt in which elites hold the people. Displacing the founding stock with aliens is wonderful, but somehow its wonders are not easily grasped by the people being displaced. Therefore, let the policy be carried out in secret.

It seems these elite public figures from the 1970s and 80s knew best when it came to deciding the future of Australia. Who gave them the right to conduct grand social experiments? No one. They gave themselves the right. They were in God Complex mode, and they will never be held accountable for the results.

It is all very well conducting social experiments if they are responsibly done and there is some damage control in place. Yet once the multicultural project had begun, it was hard to turn back. It was an experiment of amazing recklessness.

Whatever the rights and wrongs of settling Australia in the late 18th century, the new country was a majority Anglo-Celtic one. That would change, thanks to these gung ho, arrogant elites.

The post-war immigration of European migrants was not as disruptive. The import after 1970 of non-Europeans was harder. The more alien cultures would not mesh as well, and with the new policy of multiculturalism they no longer had to assimilate.

There were points in the past where the experiment might have been rolled back, but instead, those in charge seemed to double down. In the Anglo nations over the last few years, there seems to have been more immigration than ever and less tolerance of any objection to it. There has been more censorship, warnings about 'hate speech,' cracking down on dissidents, and propaganda about diversity.

Unfortunately for John Gorton's hopes of a society lacking any racial tension, Western nations today are full of it. There's a great deal of anti-white animus, counter resentment from those so targeted, and still a large number of white leftists in a real or imagined friendship with their pretend allies. There is little internal unity in any Western nation these days.

There is open hostility between ethnic groups. In France and Germany, there have been cases of immigrants openly taunting native French or German people about their replacement. This is no conspiracy theory, but a demographic reality. That has not gone down well with some of the native whites who have gradually realised what's been done to their countries.

The leaders of Western nations today are no longer in God Complex mode. They have crossed into the mode of Sorcerer's Apprentice, from the classic tale. That is, the naive young magician who played with the sorcerer's magic and was in a state of panic at the chaos unleashed. Unfortunately, there's no master magician who's going to step in and save us. Chaos is where we live.

What are the chances of achieving peace in our multiracial societies? It's hard to be optimistic. Our leaders, like most elites, live in a privileged bubble far removed from the consequences of the policies they support. Things may have to get a lot worse before they do anything different.

There are perhaps a few steps that would improve the situation.

First, our leaders could show a little humility and admit that they (past and present) got it wrong on multiculturalism. Or at least the way they went about it was wrong. They could stop insulting the white population, and blaming us for the problems they themselves have caused.

A 2024 video made by the British-Australian community even made the - perhaps satirical - suggestion that Australia's main political parties should apologise for inflicting multiculturalism on us. This was in the wake of the Labor party's obsession with apologising to Aboriginals - something they seem eager to do without hesitation.

Of course, the chance of any apology or admission of fault by the government is zero, so this is not a serious suggestion. A more realistic one is my second suggestion - that the whole anti-white, anti-Western messaging should be abandoned. Stop flogging the white guilt agenda and all that goes with it. If they are serious about wanting multiculturalism to work, they should cut out anti-white animosity in all its forms.

Third, get rid of identity politics and all the mental pathologies it entails. Fourth, stop or at least cut, the number of immigrants to Western nations, until the whole attitude has changed.

Was it Deliberate?

Five decades since the multiculturalism experiment launched, Western nations have changed a great deal. They have weakened considerably in terms of unity and social cohesion. If these nations have enemies, they are laughing.

An interesting question is whether this was done deliberately, or simply happened through a series of unplanned, haphazard events.

On the one hand, we should never underestimate the power of short term stupidity to create a long term mess. Naive idealism (the racial experiment) met with short term gain (cheap labour and economic growth) and left wing fanaticism (the anti-white program) to create today's chaotic world.

On the other hand, as mentioned in the last chapter, it is curious the number of ideas and policies that have been promoted in recent times which have in common a negative effect on reproduction and a weakening of national morale. It's interesting that all these policies came into vogue all over the Western world and at much the same time. If you want to be a 'conspiracy theorist' these days, it's really not very hard.

Still, it is possible all this happened by accident. That there was no plan or ill intent behind any of this.

Then again, how would it look any different if there was?

Oh Well, It was Good While it Lasted

What is a modern Anglo to do? Perhaps you have vague memories of a time when your country was different, but those memories should be put aside. The past is a foreign country, they say. Or is it the present? Who knows?

It's still possible to have a good life in our modern cosmopolitan cities. Embrace the moment and be a normie. You can still skate through unscathed, especially in sheltered Australia. You can get through life and have a lot of fun taking in all that exotic food and culture, congratulating yourself on your tolerance, tuning out the anti-white noise, and being blissfully unaware of the bigger picture.

That bigger picture will happen anyway, thanks to the naïve and complacent politicians of a few decades ago and the virtuous whites who've been conned into collaborating in their own extinction. Soon enough, their virtue will fade into history, as ephemeral as all that exotic food they enjoyed. Their descendants won't curse them, and the main reason for that is because most of them will never be born. We must thank Heaven for small mercies.

6

In Praise of December 31st

Before writing this chapter, I'd like to pay my respects to the first inhabitants of this land, the Dinosaurs, who were here millions of years before any humans.

Welcome to Piety

A white female politician recently posted a photo of herself online. In the photo, she's sitting with a male Aboriginal elder. As she listens with rapt attention, there's an ecstatic smile on her face. It's as if she's drinking in his wisdom and at the same time being lifted into a joyful stupor by his ancient spirituality.

In reality, he's probably just an ordinary man in his sixties, who happens to be Indigenous. You can bet that if this female politician was listening to a comparable 'white male elder' of her own tribe, her expression might be one of feminist scorn and eye rolling condescension.

The guy in the photo may be having a secret chuckle. As the author Clive Hamilton said, 'Indigenous people I have spoken with regard with wry amusement the awe in which they are held by woke activists.'

This is part of our epidemic of cringe. Australia was once said to have a 'cultural cringe' due to our excessive deference to England and British culture. There's a new cringe today, often from the same sort of people who complained about the old one. The new cringe is an excessive deference to Aboriginals and Indigenous culture.

Having said that, it's not my intention to disrespect Aboriginals. They deserve respect for themselves, and for living in this country many thousands of years. My intention is to call out the cringy

55

behaviour of white Australians with their excessive bowing and scraping, and the various pieties we are expected to observe.

Take the routine Welcome to Country rituals, or the 'respect for traditional owners' pieties. These are ubiquitous to the point of absurdity. As somebody wrote on Twitter, 'Can someone tell me what the acknowledgement of traditional owners on every fucking email I receive actually achieves?'

It achieves nothing, of course. It's simply a reminder of our Original Sin of stealing Australia from the Aboriginals, for which we must forever apologise. Cringe.

Cringing starts at the top. The prime minister, Anthony Albanese, in one of the many selfies he's put on Twitter, posted one of him sitting in his office. Three flags are on display near his desk. The Indigenous flag sits proudly in the centre spot. The Australian flag has been shunted off to one side. Cringe.

Some people think we should rename our capital cities with their old Aboriginal names. Melbourne can become Naarm and Sydney will be Gadigal. Renaming cities is a great way to show that the colonisers have lost. Cringe.

Growing up in the 1970s and 80s, I remember Australia as a confident, proud, and irreverent place, not given to ideas of guilt or piety about anything. Those who possess these traits are seen as rather deplorable these days, for modern Australia has become a centre of cringe. Righteous 'good-whites' believe in our racial guilt and demand others think the same way.

It's fine to respect other people and cultures. When you over-respect them, or disrespect your own, something has gone awry. If our present view of ourselves involves statue smashing, apologies, hand wringing, and self disempowerment, we need to locate the cause of this mental illness and cure it as soon as possible.

A basic mistake is seeing the founding of your country as a crime, as some kind of mortal sin for which you must do penance. This diseased state of mind seems to have been deliberately induced, for the same playbook has been used in Canada, the USA, and New Zealand. It contains an odd naivety about history (such 'crimes' have gone on since the dawn of time) and about how your submissive stance will be rewarded in the future.

The current chapter will examine some ideas about the origins of modern Australia and how they affect the present. But first, let's deal with another piety, which is the correct name for the people under discussion. I'll be using the terms Aboriginal or Indigenous, rather than First Nations or the unwieldy Aboriginal and Torres Strait Islanders. For those who came in 1788 and their descendants, I'll use Anglos or white Australians. It would be more exact to use Anglo-Celtic, to include all the British and Irish people, but that too is a little longwinded, so I'll use Anglo as shorthand for the lot of them.

The Main Facts

The dispute between Indigenous and non-indigenous Australians is over land, and the ownership and control of this country.

Aboriginals are thought to have lived on this continent for some 65,000 years. They were not one unified people, but a series of many smaller tribes or clans. A map of old Australia shows what looks like hundreds of 'nations.' One book says five-hundred different 'nations.'

In 1788, barely 250 years ago, Britain established a small colony in NSW, in the area that is now Sydney. From this risky and uncertain start, the British colony gradually spread to most of the habitable parts of the country. Five states and two territories were united into a commonwealth in 1901.

The Aboriginals were no longer the dominant people. As the colony grew, there was some violent conflict during the 'frontier wars' in which many were killed. Some also died from diseases unintentionally brought by the British. However, it was not all conflict. There was some peace and cooperation, and a number of

Indigenous people willingly joined the new society. There were attempts by the government to help Aboriginals, although some are now seen as abuses.

Modern Australia was an Anglo nation, mainly British and Irish, with some ethnic minorities as well. A post-war wave of immigration saw many European migrants arrive. The long standing White Australia policy was an attempt to keep the population mostly white. It began to be disbanded in the 1960s and was finally abandoned in 1973 under the Whitlam Labor government.

The policy of multiculturalism was adopted. Migration of Asians and people from Muslim countries led to Australia becoming an ethnically diverse multicultural society, especially after the 1970s.

At the time of writing, 2025, Anglo-Celts still form the largest single ethnic group, although with a far smaller percentage than a few decades ago. Many other ethnic groups are now part of the mix, and Aboriginals are estimated at roughly 3% of the population.

The Correct Response

As the British did displace the Aboriginals as the dominant people of this country, the Aboriginals were entitled to see this as an offence against them. Many of today's white leftists see it as a foundational crime for which we must do penance. If that's a poor response, how *should* we respond?

We should first remember that people have been 'displacing' each other throughout all human history. It's usually on a smaller scale, one tribe displacing another - as the Aboriginal tribes sometimes did to each other. Displacing the people of an entire country is more unusual, but is the same thing on a larger scale.

Stealing land may be deliberate - war as 'organised theft,' as Jacob Bronowski once put it - or incidental, a by-product of one group's effort to expand its territory, as the British did when they formed their new colony in 1788. They didn't see it as theft. They did not set out to make war with the Aboriginals, and were at first ordered to try to get along with them.

As the colony grew, the British must have eventually realised they *had* displaced the Aboriginals and taken control of the country. This was a sort of passive 'conquest' coming from their act of settlement, rather than a deliberate act of war.

So, what is the normal response of a 'conqueror' people to the peoples it has displaced? I'll consider this in terms of tribes rather than countries, for these displacements have mostly happened at the smaller scale. Here is a range of some of the usual options through history when one tribe displaces another - at least the first four. The fifth one is fairly new.

1. Malicious Destruction - Starting at the most brutal end of the scale, in the often regrettable history of our species, one approach to tribal warfare around the world has been to murder or enslave the men, and sexually assault and enslave the women.

2. Aloof Indifference - Once the losing tribe has been vanquished, they are more or less forgotten by the conquering tribe, who take over the contested territory.

3. Co-existence or Absorption - Although the conquering 'tribe' has come out the better, they coexist with the vanquished rather than wiping them out. They may accept them into their own group and assimilate them.

4. Attempts at Peace and Reconciliation - The victors may try to help the displaced people.

5. Guilt-induced Cringing for Social Justice - The victorious tribe feel ashamed of their history. They empower the vanquished and sabotage their own tribe in the name of social justice.

The British settlers spent most of our early history in Australia around stages two and three. They then moved into stage four. Our recent history has been spent in stage five, a phase we should be looking to end.

As for stage one, there were certainly crimes by individuals, and some battles during the 'frontier wars' which some describe as massacres. However, the British never set out to maliciously destroy the Aboriginal people as a whole. While they did displace the Aboriginals in Australia, this was a consequence of settlement rather than an act of war in itself.

While these 'massacres' are not something for the British settlers to be proud of, we should also know that the Indigenous are not blameless in this regard, as Aboriginal tribes sometimes had violent conflicts with each other. As the settlement of Australia is often seen as a moral question, this is all part of the bigger picture.

Who is Guilty?

A reminder is due that we live in the Global Progressive Regime - the GPR - which entails a set of values and a certain way of thinking. The GPR state of mind is anti-national and also anti-Western. It is hostile to 'settler' nations like Australia, New Zealand, the USA, and Canada, and favours the indigenous people of those lands. Yet it is also hostile to the indigenous people of Britain, the settlers' country of origin. From this contradiction, one can easily infer the true targets of GPR hostility.

The GPR has heavily pushed the idea that the founding of these nations was immoral, a matter for guilt and penance. In Australia, we are urged to feel guilt about the British having displaced Aboriginals when they established modern Australia after 1788.

Let's examine this concept further. Should we feel guilty for 'stealing Australia?' In answering this, I'll start by listing the main groups involved.

a) Aboriginals-Past

b) Anglos-Past

c) Aboriginals-Present

d) Anglos-Present

e) Ethnic-Australians

f) GPR Influencers

The act of 'stealing Australia' took place in 1788, more than two hundred years ago. The only people involved were groups a) Aboriginals-Past and b) Anglos-Past. If one is assigning guilt it can only go to Anglos-Past, although many of them - the convicts - had no choice in the matter, having been brought here by force.

As both those groups are long dead, they can no longer be either helped or punished. The focus today is on groups c) Aboriginals-Present and d) Anglos-Present. Attempts are often made to link them to the deceased groups. Aboriginals-Present are said to be still suffering from what was done to Aboriginals-Past, and Anglos-Present are accused of being guilty of the acts of Anglos-Past.

This is the basis of the 'Aboriginal Industry,' a system by which Anglos-Present give lots of assistance through money and social programs to Aboriginals-Present. This system is founded on two main states of mind, first, goodwill to Aboriginals, and second, guilt over having displaced or harmed them.

While the goodwill is genuine, guilt is the real driver here. It is crucial to the whole system. To point out that no present day Anglo was around in 1788 and no present day Aboriginal was displaced is to invite an angry response. The idea of 'intergenerational trauma' is vital to the enterprise, for they have to insist that Aboriginals-

Present are still being harmed today, and Anglos-Present are still responsible for it and guilty of 'living on stolen land.'

However, if that is the case, then what a wonderful boon it is that our multicultural brothers and sisters have arrived to shoulder the load. A trouble shared is a trouble halved. Thank God for group e) Ethnic-Australians. If Anglos-Present are living on stolen land, then so are all the Greek, Italian, Chinese, Thai, African, Jewish, Middle Eastern, etc people who have come to live here.

But that's not how it works. The accusation is aimed only at Anglos-Present. This is quite irrational. None of the ethnic groups settled Australia in 1788, but no present day Anglo did either. Yes, we benefit, but so do the ethnic groups. So, it is one in, all in - or none in. Either all Ethnic-Australians are 'living on stolen land' like the Anglos, or no one is.

The fact it is Anglos alone who are singled out points to the racial nature of the agenda. It would be just as 'rational' to aim the guilt propaganda at ethnic groups, but in GPR thinking, both the Indigenous and multicultural groups are seen as innocent. Guilt propaganda is reserved for Anglos.

Guilt is a tool of coercion. Indeed it has been one of the main tools used to manipulate whites in every Anglo country.

The idea of *inherited* guilt is misplaced. Each person comes into this life with a moral blank slate. However, the Marx-influenced leftists of today like to put individuals into classes and make them share the blame. This is a typical tactic of class smearing in which an entire group is blamed for the actions of one part of that group, even if that part is remote in time or space.

Guilt has its place, but is widely abused to coerce and control people. It can be used on the small scale of private relationships, or far more widely as the basis for class conflicts. Today, it is commonly used by group c) Aboriginals-Present and sometimes group e) Ethnic Australians against group d) Anglos-Present.

I have also listed another one - group f) GPR Influencers, who are only too happy to fan the flames. These are people who, for various reasons, are hostile towards Western nations and want to see them brought down. It may be those who want some kind of Marxist overthrow of society, or outsiders who resent and covet the wealth of Western nations. For whatever reason, they're happy to ferment social discontent.

Of course, none of these groups are monolithic. There's a sharp divide in group d) Anglos-Present into the good-whites and bad-whites. As mentioned in the last chapter, good-whites are those who observe all the racial pieties, buy into the idea of guilt, and always take the side of immigrants or Aboriginals on any racial issue. Bad-whites are those who do not. Good-whites are fond of chastising bad-whites for their moral failings.

Compared to What?

In a sane world Australia would be seen as a great country, but remember we don't live in a sane world, we live in the Global Progressive Regime. A basic GPR stance is the idea that the establishment of Australia in 1788 was a crime. It was an act of theft, whereby the British stole Australia from the Aboriginals, and this spiritual sin can only be absolved by heavy financial assistance and other help, regular apologies, Welcome to Countries, and miscellaneous pieties.

This is the sort of left wing thinking that dominates in the GPR. However, the black American conservative, Thomas Sowell, thinks most arguments of the left fall away if you ask three questions:

1. Compared to what?
2. What hard evidence do you have?
3. At what cost?

It's the first of those questions I'll focus on. 'Compared to what?' is something we should ask in deciding whether the establishment of Australia was a crime.

Indigenous activists want to engage in something they call 'truth telling.' As far as I can tell, this means an airing of grievances in which the activists want to chastise Anglos for stealing this land from them, and for various forms of persecution over the years.

White Australians are supposed to listen contritely, not answer back, and then make amends with yet more apologies, concessions, and billions paid to the Aboriginal Industry as a form of 'reparations.'

For truth telling to work as a form of reconciliation, however, it has to work both ways. It cannot consist of one party simply haranguing the other, who is obliged to cringe in silence. So, I am going to answer back with my own form of truth telling to put another point of view.

First, we can acknowledge that Indigenous people were here for a very long period of time - the current estimate is 65,000 years - and losing this country was for them a tragic and substantial loss. Second, there were many deaths, and some poor treatment of Aboriginals in various ways afterwards.

Aboriginal people are entitled to feel some grievance over these historical events, and have their loss acknowledged. Even so, the events don't exist in isolation from the larger patterns of history. Or if for some people they do, this is largely why the grievances will never heal, and why bamboozled whites can't shake off the ever-present scold and their supposed inferior moral status.

It is here that we need to ask *compared to what*? For example, some Indigenous people seem fixated on the wrongs done to them, and unaware that almost all peoples have suffered such wrongs - and that includes their own nemesis, the British. As the historian, Geoffrey Blainey, wrote:

The loss of their lands, their "dispossession," of course created resentment. But Aboriginal leaders tend to think they were the world's only such sufferers. In fact, the ancestors of most mainstream Australians painfully lost their lands in some faraway era and received no compensation.

Thus in 1066 the Norman Conquest of England and the actual killing or enslavement of so many people, and the raping or castration of others, was probably as devastating as the British conquest of Australia.

The Norman Conquest was nearly a thousand years ago and may seem rather remote, but there have been umpteen uprisings, conflicts, and a couple of world wars since then to inflict suffering on the unfortunate British. However, in terms of being dispossessed of one's land, you don't need to travel into the past at all, you simply have to observe what's happening today.

With the advent of immigration and multiculturalism over recent decades, most of the Anglo nations - Britain, America, Canada, and Australia - are being dispossessed of their countries. It doesn't really matter if such a process is immediate, through armed conquest, or happens slowly over a few decades. The end result is the same.

Australia in 1960 was an Anglo nation. That was the main ethnicity and culture. At the time of writing, in 2025, Australia is no longer an Anglo nation. Anglos are still the largest ethnic group - for now - but Australia is a multicultural nation of many ethnicities. Whether one thinks that is a good or a bad thing, it is indeed so.

In that case, we might observe that the time of Anglo-Australia was extremely brief - perhaps two hundred years, considering it took some time after 1788 for the new colony to rise to any real success. For the sake of argument, one might say Anglo-Australia reigned from, say, 1800 to 2000. Since then, it is increasingly a multi-culti land, not an Anglo one.

In the larger pattern of history, that is a rather brief moment in the sun. To illustrate this, compare it to the reign of the Aboriginals, who had this land for 65,000 years.

Suppose we visualise that 65,000 years in terms of a single calendar year of 365 days. In that comparison, one 'day' equals about 178 years. By the time you reach June 30th, 32,500 years have passed.

If you look at that 65,000 years as beginning on January 1st then the British took possession of this land rather late in the piece. In terms of this calendar year, the Aboriginals had it in January. They had in February. They had it in March, April, and May. Then on into June, July, August, September, October, and November. And it didn't stop there. They had it for almost all of December too. In terms of the analogy, the British arrived at about nightfall on December 30th, enjoyed a brief single day of glory on December 31st, and were then dispossessed by the new multicultural regime.

In light of that, Aboriginals should realise they are not the only ones to have been dispossessed of this land. They don't have to feel sorry for us. Indeed, they may even have a sense of *schadenfreude* at the fate of Anglo-Australia. However, if that is the case, I see no reason we should continue to feel sorry for their loss either, let alone indulge in the breast beating and gnashing of teeth that goes on today.

The Aboriginals had Australia far longer than us. Yes, they were dispossessed, but their corrupt global allies have taken revenge on their behalf, with the cooperation of our dim-witted white leaders. We Anglos are told to accept reality - *this is how it is now* - in the new land of diverse multicultural Australia. Why shouldn't we say the same to the Aboriginals? After all, they had the place 65,000 years, we had it barely 200. Stop complaining.

As for the leftist 'good-whites,' it's time to give the self flagellation a rest. In my analogy of a calendar year, Aboriginals had this land from January 1st up to most of December 30th. And now, having enjoyed one brief day in the sun on December 31st, we are supposed to bow and scrape and apologise because the people who had it from January 1st to December 30th didn't get to have it on 'our day' as well. Empathy's a two way street. I'm not sure why we have to keep crying for the Indigenous. They certainly aren't crying for us.

Compared to what? When it comes to answering that question, we are just getting started, and that will continue in the next chapter.

7

Compared to What?

There's some dispute about how long the Aboriginals have been in Australia - even among themselves. This was summed up by two t-shirts I saw selling at a recent Indigenous market. One t-shirt had the slogan '65,000 YEARS OF SURVIVAL,' while the other said 'SINCE TIME BEGAN.'

The idea that Aboriginal people have been here forever is part of their spiritual concept of the Dreamtime. While the idea of timelessness is an interesting one that requires a different mode of thinking, in a literal sense it is hard to believe Aboriginals were always here. Otherwise, they would have been around not just 65,000 years ago, but more than 100 million years ago during the dinosaur age.

There are perhaps some other motives for believing they were 'always here.' There's a set of guidelines for NSW high school teachers on how to teach Indigenous issues, and it frowns upon the idea of a 65,000 year history because it 'puts a limit on the occupation of Australia and thus tends to lend support to migration theories.'

Well yes, it does, and that raises the inconvenient truth that Aboriginals too were once 'immigrants' or 'settlers' to this land. They did not arise spontaneously from the soil at the dawn of time, but came here like everyone else, albeit a very long time ago. Current speculation is they may have come from Indonesia or India, or some other land to the north.

Therefore the slogan *Always was, Always Will Be Aboriginal Land* cannot be literally true. If the Aboriginals arrived 65,000 years ago, then they either displaced some other people who were already here, or they arrived on a continent inhabited only by animals. If the latter, then whichever species was on top at that time was supplanted by the Aboriginals. Even if they lived at the same time as the now extinct 'mega fauna,' their hunting skills would have made them the most dangerous predator.

You have to admire the Aboriginals for their survival in having lasted so long. To do so, they had to be tough, and develop an intimate understanding of the environment and the seasons. Aboriginals do claim a special relationship with Australia's natural environment. Having survived here for sixty-five millennia, there's no doubt some truth to it.

And then, finally, someone else came. It was the British, but if not them it would eventually have been someone else. It was always going to happen, once the age of technology and exploration began.

This point seems to be ignored, perhaps deliberately. Aboriginals leaders fixate on the great sin committed against them by the British, and seem to think if the British had never come, this country would still be theirs. But how could this huge continent with its natural resources and pleasant coastal climates have been ignored once technology made overseas travel so much easier than before?

Most wars or tribal conflicts are over land and resources. Whatever the rights and wrongs of that, that's how people have operated from the beginning. The Aboriginals were no exception and tribes sometimes fought each other for the possession of land, or as payback for past offences.

It is farfetched to imagine that if the British had not come in 1788, this country would still be ruled by Aboriginals. So in evaluating the alleged sinfulness of Australia's founding, we should again ask, *compared to what?*

Would the Indigenous be better off if Australia had been settled by the French, the Dutch, or some other European power. By the Russians seeking a more temperate climate? How about the Chinese or Japanese?

Perhaps the British were the least-worst option. Apart from anything else, it is their descendants who are now listening to Welcome to Country all over the place, and giving billions in guilt money to the Aboriginal Industry. Alternative settlers may not have done that. In that case, perhaps we should stop the blame-cringe cycle that's all so tiresome today.

One basic difference between the two cultures that clashed in 1788 was that Aboriginals lived in a timeless society which seems to have stayed the same for 65,000 years, whereas the British civilisation changed dramatically over a few hundred years. This was mainly through the technological advances, which of course brought both good and bad results.

Why did the Indigenous not develop such technology over 65,000 years? Perhaps they had no wish to change and were content to stay the same forever. Still, they were eventually replaced by a people who *did* change. Most of today's Indigenous use that technology. Would they willingly give it all up?

When the Indigenous arrived 65,000 years ago, they became the dominant force on this land, replacing whoever was the top species before them. After this extremely long reign, the British came and displaced them. Aboriginal activists today still complain bitterly about this. They see the creation of modern Australia as a crime, an invasion, a mortal sin. Many white leftists seem to agree.

If you follow this line of thinking through, modern Australia is illegitimate and should not really be here at all. As a white Australian myself, I reject this notion, and offer the view that the Anglo-Australia that existed in that brief window of time - December 31st in my analogy - was a legitimate country, well worthy of existence. Despite what the eternal whiners of the left would have you believe, in some ways it was a great country. In some regards, it was preferable to the confused, cringing, and conflicted Australia of today.

Compared to What?

One of Thomas Sowell's three questions against leftist doctrine was *compared to what?* Another was *at what cost?* The 'cost' of the alternate history of the British not coming here is very simple: modern Australia would never have existed. In my view, that's a hell of a cost.

It also leads to the absurd realisation that if modern Australia had never begun, neither the author nor many of the readers of this book would have existed either. Thus, in a bizarre fashion, today's white leftists crying about invasion are also protesting their own existence.

Compared to what now comes to its most direct application, and that is in comparing the intrinsic worth of modern Anglo - or multicultural - Australia of today with the pre-1788 Indigenous Australia of the previous 65,000 years. If it's a question of which has the right to be, this becomes a controversial but unavoidable idea. If the Indigenous are saying they should have been left alone, modern Australians are implicitly saying *our Australia is just as important as yours*. The comparison is inevitable.

A diplomatic answer would be that both societies were great in their own way, but so different you can't compare them. You could even say an Indigenous person might prefer the world of pre-1788, while an Anglo-Australian would prefer modern Australia.

This is a diplomatic but weak answer. As the legitimacy of modern Australia is the topic at hand, we have to ask if it was a good thing that Western civilisation came to this land in 1788, or whether it should have remained an Aboriginal country.

It is hard to evaluate the long history of Aboriginals for two main reasons. First, as it seems to be a 'timeless' culture, it stayed much the same for 65,000 years. Second, the Aboriginals never developed a written language, so historical events weren't written down and were simply passed down orally through stories or artistic forms.

We cannot, in the usual fashion, say that a particular event happened in 30,000 BCE, or that a key innovation occurred in the 45ᵗʰ century BCE. What actually happened in those 65,000 years? Can we ever know, and if we don't know, must we assume it was somehow fantastic? Or should we at least retain an agnostic silence about it?

The Teacher Guidelines mentioned earlier suggest it is inappropriate or even offensive to think of Aboriginal society as less advanced than Western ones, as this is 'based on the "progress" model of history, which many people now question.'

It's true technology can be a mixed blessing, and advanced technological societies may burn out quicker, even destroy themselves. It's possible that simpler, nature-attuned societies *might* be happier in some ways, but as a Westerner I am naturally going to view these societies through a Western lens.

With that state of mind, I am bound to see the lack of technology and "progress" as exactly that - a lack. I'm going to wonder what, in 65,000 years, the Indigenous produced in terms of scientific discoveries, technology, agriculture, written language, architecture, cities, and so on.

Some might answer that the Indigenous had no interest in such things, were quite content as they were, and in some ways were better off and happier than many Westerners.

That is a matter for speculation, and often gets caught up in romanticised anti-Western beliefs. However, I'm prepared to be agnostic and concede at least the possibility that in some odd, unknowable sense, Indigenous society was somehow better, had an elevated connection to Nature, and all the rest of it.

Having said that, I prefer the notion of Western society, something I know and value. As I have never lived in the Indigenous way, this can't be a fully informed choice, but that is inevitable.

Let's speculate further. How many people living today - Anglo, Aboriginal, or multicultural - would voluntarily return to a fully Indigenous way of life, given the chance? Perhaps an experiment could be run in one of those reality TV shows, in which twenty or so moderns were taken to live in the old pre-1788 ways for a year. At the end of that year, they could be asked if they'd like to remain in that mode of life, or return to contemporary ways.

The objection will be it's impossible to contrive those conditions for just a year, one would have to be born into it. An Anglo or multicultural person could not hope to understand. Then what of Indigenous people themselves, those who have been brought up in the modern world. They use our technology - the phones, computers, cars, electric guitars, kitchen appliances, electricity itself, and so on. Given the chance, would they give it all up and return to a pre-1788 way of life?

Maybe they would. Perhaps the pre-1788 Indigenous way of life really is superior to ours. Perhaps their pantheistic oneness with nature is an elevated state of being far beyond our own.

But if today's Aboriginals *wouldn't* go back, and actually prefer our technological world, then the endless anger over 'colonisation' is surely wearing a little thin.

The Edenist and the 'Noble Savage'

Some see the British settlement of Australia as an immoral act. Whether or not it was, it was inevitable that a more technological group was going to do it. An academic might say the idea of people being more or less advanced is a Western concept of progress. However, the fact is a people in stasis like the Aboriginals were always going to be displaced, or at least strongly affected, by a more technologically advanced group.

While the British may have had superior technology, some people have the notion that Aboriginals were superior morally or spiritually, and are perhaps still superior now.

In my view, no one group of people is innately superior spiritually to any other. This is one area where the idea of equality does hold. Europeans are neither more nor less spiritual than Aboriginals. Some suggest that Aboriginals have a special kinship with nature. They may have a special relationship to Australia, having lived here so long, but I don't see why they have any intrinsically greater connection to nature itself.

The rumours of a special, even mystical, connection to nature are hard to evaluate. You hear of their apparent veneration of the environment, concern for the balance of nature, and even the suggestion that if they hunted and killed animals it was done in some kind of ritualistic or spiritual manner.

I'm willing to be persuaded of this through more explanation, but must in the meantime remain skeptical. It seems an attempt to elevate Aboriginals onto a higher moral plane than all other humans. Killing is killing. Aboriginals were the dominant species here for all those years. Although their diet included plants, they were not vegetarians. They were skilled hunters and must have been a feared predator for many animal species. When you hear about Indigenous hunting methods of herding kangaroos into spots from which they can't escape, spearing eels, taking ants from their nests in trees, or poisoning the water to kill fish, it seems Aboriginals are just another group of carnivorous humans like everyone else.

As for whether they are more moral, for comparison, take the two main moral crimes attributed to the British - theft and murder. The British are accused of stealing Australia, and while that is more or less true, Aboriginals are not innocent of land theft themselves. Indigenous tribes sometimes stole land from one another. The Goonyandi people, for example, were displaced from their land by the Ngainan, who were part of the Walmadjari people. In 1875, the Southern Arrente in Central Australia were violently attacked by the Matuntara people and displaced from their land. So, while the British did it on a larger scale, they were not the first people on this continent to steal land.

Then we come to the matter of violence. The idea of the 'Noble Savage' has been around since at least Rousseau in the eighteenth century. This is a notion held by over-idealistic white people who have a critical view of their own society and like to see non-Western people as better. They imagine them as purer, more spiritual and in tune with nature, less tainted by civilisation, and largely free of human failings. *We're the real savages*, they conclude, with a sort of pious self criticism.

This is often a complete fantasy. The American Indians, for example, have been seen in this light, as gentle custodians of nature. They may have been so at times, but they also had the capacity for vicious, sadistic treatment of their enemies during and after battles, in both the American frontier wars and inter-tribal wars long before that.

Views of the Indigenous people of Australia may also be over idealised. An account on the Aboriginal Heritage Office website, for instance, depicts an idyllic pre-1788 lifestyle in which people lived in harmony with nature, worked just a few hours each day, and had ample time left to develop a rich culture of dance, art, and storytelling. This was in describing those living in the area which would become Sydney. In reading this sort of thing, one is tempted to exclaim *Oh my, 'tis like Eden itself!*

Then, we are told, the British came and 'brought armed conflict and a lack of understanding' as well as some disease. It's true about the disease, but as for the armed conflict, there was plenty of that before the British ever arrived.

It is possible that there might have been both an idyllic, sort of permanent holiday lifestyle and *also* armed conflict. This paradox was noted with some surprise by Edward Stone Porter, a British man who was assigned to help Aboriginals and held a sympathetic view of them. He was:

...a Methodist lay preacher who was sent to Port Phillip from London to serve as one of four assistant protector of Aboriginals. He embraced the role with gusto and much sympathy, studying Aboriginal languages and their traditional way of life. He famously remarked 'On the whole their way of life was a satisfying one, and could have been almost idyllic – but for their frequent fighting and the persistent fear of revenge.' Parker goes on to quote a well-informed Aboriginal man who argued that before the British arrived 'the country was strewed with bones, and were always at war.' Indeed 'whole tribes have been exterminated by sudden attacks or nocturnal surprises.' While Parker strongly denounced the conflict between settlers and Aboriginals, he identified that the wars between tribes were more destructive.

There is also the account by William Buckley, a white convict who escaped and lived with the Wallarranga tribe for several decades. Buckley said that he was, on the whole, treated kindly by these people and he had some affection for them. At the same time, they seemed given to petty feuds and revenge killing from time to time. At various points in his memoir, Buckley mentions violent incidents, and inter-tribal battles.

This is not to say that the British and other whites were superior, for they too were often violent, warlike, and committed atrocities. That is not denied, but the point is that we should dispense with the idea Indigenous people are above such actions or exist on some higher moral plane. They have the same capacity for violence as anyone else.

One can even find clues in a Dreamtime story, like the one about the origin of the echidna. Humans often became animals in these tales. In the story, an Aboriginal tribe was going through hard times with everyone becoming thinner and thinner - all except for one old man. Suspicious, the men of the tribe followed the old man one night and learned that he was hoarding food for himself. Enraged, they gave him a beating, broke his legs, and threw their spears at him. He crawled away on broken legs, the spears having turned into spikes, and that's how the echidna was created.

There's an alternate version of this story, different in the details, but also involving the spears into spikes transformation. It's an interesting story, even a moral parable, but also a violent one. This is not a culture to which violence is foreign or unusual.

If Indigenous people are innately gentler and more moral than whites, how does one explain the reported abuses against women and children in remote communities today? Some activists have tried to explain it by blaming it on the after effects of colonisation, intergenerational trauma, white privilege, and so on.

In other words, any violence from Aboriginals today is not their fault, it is the fault of the British from a couple of centuries ago, or even of Anglo-Australians today. Whites who believe this have a naïve and over-idealistic view of the past. There are numerous accounts suggesting violence against women was, to whatever extent, part of tribal life well before the British came. Some early settlers and explorers report seeing Indigenous women with facial wounds and bodily scars, inflicted upon them by some within the tribe. If this was done by their own husbands, as some reports suggest, it amounts to the domestic violence so condemned by feminists today but often, it seems, assumed not to exist in 'peaceful' Indigenous life.

Then, when it came to inter-tribal battles, Buckley reports that women and children sometimes met violent deaths. Therefore the idea that pre-1788 Indigenous life was a paradise, and violence a novelty brought by the British, is a complete myth.

When it comes to present day domestic violence against Aboriginal women, the attempt to blame this on the British should not be accepted. Even if one accepts the idea the 1788 settlement was a crime, it doesn't amount to a moral blank cheque which exonerates people from their own actions. Neither can the moral responsibility for those actions be passed on to those white people living today who had nothing to do with the original settlement.

In conclusion, an over idealised concept of Indigenous people is a mistake. The Indigenous have the same capacity for good and evil as any other human, and certainly the capacity for violence. They are not on a higher moral plane to which we must defer. We may well respect them as equals, but shouldn't buy into the notion they are our superiors.

They do also know how to hold a grudge. It's reported that many acts of inter-tribal violence were payback for past offences. In William Buckley's book, there are numerous accounts of inter-tribal feuds over one offence or another, often involving women. In one such case, a man went to the campsite of another tribe and speared to death a man who lay sleeping beside his family. This was because the murdered man had promised his daughter to the murderer, but then given her to someone else. This violent act in turn set off fears of further payback.

Buckley lived with these people for three decades and noted that they treated him well and kindly, but they also had this capacity to hold a grudge and act on it.

Another incident is perhaps more pertinent to our own times. Buckley describes one case where a dispute arose over a woman taken by a rival tribe. This led to another murder, which provoked first grief, then intense anger. The wronged party set out in search of revenge. Buckley writes:

> A short time after this affair we shifted our quarters,
> and, when on a hunting excursion, accidentally fell in
> with the tribe to which he (the murderer) belonged,

and a very desperate fight ensued. As is the case with them in such matters, when the parents cannot be punished for any wrong done, they inflict it upon the offspring. So now, the savages having got hold of a child of about four years of age, which this man had had by the young woman before referred to, they immediately knocked it on the head, and having destroyed it, they killed the murderer's brother, also spearing his mother through the thigh, and wounding at the same time several others, so that vengeance was heaped upon him and his tribe in a most dreadful manner.

The most relevant passage here is the sentence: 'As is the case with them in such matters, when the parents cannot be punished for any wrong done, they inflict it upon the offspring.'

Having seen that the Indigenous clearly know how to hold a grudge and understand the notion of payback, one wonders how today's Aboriginals view Anglo-Australians. Then again, it is obvious that at least *some* of them hold on to bitter grievances about colonisation. It's too late to punish James Cook, Arthur Phillip, and the early British settlers, but perhaps they can 'inflict it upon the offspring,' or in this case the descendnts, of those white settlers from the past.

And that brings us to the Voice to Parliament referendum of 2023.

8

The Eternal Voice

Most Anglo-Australians have nothing against Aboriginal people, and want them to do well. Most also want an end to racial conflict between these two groups. It is achievable, but not under the current system of Aboriginal grievance and Anglo apology. In this chapter, I'll speculate on how we might move closer to real reconciliation.

This will involve what some Aboriginal activists like to call 'truth telling.' The impression one gets is the only truth telling they're interested in is a list of grievances, to which Anglos are supposed to listen with bowed heads - but for truth telling to work, it should go both ways.

The Voice to Parliament

A major conflict happened in 2023. The Labor party proposed an Indigenous 'Voice to Parliament.' This was to be a new governing body advising on Aboriginal issues. The 'Voice' would become a permanent fixture of parliament, unable to be removed. Because of that, the question had to be put to a national referendum, in which all citizens had to vote either Yes or No. Voting Yes meant you agreed to the Voice to Parliament, and voting No meant you weren't convinced it was a good idea or that it should be enshrined for evermore.

The Voice was championed by prime minister, Anthony Albanese. At the start of the campaign, Albanese said it would be a unifying moment, something to bring Australians from all walks of life together in voting Yes. It's hard to know if he was serious, or if this was some kind of optimistic bluff. To anyone paying attention to world trends in racial politics, what followed was predictable. The Voice to Parliament debate turned into a twelve month racial brawl, with bitter animosity raging across media and social media on a daily basis.

Much of the anger was between good-whites and bad-whites. As mentioned, good-whites are leftists who observe all the racial pieties and believe in historical white guilt, but bad-whites do not. Far from being a unifying moment, the Voice debate brought this schism to the fore. Good-whites took to chastising bad-whites who expressed any doubt about the Voice. Never before had there been so much moral grandstanding on display, and it seemed to drag on forever.

As for the Voice itself, a few basic points come to mind. First, the idea of having a 'voice in parliament' would have many Anglo-Australians scratching their heads. Just as in Britain, Canada, and the USA, Anglos have watched various reforms take place against their own interests, with the secret coup of multiculturalism as the main example. Anglos are entitled to feel there is not much of a 'voice' representing their interests, and in Australia, Anthony Albanese's least of all.

Albanese seemed to check most of the boxes of the globalist politician: gynocentrism, a gung ho approach to immigration, the performance of racial pieties, and many more. In his Australia Day speech of 2024, he mentioned Aboriginals and immigrants but said not one word to acknowledge the Anglo settlers who founded modern Australia in 1788. This is textbook globalism, with its implicit anti-white bias.

Albanese once described the National Sorry Day of 2008 as his proudest moment in politics. Strictly speaking, this was an apology for the 'stolen generations' issue, but it's easy to see it as buying into a broader sense of repentance. It is an odd thing to be proud of being sorry. You wouldn't mind, say, if he felt *satisfied that honour had been done*, but he was not only proud, it was his *proudest moment in politics*.

This shows he had bought into the whole GPR program of guilt and repentance. Now he was extending that to something with real world consequences - putting the Voice to Parliament in the constitution.

For various reasons, many white leftists feel guilty about Aboriginals. This seems to be less about the 'stolen generations' than about stolen land. Indigenous activists also make stolen land the main grievance, with their *always was, always will be* mantra. Therefore the real point of contention will always be ownership of the land.

Anglos did replace Aboriginals as the dominant people in this country. Should we feel *sorry* about this? While there are *some* reasons to be sorry about displacing the Aboriginals, there are plenty of other reasons not to be. A person of good sense would explore them, and a leader with backbone would state them publicly. Now, fifteen years after the first Sorry Day, Albanese was pushing the Voice to Parliament. In so doing, he seemed to be siding with Aboriginals against the Anglo-European people to whom he belongs. Albanese didn't acknowledge any risk for Anglos in this matter. He seemed unaware of current racial politics and the precarious position of whites in the modern world. In other words he was a standard GPR leader collaborating with the globalist program.

Some things didn't add up. We were told the Voice to Parliament was 'simply an advisory body' and also that it was *urgently needed* to solve Indigenous problems. If it was urgent, an advisory body could have been set up as soon as Albanese's government came to power. Instead, they let the referendum drag on for a year in the hope the Voice could be permanently placed in the constitution. That suggests the main priority of the Voice was for the Aboriginal lobby to gain power, and solving 'urgent' Indigenous problems was a distant second.

While having no real idea how the Voice would work, or if it would work at all, Australians were asked to commit to it forever. Once the Voice was in the constitution, it could never be removed. Although no one could possibly predict the consequences of this mysterious Voice to Parliament, the government asked us to take a leap of faith that it would all work out swimmingly. Unfortunately, many people had lost faith in the government a long time ago.

The notion of permanence was a major red flag, especially as we had no idea how the Voice would work. It was like agreeing to a marriage with no option of divorce. To add to the absurdity, there were grounds to suspect the person proposing marriage had cause to hate and resent us. Only a fool would agree to that.

After a nasty twelve month racial brawl, Australia eventually voted No to the Voice to Parliament. There were many reasons the No vote won, and one of the most basic was a suspicion of the hostile intent behind the Voice. In my view, this suspicion was well justified.

The Voice to Parliament was based on a document, devised by Indigenous activists, called the Uluru Statement From the Heart. The historian, Geoffrey Blainey, made the following comment:

> The Uluru statement is militant. It offers no sentence
> of respect or gratitude to the Australian people. Yet it
> is hailed by Albanese as warm hearted and generous.
> He even announced in a memorial lecture in Adelaide
> recently that it was an invitation extended "to every
> single Australian in love and grace and patience".

It was never clear what Australians were being invited to, but an invitation given 'in love and grace and patience' sounds rather condescending.

How could Blainey and Albanese have had such different interpretations of the Uluru Statement? There's a simple explanation - Blainey had actually read it. To clarify, there are two 'versions' of the Uluru Statement. Version One is a fairly innocuous single page of just 443 words. It is often printed as a pretty poster bordered by Indigenous art, and stuck on the walls of primary schools. Version Two is twenty-six pages of printed text and contains the 'militant' content. It's partly a statement of grievance.

When asked about this, Albanese denied that there *was* a longer version. He derided the idea of the longer version as a conspiracy theory, and dismissed the other twenty-five pages as mere background notes from meetings. When asked what he thought of those other twenty-five pages, he admitted to never having read them.

This was extraordinary. Here was the man championing the Voice to Parliament who had on the night of his election said, 'On behalf of the Australian Labor Party, I commit to the Uluru Statement from the Heart in full.' Now we learned that his concept of the 'full' Uluru Statement was the pretty one page poster that's stuck on the walls of primary schools. And *this* was the depth of knowledge on which we were asked to take a leap of faith and vote in the Voice for all eternity !

It was easy enough to claim, on a technicality, that the Uluru Statement was only that first page. Some journalists did take that line, pretending the other twenty-five pages were irrelevant. Still, what did they suppose those pages were about? The collected works of Jane Austen? The latest theories in quantum physics?

Of course, they were directly related to the Voice to Parliament. They gave both the greater context and the fine print of the detail. You can say the Uluru Statement was only one page if you like, but it is wilfully obtuse to claim the other pages were irrelevant.

As mentioned, there were many reasons Australia voted No to the Voice to Parliament. Two of the most basic, however, weren't much discussed. First, despite the activists' claim to good will, many people suspected a hostile intent behind the Voice. Second, the No vote was a rejection of the whole premise of Aboriginal grievance and Anglo guilt, in which many Yes activists seemed to believe. Even after the vote had failed, a well known journalist was chastising No voters for failing to right the 'foundational wrong' that occurred when Australia was settled. But this is largely what No voters were rejecting - the idea that the creation of Australia in 1788 was a foundational wrong.

To repeat, most Anglo-Australians want Aboriginals to do well. They may have voted Yes to the Voice purely on that basis, if they'd not already been given so many reasons not to. It is the context that matters here. Albanese and the activists seemed to think they could present the Voice as a single issue without context, as if we were deaf, blind, and stupid, or had no memory of anything that had happened in the last few years as part of the anti-white zeitgeist. Well, here are some of the things I remember:

1. The statue smashing and three months of Black Lives Matter rioting in 2020.
2. Attacks on the moral worth of all Anglo nations through pushing ideas of historical guilt.
3. The infliction of mass immigration and multiculturalism on those nations, two policies that were never voted for.
4. Critical Race Theory as an attempt to blame all racial problems on white people and 'whiteness.'
5. DEI principles and identity politics.
6. The BBC's bizarre attempt to rewrite Britain's racial history.
7. Four years of hyperbolic panic about the Trump presidency and so called 'white supremacy.'
8. A general culture of complaint and victim ideology.
9. A general obsession with race and other 'social justice' issues, and the infiltration of leftist ideology into almost all our social institutions.

10. A partial and biased racial interpretation of the history of slavery, and demands for reparations by racial activists.
11. Rising left wing authoritarianism, and the increase of censorship.

In the context of all that, we were supposed to believe the Voice to Parliament was a harmless minor reform with nothing but good intentions behind it. They really must think we are stupid.

One of the authors of the book *Anglophobia*, Frank Salter, gave a series of talks on the Voice, and stressed the importance of the bigger picture.

> Context is important. Anglo-Australians who are alert to the people's needs might look favourably on an Indigenous Voice to Parliament if Australia had a manageable and stable level of ethnic diversity. If Anglo-Australians felt confident as the undisputed majority founding culture, if they were not being rapidly displaced from that status by government immigration policy. If they retained democratic control of the commonwealth ethnic policy. If their children were not being indoctrinated in schools against their own people. If they were able to express their ethnic interests without being persecuted by the mainstream media or by United Nations-mandated human rights agencies. If large swathes of land had not been alienated to Indigenous sovereignty far beyond the high court's Mabo decision. And of special relevance here, if the Indigenous rights movement was mostly a loyal partner of the Anglo nation, or if the radical wing of that movement had not allied itself with the Anglo-hating multicultural left.

However, none of these conditions apply. The reality is very different. The demand for an Indigenous voice is being made at a time when Anglo-Australia is under siege, when we have been marginalised, defamed, and hounded in the country our ancestors built.

Being targeted by the state apparatus is not unusual globally. State sponsored persecution of ethnicities and religions frequently occurs in diverse societies. Ethnic competition is a major cause of conflict and poverty around the world. Australia is in a better condition because though conflict has been on the rise since its traditional immigration policy was abandoned around 1970, the country is still wealthy. It is in this context that the likely operation of an Indigenous Voice must be evaluated.

This was the larger context in which the Voice to Parliament was proposed. Many of the Yes advocates condemned people for voting No, but I never saw any Yes advocates mention the anti-white context as a legitimate reason for people to be skeptical.

The Eternal Nagging Voice

It's easy to see the Voice to Parliament as a turning point in Anglo-Aboriginal relations, and not in a good way. It seemed to be the culmination of the whole paradigm of Anglo guilt and Aboriginal grievance. The most strident white Yes supporters were the ones most convinced of our historical guilt, and also the most critical of No voters who failed to fall into line.

Meanwhile, some Yes activists assured us the Voice wouldn't even affect Anglos, or if it did, only for the better - but talk is cheap. Be fooled in haste, repent forever. White Australians had every reason to be suspicious. After all, one of the items on the agenda was 'truth telling,' an inevitable one sided laundry list of grievances and demands. Also, we had only to recall two of the most popular phrases - *Sovereignty was never ceded* and *Always was, Always Will be Aboriginal Land* to be skeptical of the goodwill of the Yes camp.

One of the main campaigners *against* the Voice was the Indigenous senator, Jacinta Price. She rejected the victim mentality many activists seem to hold. At a key point in the campaign, Price caused a furore by denying there were ongoing ill effects of colonisation for Aboriginals. She also said there were positive effects.

This led to howls of outrage from leftists. This is because the whole Aboriginal Industry is based on the idea of the wickedness of colonisation, the sin done to Aboriginals in 1788, and the damage since. Every current Indigenous problem - lower standards of education, health, and life expectancy, higher levels of violence and jail time - is blamed on the settlement of Australia by the British.

Price's comments were given in a speech to the National Press Club, but during the Q and A period, not the speech itself. She also said, 'If we keep telling Aboriginal people that they are victims, we are effectively removing their agency and then giving them the expectation that someone else is responsible for their lives.'

This is mostly true, but didn't go down well with leftists who prefer to see people as the victims of systemic oppression.

As for Price's views on colonisation, they were pure heresy. Still, her off the cuff remarks may have been taken too literally. This is just my speculation, but perhaps she might revise her answer a little. Yes, there are *some* ongoing negative effects of colonisation, but we're bored with hearing only about them and nothing about the positive effects, and we're also bored with the whole victim mentality.

One activist wrote an angry article in response to Price's remarks. He said a key part of the Voice's No campaign was based on denying the existence of 'intergenerational trauma.' He went on to mention the stolen generation, stolen land, Aboriginal deaths in custody, suicide rates, and the rest of the usual complaints.

Remember, if the Voice had been approved, it would have been permanent. The Eternal Voice. Let us suppose that the Voice would be similar in tone to the way activists so often speak: angry, blaming, resentful, and demanding.

Now, imagine such a voice nagging you for all eternity about stolen land, intergenerational trauma, and everything you owe in compensation. An eternity of nagging, complaining, and 'truth telling.' Australia was right to reject this unappealing prospect.

'Intergenerational trauma' does exist, but many of us are tired of the monotonous beating of this drum. There seems to be nothing but complaints about colonisation, and never a mention of its benefits. For example, the activist mentioned is a successful writer and broadcaster. He's presenting his views in the 'coloniser' language, English, on the radio and in printed form over the internet, both of which were invented by the colonising culture. Is there ever a word of thanks for that among all the complaints?

This activist also seemed affronted by Jacinta Price's reference to her Irish side (her mother is Aboriginal, her father Anglo-Celtic) and Price's humorous remark that she must be 'doubly traumatised' due to being half convict, as a result of the trauma suffered by white convicts. He admits there was some convict trauma, but says it wasn't as bad as the Aboriginals' because convicts who finished their sentence were given land grants and were able to become members of the colony and build wealth.

It is strange to think someone would begrudge a convict's rise in fortunes, considering what they had gone through. Having spent time in an 18th century British prison, survived a hellish eight month sea voyage to Australia, then endured seven or more years of hard labour in the new colony, one might even be pleased at the convict's chance for a new life and some happiness. On the Second Fleet, for example, over three hundred convicts died during the voyage. However, the author can't see past his outrage that Aboriginals of the time weren't also given land and the chance to build wealth in the new Australia. While it's true the Indigenous did miss out on the chance, we might recall they had the run of that land for the previous 65,000 years.

As for the settler government, *of course* they were going to give out land. They were trying to build the new settlement from its modest beginnings, and naturally they were going to favour their own people. However, even if there was some harm done by the government, one might think the many billions of dollars since given to the Aboriginal Industry has helped to make amends. On top of this, as Blainey has noted about Aboriginal campaigners for the Voice to Parliament:

> Meanwhile, their cry of "powerlessness" is a kind of crocodile tear. In the past half-century Aboriginal groups have been handsomely recognised by their acquisition – under the Fraser and Keating governments – of ownership or certain rights and interests in 55 per cent of the Australian land mass. Few Australian voters know this fact. It constitutes one of the largest peaceful transfers of land in the history of the modern world.

To repeat, intergenerational trauma does exist, but some activists give the impression they don't realise any other racial group has ever suffered. If intergenerational trauma is all powerful, how did the Chinese come back from losing millions of lives during the famine of 1958-62? How could the Japanese return from having two cities destroyed by nuclear bombs? How did the Jews recover from World War Two, or the Germans from the horrors they also suffered at the end of that war? How did Europe survive the huge number of plague deaths in the Middle Ages, or Russians the millions killed under the Soviet regime?

So in terms of 'intergenerational trauma,' we aren't saying it's not real, only that you don't have a monopoly on it.

Some More Truth Telling

Aboriginals can tell their version of the truth if they like, but this should be a two way process. Here I'll reprise some of the truths given earlier, as I see them.

Most people would agree the Aboriginals' loss of this land after 1788 was a tragedy for them and that they suffered some bad treatment afterwards. But the people involved in those events are long dead and those alive today are not responsible for them.

Those who insist today's whites *are* responsible for their ancestors' deeds may, if they wish, take a gleeful satisfaction in the fact that those whites have been dispossessed in turn by the global multicultural coup. However, many of those whites are no longer going to buy into the blame-guilt cycle pushed by activists.

The idea that whites are forever to blame for Aboriginal problems should be abandoned. Using colonisation as the endless excuse helps no one. Far better to take responsibility for their own problems.

One of the pieties white Australians are expected to observe is the idea that the Indigenous are somehow superior to us. It can't be a technological superiority, so it must be moral or spiritual. The spiritual superiority is either innate, or a saintliness conferred by their victimhood at the hands of the British.

This too is an illusion. Aboriginals are neither better nor worse than us. They may complain about the British theft of their land, but Aboriginal tribes fought with, killed, and dispossessed each other long before the British ever arrived.

The British did eventually come, but if they had not, some other technological society would have come instead.

For all the endless complaints about colonisation, the truth few activists admit is that many of them also benefitted from it. It's even been said that the most disadvantaged Indigenous people today are 'the least colonised.' Plenty of the leading Yes campaigners for the Voice to Parliament have done well for themselves. Still, all we hear are complaints.

Many white Australians do feel guilty about the founding of this country in 1788, and feel empathy for Aboriginals and their problems. This appears to be a one way street. One rarely sees any empathy from Aboriginal activists for Anglos. This may be due to their conviction that whites wronged them and are always better off, so deserve no empathy at all.

If that's how they really think, this one sided relationship should end. In a previous chapter, I compared the time span of human habitation of this country to a single year. So, 65,000 years laid out over a calendar year. In that comparison, Aboriginals possessed this land from January 1st through to late on December 30th, before Anglo-Australians enjoyed a brief moment in the sun on December 31st.

Now the people who had the place for 364 days are moaning because they didn't have it on the 365th as well.

In the interests of truth telling, or at least inquiring into the truth, here are a few questions one might ask Aboriginal activists.

1.   Do they think that if the British had never come, Australia would still be as it was in 1788? How could that be? Or if colonisation was inevitable, who would have been better colonisers than the British?

2.   Why did the Aboriginals not form a country-wide alliance able to repel invaders, and specifically that invading British force of just 1500 people (at least half of whom - the

convicts - must have arrived in a very weakened state)? It's not as if warfare was foreign to the Indigenous. Why did they not develop - in 65,000 years - a technology strong enough to repel the invading British?

3. If they condemn the British for dispossessing them, or killing them during the 'frontier wars,' what of their own pre-1788 history of dispossessing and killing each other through tribal conflict?

4. Why is their anger reserved only for today's Anglos, rather than all the other ethnic Australians living here under multiculturalism? We're all 'living on stolen land.'

5. Aboriginals had this country for 65,000 years. Anglo-Australians had it for only about 200 before it was turned into a diverse multicultural nation. As we too have now been dispossessed, do they feel any sympathy for us? If not, why should we feel any sympathy for them?

6. On a similar theme, do they feel any sympathy for the Indigenous Britons now being displaced from their homelands by the flood of immigrants moving there?

7. Why do they always give blame for the harms of colonisation and never thanks for its benefits? If they believe there are no benefits to colonisation, should they stop using phones, computers, electricity, and other types of Western technology?

8. If the Uluru Statement was based mainly on grievance, why should non-Aboriginals support it? And if they think they're the only true owners of this land, why should non-Aboriginals support that concept of Australia?

A Small Chance of Reconciliation

It's possible there will never be full reconciliation between Aboriginals and Anglos, but for it to have at least a small chance, here are a few steps to take.

White Australians need to stop apologising for their history and their supposed sins. They need to stop feeling guilty about their own existence. They should also realise guilt is the main way they are being manipulated in the Global Progressive Regime.

White leftists should realise that their bowing and scraping and chastising their fellow whites isn't noble. It's rather pathetic. The sooner they realise it, the better.

As for reconciliation between Anglos and Aboriginals, it can't happen under the current model of grievance-blame-apology. When one side is always blaming and the other apologising, there can be no healthy relationship.

We should first acknowledge that the Aboriginals lived here for 65,000 years and the loss of the land was a substantial one.

Having said that, we assert Anglo-Australia's right to exist. We are proud of it and reject the notion of both historical and inherited guilt.

Aboriginals should also acknowledge that we had the place only 200 years before being dispossessed by multiculturalism. They can see this as payback if they like, but if feel no empathy for our loss, there's no reason we should have any further empathy for theirs.

Aboriginals should admit there have been some positive effects of colonisation and Western civilisation. If they insist there are only harmful effects, no healthy relationship is possible.

Anglos should also be open to learning about Aboriginal history, culture, and knowledge, and this may happen more easily if we move past the age of antagonism.

That concludes the three chapters about the relationship between Aboriginals and Anglo-Australia. Unfortunately the conflict in Australia is just one part of a wider global conflict around race. The next two chapters will look at the way this has played out in America in relation to the Black Lives Matter movement.

9

Kneeling for Equality

2020 was a strange year. There was the Covid pandemic, with its lockdowns, conspiracies, and general confusion. The other big event was the mass hysteria after the death of George Floyd, a black American man who died during a Police arrest in Minneapolis.

The official version of what happened goes something like this. George Floyd was an innocent black American murdered by evil police in a racial hate crime. This was part of a wider pattern of police brutality against black Americans, which in turn showed the deep racial inequality in America today. That inequality is largely due to the legacy of slavery, a heinous social evil suffered only by black people. After Floyd's death, black and white people rose up as one to demand justice. Their righteous rage justified protests and statue-smashing all around the Western world, and three months of rioting in America. Politicians and sportsmen took the knee for equality, and giant corporations pledged their support for anti-racism and the Black Lives Matter movement.

With bullshit on as epic a scale as this, it is hard to know where to start. It's a matter of breaking it down one piece at a time, then trying to understand the truth and the deeper meaning behind it. But that can wait until the next chapter. In the current short chapter, I'll try to give a relatively neutral account of what happened.

George Floyd and the Aftermath

On May 25th, 2020, George Floyd tried to spend a fake $20 note in a convenience store in Minneapolis. Police were called to the scene and tried to arrest him. Perhaps due to his criminal record, fear of the police, and being under the influence of drugs, Floyd became agitated. After Floyd refused to be handcuffed, Derek

Chauvin, one of the four police officers, restrained Floyd on the ground, partly by kneeling on his neck. This went on for eight minutes during which Floyd died.

This was all done in broad daylight, in front of witnesses, and captured on film. The footage went viral. It was quickly picked up by the Black Lives Matter movement, the far left group Antifa, student radicals, and other leftists.

This led to riots and looting in many American cities, which went on intermittently for over three months. The protests spread to other Western nations, and became part of a broader protest about race. A key part of this was smashing statues of historical figures thought to have ties to white racism against black people. Therefore, the death of George Floyd became linked to British colonialism and other alleged historical sins.

These riots didn't just happen. There was a greater context. For a long time leading up the Floyd incident, there was an obsession with race. The Obama presidency had done nothing to end this, as many had optimistically thought it might. Then, during the four year Trump presidency, there was a constant focus on racial issues. Much of it seemed contrived, a deliberate attempt to keep racial hysteria always on the boil. Trump himself was portrayed as a white supremacist. There was no end to it.

After the Covid lockdowns, and leading up to the 2020 US election, the unfortunate death of petty criminal, George Floyd, was the cue for mass hysteria, as well as opportunism from race hustlers and politicians. The three months of rioting was supposedly a revolt against the oppression of blacks. The statue smashing which took place around the Western world was a protest against the historical sins of slavery and colonialism.

The Black Lives Matter movement pushed the rioting, and ran a campaign of activism to which all capitulated. Top politicians 'took the knee' to show their support. Most media accepted the BLM story without question. Big corporations are said to have donated billions to the BLM cause, as well as forcing mandatory anti-racism training on their employees.

The Cultural Revolution

To an outside observer, three months of riots and looting, and a corporate shakedown for billions of dollars might seem an overreaction - and it was. It was a sort of Cultural Revolution of the type seen in Maoist China. Although, of course, not as violent or extreme, there was the same sort of frenzied upheaval, the pushing of false ideas, and the fanatical punishment of dissenters.

As a sign of the cult-like nature of it all, there was the absurd canonisation of George Floyd. An undistinguished man to say the least, after his death he became a martyr, celebrated with statues and street murals. He was given three funerals and buried in a gold coffin. His family received a $27 million pay out from the government.

Floyd's death was supposedly a watershed which symbolised the plight of black America. We were expected to believe his death would be a turning point as we began to heal. Floyd's death was a *Never Again* moment.

All this was greeted with po-faced solemnity by governments, media, and universities.

One might reasonably wonder what the behaviour of a small time criminal and his local police have got to do with the other 200 million American citizens, let alone people on the other side of the world in Britain or Australia. But that would be to misunderstand the nature and scope of the Cultural Revolution, and its attempt at a global coup.

All this was allowed to happen by governments who were either quislings, cynical opportunists, or useful idiots silly enough to believe it was all real.

Let's recall that not long before Floyd's death, most countries had been in lockdown due to the Covid pandemic. These lockdowns were so strict people were confined to their homes, and in the rare circumstances they could go out in public, had to 'social distance' from others. Then that was forgotten and suddenly it was fine for thousands of people to go out on a street march together to protest racism.

Truly absurd!

As mentioned, the whole race obsession had been pushed for years. Meanwhile, something called 'Critical Race Theory' had emerged as the theoretical arm of the revolution. It was a doctrine based on the idea that all current black problems and failings are caused by invisible racist structures built into society. Formerly an academic theory, CRT entered the mainstream after George Floyd's death. Corporate employees were forced to take anti-racism training, admit their racial privilege, and so on. Anyone refusing to go along with this could be sacked.

Universities, had been heavily left wing for a long time, and it's hard to think of a single academic who dared speak up against BLM during the post-Floyd hysteria.

This racial Cultural Revolution was an excuse for an outpouring of anti-white aggression. Many whites were forced, or coerced, into 'taking a knee.' They were kneeling for racial equality.

Of course, the idea of kneeling for equality is classic Orwellian nonsense. You don't kneel for equality. You kneel for submission.

In any case, it's hard to believe no one was triggered by this gesture, considering it was allegedly Derek Chauvin's 'kneeling' which had killed George Floyd. Still, a symbolic gesture means whatever the authorities tell us it means.

What were the cultural revolutionaries hoping to achieve? Those who were sincere were presumably trying to create a more racially equal society. To achieve this, however, no accountability was assigned to black Americans for their lives. Little criticism was aimed at other non-white ethnic groups either. No, all this 'inequality' was blamed upon whites, who were collectively asked to take a knee, renounce their privilege, listen to the tales of woe from black Americans, and pledge the rest of their lives to ending racism once and for all.

As for those at the top, the racial hysteria of the BLM era seemed to suit the Democrats, at least. Let's not forget America was just six months out from the possible re-election of arch villain Donald Trump. The frenzy over race had raged for Trump's entire term. Here was the climax.

It is to the great discredit of our institutions that they collaborated in this absurd Cultural Revolution, and they lost a lot of credibility in so doing. I can barely recall one politician, academic, or journalist who dared to stand up to BLM or query their claims. The next chapter will look at the some of these claims in more detail.

10

I Stole this Cake for George

The race riots, the corporate shakedown, and the whole cultural revolution were based on the notion that black Americans are uniquely victimised: in the past through slavery and segregation, and in the present by racist police, prejudice, and deeply engrained systemic racism.

I'll start by dealing with the various myths that make up this story: slavery, 'racist police,' George Floyd's death, Black Lives Matter, and Critical Race Theory. All these topics could be the topic of a chapter on their own. As space is limited, I can discuss them only briefly here.

1 – Slavery

Let's start with the alleged historical source of black problems - slavery.

As a slightly odd prelude to this topic, let's first consider lynching, another topic for which history has been rewritten. To the modern mind, the idea of lynching suggests a black man being strung up by an angry white lynch mob in America's racist past. Yet as the historian Simon Webb pointed out, just a few decades ago lynching was at least as much associated with white people being hung in the Wild West, as in Western films like *Hang 'Em High*. For some reason, the idea has now been re-imagined as racial.

In a similar way, the idea of slavery has also been recast as a racial matter, affecting only black people and perpetrated only by white people. Many people have been taught to think of it only in terms of the trans-Atlantic slave trade in which Africans were brought to America as slaves for whites. This is a foundational myth which supposedly explains the origins of US racism, and the problems of black Americans today. It is behind the call for reparations and other types of compensation. The notion of slavery as a white racial sin against blacks is used by some as a permanent excuse for any failings, and as an ongoing weapon of grievance against whites.

However, the notion of slavery as a racial crime for which whites must do penance and pay trillions of dollars in reparations is a myth. Here are nine reasons it should be abandoned.

(i) Slavery's Long History

Slavery was not invented by 17th century whites as a way to racially oppress Africans. Slavery has existed for most of human history. It existed, for example, in Ancient Greece, Rome, and Egypt. It has existed in Africa, and in various Muslim countries. Therefore, the idea of slavery as some kind of unique crime against blacks in America is a mistake.

Nor is slavery racial in nature, as it has often been practiced within the same racial group. The idea of slavery as a race-based practice is simply not true.

(ii) Whites Were Also Enslaved

Whites have also been the victims of slavery. A great many Europeans were captured and sold as slaves during the Barbary slave trade of approximately 1500-1830. They were taken from European countries to be used as slaves in parts of the Muslim Ottoman empire. Ironically, in the context of this discussion, the Barbary states where the slaves were taken were in Africa.

(iii) There Were White Slaves in America

Neither was slavery confined to blacks even in America. A great many whites were taken from Britain and Ireland to America as 'indentured servants.' Many were taken on the basis of false promises of a better life, and some were simply kidnapped. It is easy on a technicality to deny they were slaves, but they were treated much the same way, or worse, than the black slaves. Many were worked to death. They are the forgotten white 'slaves' of early American history.

(iv) Africans Sold Slaves

Most of the slaves coming from Africa were sold to white traders by other Africans. Therefore, black Africans collaborated in the slave trade and benefitted from it. If modern day black Americans are looking for reparations, they had better take it up with Africa too.

(v) Whites Didn't Start Slavery. They Ended it.

The idea of whites as uniquely responsible for the evils of slavery is false. As mentioned, slavery existed long before America did, and it has been practised by many non-whites. Even more to the point, whites played a major role in *ending* slavery. The abolitionist movement in Britain and America was set up to end slavery. Britain also spent considerable effort in standing against the slave trade after it officially ended, when some other people wanted it to continue. Britain's powerful navy, for instance, helped police the ending of this trade.

In light of this, the idea of whites as uniquely responsible for the evils of slavery is absurd. While whites of the past have participated in slavery, they have also been the victims of it, and they *also* played the major part in ending it. So, if one is going to play the leftist game of assigning group responsibility for a historical evil, one must take into account the great virtue of having ended the practice in question. Still, that's not going to help the case for reparations, is it?

(vi) Other Racial Groups and Trauma

It is commonly claimed that the current problems of blacks - individuals and groups - are partly the result of ongoing trauma and inequality caused by slavery. We should note that this is from the same playbook used by the Australian Aboriginals about colonisation.

While historic events do have ongoing effects, the idea is clearly overplayed and serves as the foundation of a permanent Excuse Culture. Social problems or individual failures? Just blame the legacy of slavery.

We should ask why other racial groups do not do this. There can be very few racial groups who have not suffered traumatic events in history. The Chinese, Japanese, or Jews, for example, have had their share of trauma. As for white people, there's the small matter of a couple of world wars, or having a third of Middle Ages Europe wiped out by the plague. All racial groups have suffered horrible episodes - but not all of them obsess over them. You have to move on.

(vii) Only a Few

In the days of American slavery, only a small percentage of whites owned slaves. Yet today's black activists want to make the entirety of white America pay reparations, including those whose ancestors never owned slaves, as well as those descended from the 'white slaves' known as indentured servants. Some of today's black Americans may even have racial ties to those Africans who sold slaves to the slave traders. Maybe they had better pay reparations to themselves.

(viii) Blacks Better off in America

For all the complaints about slavery, in the long term blacks are actually better off living in first world America rather than in Africa. This very obvious fact tends to be overlooked. In the words of boxing champion, Mohammed Ali, 'Thank God my granddaddy got on that boat.' So, if you take the emotion out of it, they have actually benefitted from the slave trade. Still, if black Americans really would prefer to be in Africa, they can always go back. No one is stopping them, and plenty of Africans would gladly take their place.

(ix) Reparations Have Already Been Paid

See section five of this chapter.

2 – The Police

One of the key triggers for the 2020 race riots was the belief that police prey upon innocent black men for no reason, even to the point of killing them. However, there are good reasons to doubt this idea and to suspect it has been deliberately pushed.

In 2016, four years before the Floyd riots, a Harvard professor named Roland Fryer published a study showing that there is no evidence of racial bias in police shootings. He was warned not to publish as it would ruin his career. When he did, he lived under protection for a month due to death threats, which suggests how committed some people are to the theory of racist policing.

Then, in 2020, at the height of the Floyd frenzy, Zac Friedman, a data scientist working for the Reuters news service, began to question the whole narrative about police victimisation of blacks.

> During his leave, Kriegman used his skills as a data scientist to conduct a careful statistical investigation

comparing BLM's claims on race, violence, and policing with the hard evidence from a range of academic and governmental sources. The result: a 12,000-word essay, titled "BLM is Anti-Black Systemic Racism," that called into question the entire sequence of claims by the Black Lives Matter movement and echoed by the Reuters news team.

Kreigman disproved the three main claims of BLM: 1) that police kill black Americans at a higher rate 2) that black neighbourhoods are 'over-policed,' and 3) that removing police from those neighbourhoods will reduce violent crime.

Kriegman's article made a strong case against each claim. If the idea of racist policing isn't true, that would surely be good news for the black community. However, it is in the interests of various groups to believe in this myth. In fact, his own employer, Reuters, sacked Kriegman for writing the essay.

Many black parents believe they are racially targeted by police, and are said to give 'The Talk' to their teenage sons about what to do if stopped by the police. The parents advise their sons to stop the car straight away, not make any sudden moves, talk politely, and avoid arguing even if they feel they've been unfairly accused. In other words, to fully cooperate with the police.

If that is 'The Talk,' it seems to be good advice for a person of any race stopped by the police. It's worth noting that it doesn't seem to have been followed in some of the high profile police shootings of recent times like Michael Brown, Trayvon Martin, and others. That doesn't mean any of these people should have been shot, but it suggests the shootings could have been avoided if the victims had followed the advice.

3 - George Floyd

We now return to the unfortunate death of George Floyd, the event that sparked the race riots. The popular idea in 2020 was that Floyd was an innocent man killed during a police arrest when Derek Chauvin restrained him by kneeling on his neck, and this was the racially motivated act of a white police system. There are a few points to make about this.

First, George Floyd was not the saint he was posthumously portrayed. He had a long criminal history ranging from petty crime to armed robbery. At the time of his death, he was being arrested for trying to pass a fake $20 note at a convenience store. There were several other dubious aspects of his life. None of this means he deserved to die that day, but it is odd the way Floyd was depicted after his death. He was no model citizen, let alone a saint.

Second, the actions of Derek Chauvin in arresting Floyd weren't that unusual, or far from normal procedure during an arrest. Chauvin had tried to cuff Floyd, which he resisted, which led to Chauvin trying to restrain him by kneeling, once Floyd was on the ground. If Chauvin's actions were against procedure, he should face punishment, but they don't seem to have been that unusual. George Floyd was a large man, over six feet tall, acting strangely and unpredictably, and Chauvin was trying to arrest him.

Third, Chauvin's kneeling actions were part of what caused George Floyd's death, but were far from the only causes. A major factor was that Floyd had traces of fentanyl and meth in his body and these drugs, combined with a heart condition and having recently had Covid, contributed to his death under the stress of the arrest. In fact, Floyd's death certificate showed the cause of death was heart failure, not suffocation.

The drugs may also have contributed to Floyd acting erratically on the day, panicking, and resisting arrest, which led Chauvin to have to take steps to restrain him.

Fourth, there is no reason to believe Floyd's arrest was racially motivated. Chauvin may well have treated a white suspect exactly the same way if he had behaved like Floyd. Two of the four arresting officers were non-white. What's more, all police are well aware of the racial connotations of policing in recent times, including Chauvin with nearly twenty years on the job. It makes little sense to think Chauvin would have acted in a racist way in the arrest, which was done in broad daylight in front of witnesses and on camera. So, the assumption of a racial motivation, which drove the riots, may be quite wrong.

Fifth, as mentioned before, the idea of racist policing - that blacks are treated differently - is probably a myth. So the Floyd incident was not some revelation or watershed as was widely believed. However it was used to justify worldwide protests and over three months of rioting in the US, not to mention the huge financial shakedown, and all manner of foolishness from once-respected media outlets.

4 – Black Lives Matter

The Black Lives Matter movement began in response to the alleged police victimisation of black people. Like most movements, Black Lives Matter (BLM) may have been founded on good intentions. At the same time, there is reason for other people to see them as hostile, mistaken in their views, and of questionable honesty.

One of the founders of BLM admitted to being a trained Marxist. That training may have been put to good use in all those riots, and in the terror tactics used against businesses and individuals to make them obey the racial revolution.

In the aftermath of Floyd's death, there was a shakedown of epic proportions with billions of dollars extracted from government and corporations for the BLM cause. Some of that money may have been used well. But eyebrows were raised when rumours surfaced about a BLM leader having bought a six million dollar house.

In order to pull off that shakedown, BLM had to use the racism narrative to full effect. Any critique of the idea would have harmed that cause. So, in an odd sense the idea of black victimhood was far preferable to them than any notions that black people weren't really oppressed. As it turned out, during the hysteria of that time, very few people were prepared to challenge BLM's views.

There is good reason to doubt the sincerity of the claim that 'black lives matter' if only a portion of those lives are given attention. Most black victims of violent crime are the victims of other black people, not of whites. If BLM was sincere, why weren't there riots over those deaths? BLM's exclusive focus on the minority of cases with white killers suggests this was purely a racial shakedown, rather than a concern for black lives in themselves.

The lazy answer favoured by Critical Race Theory, is that even black on black crime is the indirect result of racist social structures. This excuses individuals from their own violent actions.

Then we have BLM's call to 'defund the police.' With their deep conviction that the police seemed to persecute black people for no reason, the idea spread that they'd be better off without the police altogether. Although the movement to defund the police did not succeed, there was certainly a decline in policing after George Floyd's death. The results were not good for black people. Crime went up, and one source estimated a 30% rise in violent deaths among blacks due to the reduction of policing.

Ironically, the area where Floyd died, since renamed as George Floyd Square, became a criminal hotbed because police avoided it. In becoming such a dangerous area, few ordinary people wanted to go there. A couple of years later several local businesses sued the city for not policing the area, which had led to them losing most of their business. The area had become a No Go zone. You can't make this stuff up.

Due to the disastrous side effects of BLM's stance on policing, one would suspect that BLM is either insincere in wanting to protect black lives, incompetent in doing so, or simply mistaken in the idea that police persecute blacks and make their lives worse.

In general, a neutral observer would have to view BLM with a lot of suspicion. They played a major part in the race based turmoil after Floyd's death, and extracted a great deal of money as a result. Yet have black lives improved as a result of their efforts? Have race relations improved? No, of course not.

5 - Reparations

We now cut to the bottom line of the great racial shakedown, which is the idea that black Americans should be paid reparations to compensate them for slavery.

Let's imagine a hypothetical young black man who went to university, studied hard, then got a high paid job and was a success. He wouldn't need reparations. Now let's imagine another hypothetical young black man who hardly ever went to school, was apathetic or aggressive when he did, then dropped out to begin a life of petty crime, spending short periods in jail as a result. If the reparations bill were ever approved, this man could become an instant millionaire. All his personal failings could be excused, blamed on the legacy of slavery. Would his newfound wealth be a heart-warming tale of racial justice? Not particularly. It would be a joke.

Many people believe there are far more of the second type of man than the first only because of slavery, discrimination, and systemic racism. That is, at best, a theory. Besides would not the first man only have succeeded by conforming to Western behaviour standards or, as some black people derisively call it, 'acting white?' Reparations sounds like a much easier path to success.

One estimate for reparations calculated it at 14 Trillion dollars. Presumably this enormous bill would come from taxes. So, would it come from the taxes paid by wealthy Asians, Indians, or Jews, for example - all of them higher average wage earners than whites - or would it come only from the taxes paid by white people? As Asians, Indians, and Jews did not found America, they aren't responsible for starting slavery. Then again, they also benefit from those invisible structures of white supremacy mentioned in Critical Race Theory, so perhaps they should chip into the reparations fund.

What an administrative nightmare it would be figuring out who owed what to whom. You would have to work out the entire ancestral tree of every modern American. What about whites whose family never owned slaves? Or those who were slaves themselves in the form of 'indentured servants'? How about blacks descended from those who helped sell slaves in Africa? What about Africans who moved to America in the 20th century after slavery had ended? How about a modern American of mixed racial descent, say, someone with a black father and a white mother? What's he going to do - pay reparations to himself?

We've already seen that the idea slavery was just a white on black phenomenon is a myth. So, if reparations are for slavery, we need a far more accurate understanding of slavery than the false idea of it that many believe.

When it comes to reparations, some would argue that whites have already paid plenty. This was in the form of white lives lost fighting the civil war, which helped end slavery, and English lives lost policing the end of the slave trade after it was finally abolished.

Then there are all the other bills whites have already footed: welfare, legal and policing bills, health costs as well as pro-black policies like affirmative action.

Apart from that, whites have had to endure endless 're-education' about slavery, racism, and other sins, with the Critical

Race Theory craze in 2020 just the latest version. All this re-education has led to flow on effects for policies harming whites, not least the coming loss of white majority status in America. In other words, whites have already paid plenty for their real or imagined sins.

Almost all countries have done terrible things in their history, but few are prepared to apologise for it, and even fewer are going to pay any reparations. Only white people are silly enough to take the idea seriously.

As mentioned, in terms of consequences, one might ask who is better off: the average black person living in First World America, or those living in Third World Africa? For all the historical evils of slavery, the end result of the Trans Atlantic slave trade is that black Americans live in America instead of Africa. On average, most are better off.

The idea of reparations for slavery is an obvious rort. It is tied to Critical Race Theory which claims all black failings are due to inherent racial structures which benefit whites and harm blacks. This provides a permanent Excuse Culture in which any black problem can be blamed on whites, 'whiteness,' and racism. As a genuinely great black American, Thomas Sowell, has said:

> Have we reached the ultimate stage of absurdity where some people are held responsible for things that happened before they were born, while other people are not held responsible for what they themselves are doing today?

Or to put it more succinctly, an online meme about reparations says: 'I never owned slaves and you never picked cotton. I don't owe you shit.'

6 - Pathetic Behaviour

During the hysteria of 2020, both blacks and whites behaved pathetically. Not in the sense of pathos and inspiring compassion, but in behaving contemptibly and without honour.

In the case of blacks who rioted, we are supposed to believe they were so profoundly moved by the fate of George Floyd that they rioted and looted for weeks on end to express their grief. It was a howl of racial anguish at the plight of black Americans and their endless suffering.

First, let's for a moment pretend it was true that blacks are permanently victimised, the legacy of slavery lasts forever, white cops randomly kill black people, and so on. Even if that were true, how is it a sane response to trash buildings and businesses, and loot department stores?

One might forgive a street march, a public lecture, a well written article, or something else that was a sane expression of your cause. Yet it is hard to see any real connection between grief over the death of George Floyd and the looting of shops for personal gain.

Are we to believe that the howl of brotherly anguish over George's death could only find consolation in the theft of an expensive pair of Nikes or a top range laptop? Grief can have strange effects, but it seems to manifest in people differently. White people too sometimes suffer the loss of a loved one through cruel circumstances - a car accident, a murder, a random illness - but it is rare for mourners to find solace in stealing expensive electrical goods from department stores.

There was a lot of footage of the riots on social media in 2020, much of it disturbing, but as always there was some dark humour to lighten the mood. One meme showed a photo of an attractive young black woman walking out of a looted shop holding a very large cake. *I Stole This Cake for George* was the headline on top of the image.

Of course, the idea that stealing an enormous cake has anything to do with mourning George Floyd shows the farcical nature of this whole period. While many black Americans were no doubt upset by Floyd's death, others saw it as the chance to smash things up or steal as much as possible while they could.

This was either cynical opportunism and therefore dishonest, or a genuine cry of rage which seems a purely emotional response with no rational thought.

It is also lazy. At least the black university activists went to the trouble of writing a book or article, or giving a speech, about their cause. Maybe it should have been a precondition for the rioters to at least write a two-thousand word essay, or give a ten minute talk, before they were allowed to go loot a department store.

But no, far easier to just accept the simplistic notion of racism as the cause of all social and individual problems, then smash everything up and steal a toaster.

As for the behaviour of whites, that was pathetic for different reasons.

It was also a purely emotional response, but in this case the induced hysteria from years of indoctrination about slavery and race. The racial guilt they had been taught found exorcism through the aggressive virtue signalling of street protests, or the even more pathetic act of apologising or taking a knee.

Most of these people thought they were being righteous, rather than the pawns in a cultural revolution. They were probably unaware that many of the black protesters despised them, or that the revolution would harm their own long term interests.

Other whites watching the protests with a certain horror and trepidation made a cowardly surrender to it all by saying nothing.

Then you had the po-faced reporting from the ABC, BBC, and other 'serious' broadcasters, with not a word of criticism, as well as the capitulation from the corporate world.

What a farce.

7 – Critical Race Theory

For a while, many white people had assumed the best way to practice racial equality was to treat everyone the same. That is, to adopt an idea that many leftists claim to believe, which is that race doesn't really exist and we are all the same beneath surface appearances. This approach - being 'colour blind' - would seem a fair one.

This is not enough for those leftists who promote Critical Race Theory (CRT). The advocates of CRT believe that racism is woven into the very fabric of society. Every institution, every thought, every social interaction is built upon racial ideas. These are so taken for granted they become invisible. Therefore to try to be colour blind is to ignore this ingrained racism, which allows it to continue.

What Critical Race Theorists want to do is bring all this hidden racism into the light. Expose it, denounce it, then transcend it to achieve true racial equality.

These theorists also believe that all racial content works in favour of the dominant racial group - whites. However, they are not just concerned with white *people*, but an abstract quality called 'whiteness', which is mainly just the ways white people tend to think and behave in normal Western cultures.

Criticisms of CRT:

Critical Race theory is a big topic, but there is only space to discuss it briefly here. There are many problems with CRT, of which I will list just a few.

A core problem is that CRT is completely obsessed with race, and with seeing racism everywhere. At the same time, on every single racial issue, CRT will invariably take an anti-white and pro-black position. CRT says that white people are the most powerful, and 'whiteness' is the dominant norm all people are meant to adhere to. So, as CRT wants perfect equality, it will always be trying to undermine white people and whiteness.

As a result, this 'anti-racist' movement seems rather racist in itself. Its main advocates may deny this and say they simply want racial equality. We should recall that CRT had to change the definition of racism to mean not just *prejudice*, but *prejudice plus power*. As they claim only whites have social power, this means anti-white racism is impossible, in their eyes.

This devious manoeuvre should give some idea of the true nature of CRT. But there are other reasons for white people to reject it. For instance, CRT assumes social equality should be everyone's main goal. That's a false assumption for a start. But let's suppose whites *were* the most powerful group, it's up to CRT advocates to tell them why they should give that up. Why, for example, should white people in Britain want to give up their status as the main ethnic group, especially when the multicultural system was forced on them without their consent? More to the point, you could easily make a case that whites are no longer the most powerful group in the various Anglo countries, so the premise is false. Whites certainly aren't the top income earners in America, for a start.

CRT advocates believe society is steeped in invisible racist structures, and the only way to achieve equality is to hunt them all out, including the racist attitudes we unconsciously hold. Therefore, they want to force their race obsession on the rest of us, so that we go through our day seeking invisible racism that is apparently all around us.

Even though equality and invisible racism may be of obsessive interest to CRT advocates, there is no reason anyone else has to share it. There are surely more interesting things to spend all your time thinking about than race.

Apart from the antagonistic nature of CRT, there's also its one dimensional nature. Helen Pluckrose and James Lindsay, in the book *Cynical Theories*, say that CRT is just another form of Marxist subversion. Like similar doctrines gender theory or queer theory, CRT:

> ...does the same thing over and over again: look for the power imbalances, bigotry, and biases that it assumes must be present and pick at them. It reduces everything to one single variable, one single topic of conversation, one single focus and interpretation: prejudice, as understood under the power dynamics asserted by Theory.

CRT does this through a fixation on race.

> (CRT's) hallmark paranoid mind-set, which assumes racism is everywhere, always, just waiting to be found, is extremely unlikely to be helpful or healthy for those who adopt it. Always believing that one will be or is being discriminated against, and trying to find out how, is unlikely to improve the outcome of any situation.

As this quote suggests, in the end CRT is not likely to help black Americans. How could it when it is based on envy and grievance, and insists on seeing everything in terms of power?

Lindsay, says elsewhere that CRT is not necessarily an attack on white people themselves, but on 'whiteness' which really just means Western norms. So called whiteness is often just the normal behaviour needed for success. One BLM-friendly museum exhibit from a few years ago included the following as traits of whiteness:

Rugged individualism and self reliance; traditional family structure; scientific method, objective thinking, study of cause and effect; Protestant work ethic; 'future orientation' i.e. planning for the future, delayed gratification; following time schedules, punctuality.

This extract, critical of 'white' norms, verges on parody. Many of these traits are just basic requirements for success, or at the least, are helpful in achieving it. Adhering to these too strictly might be stifling, but you can't deny these traits lead to success as most people understand it. You can, of course, choose to reject these behavioural norms, but it shouldn't be any surprise if there is a gap in outcomes with those who accept them. This is especially true averaged out over a large statistical sample. A few people can achieve success while rejecting these aspects of 'whiteness' but most will not.

One of the most basic requirements for social success is education. A small number of high school dropouts have gone on to become CEOs, but they are outliers. On average, few people can reject education and hope to gain high social success.

As a result, it is no surprise that Asians, a racial group that takes education seriously, is doing better than black Americans, a group whose members often do not. You can say the poorer schools many black Americans attend are a sign of racial inequality. Even if that is true, the individual still has agency. The individual can choose to show up to class, listen to the teacher, and study. Some black American students do that. Plenty of others do not. Some go to class and spend the time speaking on their phones, abusing their teachers, and openly rejecting learning. Many don't show up at all. Some shame their fellow black students who do try hard in school for 'acting white.' So, on the one hand some want to reject these apparent traits of 'whiteness' then later wonder about lower economic status.

These sort of behaviours show a complete contempt for education, in contrast to, say, Asians' vigilant respect for it. If they choose to show contempt for education, so be it, but they can't then be surprised at a gap in outcomes.

At a basic level, CRT denies personal agency and accountability. Everything is seen as being caused by external factors, those invisible structures of racism. In denying agency, CRT also denies accountability. Nothing is the fault of the individual. It is all down to the system.

In denying personal agency and accountability, CRT does not empower black Americans. If CRT really did care about empowering them, it would give some hard truths about the so called traits of 'whiteness' being basic requirements for success. Instead, CRT coddles them and offers an Excuse Culture, at the same time as making hectoring and irrational demands upon white people.

Thus, CRT is not about empowering black people by giving them agency. It's a neo-Marxist shakedown in which 'privilege' is not something earned, but simply demanded in the name of equity.

It's all so tiresome.

8 - How Should Whites Respond?

CRT advocates may mean well, and fully believe in their mission. Some of them are sincere, but others are little more than race hustlers. Even for those who are sincere and can make a case, I can't share their vision of a perfectly equal society as a desirable goal, even if it were possible.

Older white people may remember a time when race was not forced on them on a daily basis. Those halcyon days have gone, and we have had to hear endless talk about it for quite a while.

We have also heard that diversity is our strength. Clearly it is not, if diversity produces nothing but racial stress. Critical Race Theorists want us to becomes as race obsessed as themselves, and to see it in everything. At the same time, they want to see every racial interaction through a pro-black, anti-white lens. If those are the terms on which we are expected to base a mixed race society, it is doomed to failure.

If we are going to have diverse societies, the only hope is to go back to a colour-blind approach, if for no other reason than it will allow us all to get on with our lives without a fixation on race. No one, apart from CRT advocates, has time to go around seeking out invisible racial demons everywhere they look.

9 - The Cultural Revolution, and Reasons to Think This was Deliberate

We now return to the hysteria of the post-Floyd period, when a type of Cultural Revolution took place in relation to race. There was rioting and looting in American cities for three months. Other Western nations joined in, with protesters tearing down statues supposedly linked with a racist past. White people 'took the knee' for racial equality, either voluntarily or through coercion.

Remember also that all this took place during the year of Covid and its lockdowns, and leading up to the 2020 US election after four years of hysteria about Trump.

There was a mass mental conformity with a forced acceptance of the BLM race narrative. Academics at every university had to toe the line. Barely any dared speak out against the BLM view.

There was an anonymous letter written by an American academic condemning BLM's version of events. Its author, although non-white himself, admitted he would not dare publish it under his own name. This letter shredded *every* aspect of the post-Floyd fiasco, pointing out its farcical nature. However, the atmosphere of fear and intimidation meant any public figure speaking against BLM would have been sacked.

Meanwhile, almost all the mainstream media I saw accepted the official line. The Australian ABC for example, a supposedly impartial source of news, barely bothered to hide its far-left nature during this time. One day in June 2020, for example, I logged on to its news site and noted stories on the following topics: tearing down statues, BLM protests, banning racist TV shows, police violence, anti-Trump stories, pro-Jacinda Ardern stories, pro-Aboriginals, pro-immigration, slavery, warnings about the far right, and of course feminism. Although feminism had to take a backseat for a while during BLM-mania, the ABC kept the torch burning.

In Britain, the BBC apparently took up the BLM cause with equal fervour. Did either of these 'national broadcasters' take the slightest critical look at BLM, or stand up for Western nations and their history while crazed protesters were smashing statues? Of course not.

Meanwhile, there were many lies of omission, and some white victims of racial crime barely got a mention. Who, for example, heard about Cannon Hinnant, a five-year old white American boy shot dead by a black neighbour on August 9th, 2020? Who heard about Jessica Doty Whitaker, a 24 year old white mother in Indianapolis killed by a BLM thug for saying 'all lives matter'?

What are we to make of this period of mass hysteria?

On the one hand, it was an epic shakedown on the part of BLM and other activists. George Floyd's death provided the opportunity for that, and so much more. It also enabled an outpouring of hostility against white people, as well as the chance to hurt and disempower them. Collaborating in this process were gullible white leftists who thought they were being noble.

Here was the chance to smash white people and crush their morale. We should remember the wider racial conflicts going on at this time - struggles over illegal immigration, DEI, and multiculturalism. The hysteria of 2020 was the chance to stir conflict and further erode social cohesion.

There are reasons to suspect this was deliberate. For some people, the social chaos, the harm, the damaged morale was all part of the push to destroy then later re-mold society. For both the race hustlers and Marxist reformers, the idea of black victimhood at the hands of white society was a way to advance their cause.

I said earlier that if Critical Race Theorists really wanted to empower black people, their message would be very different. Instead of making them obsessed with racism and telling them external forces controlled their lives, they would stress personal agency.

In the same way, if politicians really cared about black lives, they wouldn't play along with the fake BLM narrative. Instead of accepting ideas about racism, they would challenge them. They would look with calm detachment at claims about racist policing, white privilege, systemic racism, slavery, and the rest of the package.

But they do not. What they do instead is clamp down on those who *do* try to challenge those myths. They censor such people, ban them, or smear them as 'far-right' or white supremacists.

What this suggests is that either the people in power are rather stupid and credulous or, more likely, the fake narrative is more useful. The purpose may either be a short term one as, for example, when a politician sells people the idea they are victims and need his help. The purpose might also be a longer term and more sinister one of wanting to ferment turmoil in the hope society will break down.

It is strange to consider that some people see this as a desirable goal, but bizarrely, some do. This goes back to Marxism, which is all about stirring up bitter class struggle in order to create as much chaos as possible, in the hope society will collapse and then be reformed. 'Build back better' was a popular slogan in 2020, after all, as part of a rumoured 'Great Reset.'

This is not as far-fetched as it seems. It actually happened, for example, in Mao's China during his various purges and especially the Cultural Revolution. This details of what happened were little known in the West, but rather boggle the mind once you do hear about them.

In light of all this, one should view the aftermath of George Floyd's death quite differently. Supposedly the riots were a response to racist policing and a cry for racial justice. Instead, it was a case of induced mass hysteria in which many people were duped into joining in someone else's fake morality play.

10 - Conclusion

We now come to the end of this part of the book dealing with Racial Sacred Cows. It's easy to see some common themes. The first chapter discussed Anglophobia. Then there was multiculturalism, the society-transforming policy no one voted for, which appeared in all Anglo nations at around the same time.

We then looked at the case of the Australian Aboriginals, their grievances against the British, and the attempted coup of the Voice to Parliament. Finally, we considered George Floyd's death, Black Lives Matter, and the contrived Cultural Revolution that followed.

What should be clear is the widespread hostility towards white people and the Anglo nations. It's about time people put the whole picture together. This is all part of the Global Progressive Regime and its dubious agenda - which many white leftists have been conned into supporting.

Still, among all these concerning trends, perhaps we can look to a happy ending. The American Dream may not be dead after all. Just consider George Floyd himself, a suffering black American who led a troubled life including stints in the systemic oppression of jail. It's true that his tragic death was unfair, but at least he ended up being celebrated in street murals and statues, even as the statues of founding white Americans were torn down in the name of racial justice.

More to the point, George's family, including his five children, received a $27 million payout from the government. George went from a man in such financial strife he was forced to pass a fake $20 note to a man who provided his family with $27 million just so they could live.

We can only hope that every black American family will also receive $27 million one day as compensation for slavery. Let there be reparations. Then the complaints about whiteness will surely at last come to an end.

Part Three

Sacred Cows:
Gender

11

It's Not a Lie if You Believe it

In the Global Progressive Regime, race is the main area of conflict, but gender is not far behind. Gender is a tremendous source of conflict, mainly between men and women. There is also the trans issue but that won't be discussed here. The next few chapters will consider male-female relations at the current time, and especially the influence of feminism upon them.

Feminism

Most fair minded people would agree to a few simple points about women's rights. Women should be able to choose their education, their careers, and whether they want to marry or have children. They should not be forced to behave in particular ways because of their gender and should be assumed, until proven otherwise, to have the same abilities and potential as men. They should also be able to go to work without being sexually harassed, in the ordinary sense of that term.

And that is basically it.

In first world Western nations, the feminist war was won many years ago and we should have been able to forget it and move on. But for feminists, the war is never won. They seem to think women's struggles for equality are more dire than ever, and the need for reforms has never been more pressing.

In other words while the real war ended some time ago, we're now immersed in the phony war contrived by 21st century feminism. The whole charade is propped up by false premises. Chief among them is an idea of male power and female disadvantage. This leads to a misplaced envy towards men, and other harmful states of mind, mainly resentment and a lack of empathy. You cannot feel empathy towards those you envy.

Feminism today requires us to collaborate in the idea that Western women are still oppressed, chiefly by some nebulous force called the patriarchy. 'Patriarchy' is the idea that society is set up for the permanent advantage of men and the disadvantage of women, and that men have more power than women. This idea bears little relation to the facts. Women may in some ways have been disadvantaged in the past, but they are not now. While there are some non-Western countries where 'patriarchy' still prevails, it's absurd to think the position of Western women is anything like it is for the women living there.

If feminism was just an academic field it wouldn't matter, but its ideas are mainstream and cause real world problems for both men and women. The main problem is a deep antagonism between the sexes. In a healthy society, men and women would get on well, but instead we are suffering this contrived gender war.

As a pseudo-moral campaign peddling grievance and the promise of 'justice,' feminism is a key pillar of the Global Progressive Regime. It has done a wonderful job helping create the dysfunctional society we fail to enjoy.

Feminism did some good in freeing up gender roles and career options, and changing some sexist attitudes that existed in, say, 1970. Having done that and raised a few other legitimate concerns, feminism has largely made itself redundant. Instead of retiring, feminism insists on hanging around causing endless collateral damage through the pursuit of its phony war. In the next few chapters, I'll try to explain what this means.

If some of their key ideas are wrong, I'm not saying feminists are lying, only that they may be mistaken. It's not a lie if you believe it. Many children, especially girls, come through the fem-friendly education system and have no idea there could even be another perspective on these matters. They have been taught to believe in it. My role in the next few chapters is to say why I don't, and why it would be better for everyone if Western women stopped pretending they're oppressed.

Two key mistakes are the ideas of male privilege and patriarchy. Male privilege is the belief that in nearly every aspect of life, men are better off than women. Patriarchy is the notion that society was set up by men for their own benefit, and that they have more power than women.

At first these two ideas seem almost the same, but they are subtly different. Male privilege says life is easier for men. Patriarchy says that this situation was deliberately set up and maintained. In any case, both ideas are wrong.

Male Privilege

The core premise of feminism is that women are worse off than men. Hence their fixation with 'gender equality.' As a result, we are supposed to feel special sympathy for them and constantly look for ways to improve their lives. The flip side of this is the idea that men's lives are much better and easier - so called 'male privilege.'

My book, *The Vast and the Spurious*, made a detailed case that this idea is false. Yet whole generations of girls have been taught to believe it. To repeat, it's one reason there is so little empathy from women towards men. You can't empathise with someone you've been taught to resent. When your whole belief system is founded on a sense of envy, you are not going to feel well disposed towards the people you've been told are so much luckier and better off than yourselves.

In 2021, the ABC in Australia broadcast a four part series called *Why Women Are Angry*. The core idea was that women are unfairly treated and disadvantaged compared to men. The series concluded with the claim that for every woman in Australia, men at a similar socioeconomic level are better off. Thus, male privilege.

As it happens, men have at least as much cause to be angry. There are many reasons for this, and one of them is that our national broadcaster would never permit, let alone produce, a comparable program called *Why Men Are Angry*.

Some feminists believe that the backlash against them is because 'privileged' men resent losing their power. Instead, it is the false idea that they are privileged in the first place which many men find obnoxious.

To refute the idea of male privilege you could simply point to higher rates of male homelessness, incarceration, and suicide, or to lower life expectancy and success in education. You could mention the routine denigration of men and masculinity and wonder how that equates to privilege. You could consider how some men are treated during divorce, or indeed during marriage. You could check which gender is most represented in the workplace - not the prestige jobs like being a CEO, but the dirty or dangerous jobs like garbage collecting, plumbing, fishing, or logging. As Jim Goad said, there's the gender pay gap and there's also the gender death gap: the glass ceiling and the glass coffin.

On the topic of work, we should also look at one of the most basic feminist concerns, about education and careers. This is the idea that women are held back and prevented from reaching their full potential. This may have been true sixty years ago, when gender roles were more limited and most professions male-dominated. It isn't true now. In the Girl Power era of recent times, doors have not been slammed shut, but thrust open and women urged to travel through them.

As for the general notion that women are being held back let's consider the following quote from a conservative You-Tuber who calls herself 'Blonde in the Belly of the Beast.' At the start of one video, she said:

I'm often asked do you feel like you've ever been discriminated against because you're a woman? And if I'm evaluating my life honestly I have to say no. In fact I believe that I've been given countless opportunities that I did not earn, second chances that I didn't deserve, many of which I ungratefully squandered. All because I'm a woman.

Truthfully it's been a lifetime of me being told that I'm awesome for relatively mediocre achievements, kind of a tough pill to swallow but it is the truth so I would imagine that many other slightly above average American women have had a similar experience whereby they coast on their moderate intellect and minor achievements which are then leveraged to attain various undeserved positions and accolades.

Millennials grew up in a participation trophy era in which all students were praised merely for showing up. Additionally, millennial women had this secondary positive reinforcement strategy laid on us. We were taught by parents, teachers, counsellors, and society that girls can do anything that men can do, that our potential is boundless, that we're amazing just the way we are, that merely by virtue of being female we bring goodness to the world. Because we were born with this value we cannot fail, and if we do, it must be someone else's fault.

While, this account won't reflect the experience of *all* girls, it does fit the general tone of our You Go Girl age of female empowerment. It's really about time we stopped pretending Western women are being ground underfoot by oppression.

Patriarchy and Gynocentrism

The theory of patriarchy is that society is run by men for the benefit of men. There's an alternative theory, less well known, that society is 'gynocentric,' meaning it exists largely for the benefit of women, or least prioritises their needs.

These two theories - patriarchy and gynocentrism - contradict each other. Society cannot exist mainly for the benefit of men and also mainly for the benefit of women. So, which is the more plausible theory?

The question of which gender is better off is usually seen in terms of which one has the most power. What is 'power'? You might say it's the ability to act effectively in the world. But you could also say it's the ability to have others act on your behalf.

The majority of men have usually been obliged to exercise 'power' not for their own sake, but on behalf of others, whether that's an elite class of males or a protected class of women and children. Whether it is fighting wars, earning a living, or maintaining critical infrastructure, men have had to do the dirty work. This has often been an obligation, not a privilege. As author, Tim Goldich, has said:

> What I'm alluding to is men marching off to war and thinking of it as 'power.' Men devoting themselves to earning money others will spend and thinking of it as 'power.' Men set in fierce competition to perform, achieve, and succeed their way into having what women are empowered to demand of them and thinking of it as 'power.'

Consider a British working class man born in the 1890s. His time of birth would have earned him the privilege of enduring years of trench warfare, and if he'd been lucky enough to survive that, he may perhaps have gone on to a post-war career in a factory or down a coal mine. Some 'power.'

Moving to the other end of the social scale, we can visit the world of princes and princesses, albeit in the archetypal form of fairytales. Consider the classic fairytale princess whose hand in marriage is the prize offered to hundreds of male suitors, one of whom will win it by going on a quest and performing mighty deeds.

This is an example of women as 'human beings' and men as 'human doings.' The men's worth is measured by their strength, bravery, or intelligence. The princess, on the other hand, only has to show up. A feminist would say the men are performing their deeds for the right to posses her, and she is simply being given away as a prize by one patriarch, the king, to another, the successful prince. However, the fact is that all this 'power' is being conjured because of her. It may be a passive sort of power, but power it is.

The feminist might see this princess quest as patriarchy in action, as the powerful male suitor takes possession of her. But through a gynocentric lens, we can see a large number of males exerting themselves so one powerful woman can achieve her dream husband.

To realise the myth of male power, to use Warren Farrell's phrase, we should take a step back and consider the *apex fallacy*. Suppose there are one hundred men competing for the princess's hand. Only one man will succeed, so those one hundred men will contain 1% winners and 99% losers. The rest of the top 10% of men might marry other high ranking women, and the next 20% may marry women lower down the social scale. That still leaves 70% unmarried, and many of the bottom half might be killed or maimed in their failed quest to win the princess.

Under the spell of the apex fallacy, we see only the winner, and perhaps the rest of the top 10%, but fail to see the other 90%, the 'losers.' Then we mistakenly equate the top 10% with the whole male gender.

This is what happens in our own world, and it is the key source of the false idea of men's power. Feminists often cite the higher proportion of male politicians and CEOs as proof of male privilege. But while it's true most national leaders and CEOs are men, it makes no sense to think the power enjoyed by these elite males is shared by the other 90% of men.

A truer model, held by a gynocentrist, would see society as made up of be an elite five or ten percent of men (and some women) at the top, then most women (and some men), then the rest of the men to serve both the elites and the women. Of course, this is an over simple generalisation, but it is more accurate than the idea of universal male power.

It could be said that discussing a *princess* is also a form of the apex fallacy, for not all women have the social power that comes with royalty. That's true but it leads to an interesting point about the way feminists see power. Under the theory of patriarchy, it is assumed that men are more powerful than women at *every* level of society. One feminist quoted on Twitter a definition of patriarchy as 'a system in which men have power over women, deriving benefit from doing so, at women's expense.'

I replied, 'Which women do I have power over? I can't think of any.' This received no answer. Of course, I have neither the expectation nor the wish to have 'power over' any person, but the idea that patriarchy bestows such power would come as a great surprise to many men.

Feminists believe patriarchy gives men power at *all* social levels, not just the top. They see the heterosexual family as the smallest social unit, and assume that the father rules it as his patriarchal mini-regime. While that model may perhaps operate in, say, Islamic countries, among some orthodox Christians, and in some other families, it isn't true this is how most modern families work.

It takes only the most basic life experience to know that plenty of families are dominated not by the man, but the woman. The hen-pecked husband is a well known trope, and as a reminder that this is nothing new, we could go back at least a couple of centuries to the tale of 'The Fisherman and his Wife.'

I recently read a Jewish Joke Book. Now, this was a book written by and for Jews, so there can be no question of anti-Semitism! The book was full of jokes about husbands and wives, with recurring motifs of the wife or mother-in-law as a pushy, domineering, and demanding woman, and the man as their hapless and long suffering servant. You could say these were stereotypes, but stereotypes usually have some basis in truth.

The upshot of all this, and a thousand possible anecdotes, is that the idea of families as the smallest unit of patriarchy in which men rule over women is largely a myth, at least in the Western world. There are *some* families like that, but the idea that it's some kind of universal norm is absurd.

Another key area of alleged male privilege is the world of work. In older style marriages, the husband worked and the wife stayed home. While those gender roles were too limited, it's a mistake to see the husband's role as necessarily a privileged one. Some men might have liked to stay home and send their wives to work instead. To have to go out and do a job that may be dull, difficult, or even dangerous is a strange sort of privilege. When all's said and done, and as many women have found out since their 'liberation,' having to earn a living can be a burden rather than a blessing.

Gynocentrism

Gynocentrism is the idea that society places a greater priority on women's wellbeing than men's. Patriarchy is the theory that society exists mainly for the benefit of men. These theories can't both be true. In an odd way, the paradox can be partly reconciled by realising the *apex fallacy* does lead to an illusion of a patriarchy.

If most of the leading roles in society are taken by men, feminists falsely attribute this elite power to the male gender as a whole. As a recent online comment said, 'With the Patriarchy theory, feminists believe half the population are part of the 1%,' which drew the reply that, 'It's because most men are invisible to them. It's the same reason they think they can survive without men.'

To repeat, it has usually been men who've taken on the dirty and dangerous jobs for the benefit of society's protected classes. It was men who were expected to give up their proverbial seat in the lifeboat, to put women and children first.

As for the origins of this, one might tie this to child rearing. I don't normally use evolutionary explanations, but it makes sense to say a tribe which protected its women was more likely to survive, given women's role in reproduction. On a larger scale, societies with high birth rates survive. For this, men were relatively disposable, and were often expected to make sacrifices for the greater good.

Women were usually spared from making those sort of sacrifices. It wasn't the women who were asked to fight in wars, go down the coal mines, or construct and maintain tall buildings. From a feminist point of view, one might say that by being confined to mainly the domestic or parenting sphere, women were denied full participation in public life, which was another form of sacrifice. That's a fair point but even if women's role was limited, they were still largely the protected class compared to men. Thus gynocentrism seems more plausible than a theory of patriarchy. 'Patriarchy' here could only refer to a small elite group of men at the top of the social pyramid, not the male gender as whole, most of whom were doing the hard yards on behalf of everyone else.

Of course, many feminists won't see it like that. The way people view the traditional marriage set up is really something of a *Rorschach test*. Feminists tend to see it as a form of legalised slavery with the woman servicing a privileged male lord. This cartoonish view of marriage may depict some marriages, but hardly all, as the power dynamics in many marriages are nothing like that. In terms of 'slavery' the husband in a traditional marriage was both duty and legally bound to provide for his wife and children, often having to endure a boring or stressful job to do so. Many's the 'working stiff' who suffers in silence for years for the sake of his dependants. Some will see marriage as patriarchal, but others will see it as largely gynocentric.

Deep Gynocentrism

There seems to be an unconscious gynocentrism in women as a class. This manifests in various ways. One is the expectation that women are to be protected and provided for. This may seem a reasonable expectation. It's worth noting, however, that men as a rule do not have it. Men are not generally raised with the belief they will be either protected or provided for, but that they will perform this service for others - especially women. At the very least, men are expected to be self sufficient. A recent YouTube video about bullying drew one anecdote in the comments.

> (As a young boy) I got bullied at school and my mother told me if it happens again tell the teacher and try to avoid the bully. My dad told me don't tell the teacher because no one likes an informer, and then he got some boxing gloves and gave me some tips on how to box and said go into school and pick a fight with the bully and keep punching him on the nose till he stops. So that's what I did. My old father went to sea in WW2 at 14. He said he was 18. It's a pity more people didn't have someone like him to advise them. After picking a fight I was never bullied again.

It's interesting to note that the mother believed the authorities would protect the weak, but the father knew they wouldn't and advised self reliance. That says something about which gender is the more protected in our society.

Another way this manifests is in women's demand for safety. This has come about in the wake of some recent murder cases, after which some feminists made outraged demands about women's safety. They believe a safe environment is their right, and imply that such crimes violate an unwritten social contract.

Some of them have tried to blame men-as-a-class for the crimes of rogue individuals, and demanded men-as-a-class prevent it happening again. In this demand we see again the feminist view of the male gender as some kind of gestalt entity. With the apex fallacy, they attribute the power of the top 5% of men to the male gender as a whole. In a similar way, they attribute the crimes of the bottom 5% of men - morally - to the male gender as a whole. They use a broad brush of shame and demand that *men* stop doing it. How this could be achieved is a mystery.

Feminists might suppose that murders of women are a sign of men's patriarchal power, but patriarchy was usually about protecting women. Of course, this trait can be abused, as in the figure of the 'controlling father' within the family, but the basic instinct is protective. Women's demand that murders never be allowed to occur shows that women believe they are owed protection. Men don't believe that they themselves will have any such protection against violent crime, other than the laws already in place.

On one hand, feminists complain about patriarchy controlling their lives. At the same time, they make the gynocentric demand for patriarchy to do everything possible to help them, and provide a safe environment. If it does not, the patriarchy has failed in its protective duties.

Observing the many women's public protests in recent years, you get a sense of the unconscious gynocentrism behind it. Those walking in angry women's marches assume that they matter, that they will be both heard and helped, and that there's a patriarchy that bothers to oppress them in the first place.

On the other hand, adult men learn that the world is largely indifferent to them, and they'll have to solve most of their problems themselves.

Gynocentrism and Feminism: a Toxic Brew

Gynocentrism far predates feminism. It may go all the way back to that tribal mentality, where survival of the tribe was tied to reproduction. This led to more limited life choices for women, but also to protection and special treatment. This continued through the ages manifesting in chivalry, 'first seat on the lifeboats,' and various other forms of privilege.

Onto that base of innate gynocentrism, you then add feminism, a grievance-based belief system that tells women they've been short changed and are owed reparations in the form of new kinds of special treatment. This has led to a series of demands that ever more be done for women.

If we did live in a patriarchy these demands would never be heard, let alone agreed to, just as feminism would never have begun in the first place. Because our society does have a strong gynocentric bent, such demands are taken seriously.

This is why the recent push for 50% female politicians is a mistake. It's based on the idea that male politicians govern in favour of men, a premise that is clearly false. Male ruling elites have always used and sacrificed men when convenient. If they governed in favour of men today, we would not have the anti-male bias in the family law court system through which husbands and fathers suffer after divorce. We would not have the anti-male slant in media or education. If we lived in a patriarchy, terms like 'male privilege' and 'toxic masculinity' would be banned.

Far from being biased towards men, most governments are heavily gynocentric. To take a recent example, Joe Biden's 2020 US election pitch, 'The Biden Agenda for Women' was fawningly aimed at that demographic. In Australia in 2022, the Labor party was equally shameless, making the alleged woes of women the central part of its election policy. After he was elected prime minister, Anthony Albanese toed the feminist line on every issue - domestic violence, the 'gender pay gap,' the urgent need for gender equality, and so on.

It's amusing to note that despite being the most gynocentric prime minister in Australia's history, it still wasn't enough, and Albanese found himself under feminist fire a couple of times for getting it wrong.

With political parties *already* heavily biased towards women, one can only suppose that having 50% female MPs would make governments more gynocentric than ever. This is not something to look forward to, and there should be no illusions about the sort of 'gender equality' they would be aiming for.

If feminists think we live in a patriarchy, they might ponder why so few mainstream politicians ever dare speak up for men as a class, raise a men's rights issues, or substantively argue with a feminist talking point. Most male politicians are craven gynocentrists, or at least pragmatic enough to realise who has the cultural power in the gender war.

How refreshing it would be to see a politician stand up to feminist bullies rather than kowtowing to them. It's unlikely to happen anytime soon in the Anglo countries, although Javier Milei has done so in Argentina.

In terms of which gender has the most social power, some light is shed on the matter by a fellow who calls himself 'Eccentric Hat' on Twitter. In one of his pithy tweets, he said 'The actions women fear most from men tend to be illegal. The actions men fear most from women are not only legal, they are often encouraged.'

Mr. Hat is even more succinct in remarking that 'We live in a patriarchy where even daring to say children need their fathers is a highly controversial political statement. In other words, we don't live in a patriarchy.'

And there you have it, the *reductio ad absurdum* of patriarchy theory. As mentioned in Chapter Three, if patriarchy is the demon feminists fear, it is an astonishingly weak one.

That is not to say patriarchy, to whatever degree, did not exist in our past, or does not exist now in some non-Western cultures. But it's about time to stop pretending that our current reality has any resemblance to them.

It's not a lie if you believe it. Many feminists are not lying, and they do believe in *the Patriarchy* - but this belief can only be maintained by a skewed and selective reading of the evidence.

Feminist reformers will continue to believe in false concepts like male privilege, and continue to push for ever more reforms in favour of women. Never mind the damage done to men or society overall. As long as they're perceived to be good for women, that's all that matters. Such is gynocentrism. Any question of male problems seems to be a matter of complete indifference to them.

As mentioned earlier, there were some good reasons for feminism in terms of freeing up gender roles and choices, but there was far more to it than the simple liberation tale many of us were told.

When it comes to power, there *are* some valid reasons behind feminist reforms. As discussed, one might say there are two kinds of power. There's 'active power' which is the ability to act, and 'passive power' which is the ability to have others act on your behalf. For much of history, women may have had more of the latter and not enough of the former. Where the feminists have a point is that women wanted to move into the realm of active power - as in taking a greater role in public life, the workplace, and so on.

This is understandable but what they should *also* do is stop pretending women in history had no power at all, and that men as a class had it all when the majority of men pressed into service roles often had less of it than women.

In speaking of power, we'll now consider another form of it in the arena of sexual relations. While some women were publicly saying ME TOO, men were privately saying MGTOW. As we will see, both were responses to the apparent power of the opposite gender.

12

From ME TOO to MGTOW

Some time ago, a feminist posted a comment online about sexual assault:

> Perpetrators are made, not born. When a man assaults a woman, this is the predictable result of lessons about manhood as he grew up, the sexist cultures in which he participates, and the gender inequalities woven into his everyday life.

This quote implies that in a 'state of nature' rape wouldn't occur. If assaults are the result of socialisation then in the pre-social era of early humans, they wouldn't happen. Thus Neanderthals or Cro-Magnon (wo)man never suffered this problem.

It seems an act of nature worship to believe rape never occurred in the world of early humans. Can even the most fanatical Edenist believe this? Yet that is the implication here.

Biology plays a role in sexual assault. Hormone-driven sex urges help drive an immoral man to rape. These urges existed before civilisation. In that case, one might suppose it was civilisation which helped prevent rape, rather than inventing it.

This is a problem for feminists, for it suggests society was also for the protection of women rather than their oppression. Feminists tend to see rape is an expression of patriarchal control over women, a misogynistic act of male dominance. It no doubt is misogynistic in some cases. In others, it might be a mindless response to biology. Feminists assume there is thought involved in these crimes. In some cases, there may be very little of it.

Civilisation has done many things, for better and worse, and one of them is to help people live by a moral code rather than

141

simply acting on impulse. Having said that, let's take seriously the feminist premise that sex and /or sexual assault is really about power. Of course, sexual power does relate to social power, but it's hard to see how anyone could say this is all on the male side.

The idea that sexual power is the sole property of men is obviously untrue. The simple quality of being sexually desired can bring power. It can bring problems, of course, but also power - and women are easily the most desired gender, especially when young. Just compare the number of male and female incels. On the hookup site, Tinder, apparently young women 'swipe right' on less than 5% of matches while young men swipe on at least 30 or 40%. As someone also commented on YouTube, dating for men is like a job interview, but dating for women is like shopping - and for an attractive girl, it's like shopping with an unlimited credit card.

In suggesting the balance of power favours women, I'm not referring to actual patriarchies outside the West, or to however it may have worked in the past, but to normal male-female relations in Western countries today. As the odds clearly favour young women in the dating scene, it makes no sense to pretend sexual power is all on the male side.

Another basic mistake is in seeing male sexual desire for women as inherently bad, as some kind of convenient method of hurting or controlling them. Strange as it may seem, many men are attracted to women because they like them and want to be loved by one of them.

To make themselves worthy of female love, men have pursued careers, launched companies, begun perilous voyages, or tried hundreds of other difficult endeavours in the hope of winning a woman's heart. This too is a form of female power - to be able to inspire action in men.

It is also the case that many women have, through all history, been able to use their attractiveness for social gain. They have the ability 'to use their sexuality as a means of upward mobility,' as one honest female academic has said. This is just another part of the spectrum of sex and power which we must factor in to understand the full picture.

If sex is connected to social power, this power is clearly not just the property of men, and in many ways women have the advantage. Men have often tried to affect this power imbalance by achieving wealth or social status, which gives them more power in the sexual arena. Like most forms of power, this can be abused. That brings us to Me Too.

Me Too

The Me Too movement started in 2017 as a protest against powerful men pressuring women for sex in exchange for career advancement. The Harvey Weinstein accusations seem to have been the launching point. Anger over this specific case then broadened into a protest against sexual harassment of all kinds, then to a wider agenda about alleged misogyny and women's lack of power overall.

No one need disagree with the basic premise of Me Too - that women should be free from obvious sexual harassment at work, and bosses should not use their status to put sexual pressure on those beneath them. The Me Too movement had some valid concerns in protesting abuses by powerful men. For example, the notion of the casting couch put a stench over Hollywood for a long time. There have also been abuses in more mundane work settings.

Having said that, there's always more to the story. What, for example, of the women who *do* use their sexuality for social gain? As Janice Fiamengo pointed out, they too are *abusing their power*, at the expense of more ethical women who refuse to do so, or those who lack such power in the first place, like less attractive women, or indeed men.

There are many real victims, but not all 'victims' are the same. In one high profile case, a powerful man preyed on a succession of young women. While most were genuinely abused, one 'victim' was allegedly raped by him then had a consensual relationship with him lasting years, using it to advance her career. The relationship seems to have been transactional rather than abusive. The 'victim' had her cake, and later vomited it up and ate it again when Me Too began, jumping on the bandwagon when convenient. So, there were the ill gotten gains of the first phase, then the contradictory ill gotten gains of the second phase.

The Me Too frenzy raged for a couple of years in an apparent revolution against male power. It went strangely quiet during the Black Lives Matter hysteria of 2020, but was soon back on the horse again, and continues to wax and wane to this day. However, Me Too did not emerge from nowhere in 2017. It was just a more public manifestation of feminist efforts that had been going on for decades.

This was documented as far back as 1998 in the book, *Heterophobia*, by an academic named Daphne Patai. The book was a detailed critique of what Patai called the 'Sexual Harassment Industry' in universities.

This book deserves to be better known. Indeed it should be required reading for all who force mandatory sexual harassment training on men, and for those in the media who uncritically supported Me Too.

Patai spent ten years in a women's studies department and got to see the Sexual Harassment Industry (hereafter, SHI) in action in the university as a whole. She describes several cases of male academics being accused by young female students under this system.

SHI activists believed women at universities faced 'systemic sexism.' They saw sexual harassment as a weapon by which men preyed on women and kept them in their place. This belief led to a hyper vigilance about harassment - actively looking for incidents and taking them seriously. The SHI aimed to wipe out such incidents entirely. This was part of their war on patriarchy.

Daphne Patai saw several problems with this. First, rather than creating a safe environment for female students, as it intended, the SHI created an atmosphere of fear for both sexes. The 'heterophobia' of her book's title describes a heightened fear of male-female relations, in which normal interactions were to be viewed with suspicion, even paranoia. This led some students to look for incidents of 'harassment' and exaggerate them.

This was all enabled by the SHI, which seemed determined to find such offences by any means necessary. For example, feelings were now seen as evidence, so if a given student 'felt uncomfortable' this might amount to harassment. Some incidents were also reinterpreted in hindsight.

Second, the SHI believed harassment was an expression of male power under patriarchy. This dubious theory led some cases to be pursued with vigilante zeal, as part of a wider agenda. Incidents were not treated on their merits, but as small battles in a greater cause. If there was any collateral damage - like falsely accused men - too bad.

Third was the very obvious anti-male slant of the whole business. Men were viewed as threatening, by definition, and as gender enemies under the system of patriarchy. Some of the more radical feminists, like Andrea Dworkin, had in the past said all male-female sex is a form of rape. While SHI would never publicly endorse such an extreme view, there's a whiff of it around the whole enterprise. Men's natural attraction to women would at the least be viewed with suspicion.

Fourth, the Sexual Harassment Industry held faulty assumptions about who had the sexual power. Alleged harassers were 'assumed to have "power" by simply being male and "victims" by contrast are always innocent and, by definition, weak.' Patai noted that all SHI literature was written by its members and seemed to share the same biases, namely:

> '…unexamined notions of male "power" and predatoriness; a belief in women's perpetual "silencing." The persistent… delegitimization of male fears of false accusation; and the automatic assumptions about female honesty and goodwill."

In terms of sexual power, Patai seems rather more worldly than her colleagues in noting that:

> Of course, the one kind of power never mentioned at all is the lure of sexual attraction, a power women have always understood and used. The SHI, playing innocent for the purpose, pretends that women do not employ this traditional asset.

On top of this natural power, female students were also 'empowered,' if you will, by a system that regards them as saintly beings incapable of any wrongdoing. In discussing one SHI paper, Patai critiques the author's claim that accusers must always be protected from 'retaliation.'

> (The author) doesn't consider the possibility that charges may stem from 'a complainant's own desire to "retaliate" - say, because of a poor grade, an ideological disagreement, an unrequited infatuation, or a personal conflict.'

> (And)… 'there is no awareness that the complaint process is itself a powerful weapon in the hands of - supposedly powerless -"complainants," regardless of the merits of their charges.'

To compound this injustice, the SHI had a cavalier disregard for the fate of men who may have been falsely accused. As Patai notes about another SHI paper:

> Not a single cautionary account is given of how an accused person's life was "transformed" by made-up charges... and no words of warning are uttered against students who find in allegations of sexual harassment an effective weapon against their professors or against one another.

Patai notes in passing that female on male, or female on female, harassment challenges the dogma that harassment is a tool of patriarchal intimidation. However, one of Patai's main concerns is the end result of the SHI's vigilante pursuit of its agenda. This would likely be a sterile, uptight, and rigidly controlled university environment which would be bad for both men and women.

At this point, we can recall Thomas Sowell's idea that most leftist arguments collapse by asking three simple questions:

1. Compared to what?
2. What hard evidence do you have?
3. At what cost?

In terms of that third question, the 'cost' of the SHI's attempt to create a perfectly safe environment for women is that they are creating one that is both poisonous and sterile. Poisonous in that men and women become paranoid about interacting with each other, and sterile in that many will opt out of those interactions as a result.

The SHI began with good intentions. In the past, there was a more permissive approach to teacher-student relationships. This opened the possibility for power abuse by *either* party, the teacher through predatory behaviour and abuse of rank, but also potentially by the student in an attempt to gain advantage with a given teacher.

It may have been right to make this sort of behaviour out of bounds, but in trying to do so, the universities went too far the other way, affecting students' behaviour with each other as well. The changes have not necessarily been for the better. There have been bad consequences for both men and women.

Me Too II

To return to the more recent Me Too crusade, we can again agree that the *basic* premise of Me Too is sound, which is that women should be free from obvious sexual harassment in the workplace. A problem, however, is that the definition of sexual harassment has become, as Janice Fiamengo said, 'outrageously elastic.'

As she recounts, Fiamengo initially understood sexual harassment to mean 'a specific kind of threatening behaviour involving coercion… when an employer or teacher, someone in a position of power, extorts sexual favours by offering something in return.' The Sexual Harassment Industry has since expanded their definition of the term to include all sorts of other, less serious behaviour. 'Harassment' can now include jokes, comments, looks, unwanted date invitations, and various other words or actions which can be perceived as sexual or harassing in nature.

Still, that is only one of several dubious issues. In the Me Too crusade, many of the same problems Patai sees in the SHI are at play. Chief among these is the denial of women's power, and the assumption of their permanent innocence.

Female beauty is a mixed blessing. It can bring the risk of harassment and unwanted attention. It can also bring advantages, such as help from men who are drawn to it. In the workplace, it doesn't necessarily give a woman advantages, but it certainly *can*. Me Too crusaders want to focus on the problems but ignore the advantages. As Chapter Fourteen will explain, this is an example of what you could call the 'buffet approach' to equality. They also never seem to think of those who lack such advantages, such as plain women, or men. They focus only on the drawbacks.

Sexual attractiveness *is* a form of social power. It exists in private life and, for better or worse, it can function in the workplace. Complaints about power abuses by Me Too and the Sexual Harassment Industry would be more credible if they didn't pretend this power was all in the possession of men.

In pursuing its agenda, the Sexual Harassment Industry is also playing a power game, with its barely concealed war against the patriarchy. So too is the more recent Me Too movement. Beginning as a protest against sleazy bosses, it soon turned into a more general crusade against 'misogyny' and targeted more specific, and frankly irrelevant, causes like a 50/50 gender quota in government ministers. Despite claims about systemic power, Harvey Weinstein's sexual predation on young actresses has nothing to do with achieving 50% female MPs in Australia or anywhere else.

To digress slightly and return to the topic of gynocentrism, the idea of having 50% male and female MPs is based on the false premise that majority male governments govern in favour of men. This would come as news to those men sent off to fight in wars, or to work down the mines. Even in peacetime, governments do not favour men, and certainly not in recent years.

As mentioned in the last chapter, this was clear in Joe Biden's US election campaign of 2020, in which his pitch for the women's vote was shamelessly gynocentric. In Australia, the Labor party's push for election in 2022 did the same, pandering to women to the fullest possible extent.

As part of this, the Labor government enthusiastically jumped on the Me Too panic leading up to the election. Taking centre stage in this was the alleged rape of a young woman in Parliament House in 2019. The accused man denied it and there was no conclusive evidence. Even so, the case became a national obsession and was used by the Labor party in its campaign.

The young woman was scandalously allowed to give a National Press Club address - broadcast on TV - long before the case ever went to trial. It seems absurd that this was permitted, but it was part of the Me Too mania of the time and the Labor party's efforts to get elected - which they did, a few months later.

Concern for alleged rape victims is one thing. Cynically using them for political gain is another. As the journalist, Miranda Devine, wrote:

> This line of attack to soften up the government pre-election was Australia's version of Black Lives Matter, without the riots.

> Leap on a couple of scandals, blow them up out of all proportion, lie about them, then hang them around the neck of a hapless Liberal minister, turn the "victims" into prime-time heroines, paint the PM as the enabling villain because he didn't fire the "predators," depict the Liberal Party as irredeemably misogynistic, enlist mothers and daughters in your cause and disable the men in their lives.

I mentioned this to a Canadian academic, and she said the feminists had used exactly the same playbook there.

Such a campaign was hardly subtle. One article in *The Sydney Morning Herald* boasted about a new female power rising in politics, all around the world. In other words, we got to see that the Me Too campaign wasn't just about blushing actresses fending off beastly old Harvey Weinstein, it was about the feminist campaign to smash the patriarchy once and for all.

From ME TOO to MGTOW:
The Unintended Consequences of War

Women's attractiveness is, it seems, a problem. It's a problem for them and now, apparently, for everyone else as well. Of course, you can only solve a problem if it's honestly diagnosed, so the pretence sexual power is only a hindrance, rather than a benefit, is a poor place to start.

As Thomas Sowell said, when it comes to solving difficult problems, 'there are no solutions, only tradeoffs.' In a complex world, there are no simple answers. Actually, there *are* some simple answers that have been tried - cloaking the whole female gender in black from head to toe, for instance - but that's not the sort of solution we're looking for.

When you do try to fix a problem, new problems may arise. There have been unfortunate side effects of the Sexual Harassment Industry's vigilantism and the Me Too Crusade. Here are a few of them.

The first consequence is some variation of what have been called 'Mike Pence Rules.' The former US vice president had a strict rule never to be alone in a room with any woman other than his wife, lest some kind of spurious charge be made against him for political gain. Some would call this paranoid, others would say prudent. It's a matter of risk management.

A variation of this is the reluctance of male bosses to mentor young female employees. There was too much risk of some kind of charge being laid if the working relationship soured or if, for example, the employee was later passed over for promotion.

While the chances of this are unlikely, and would probably never occur for, say, nine out of ten women, it is the tenth woman who cruels it for the other nine.

Daphne Patai, in *Heterophobia*, mentions the case of a male academic who faced a spurious harassment charge. After a three year battle to clear his name, he explained how his behaviour at work had changed.

> I still avoid interacting with women I don't know and trust... I still avoid meeting female students in my office, unless I know someone else will be there. I definitely treat my female students differently now than I do my male students.... A lot of professors are being very careful with what they say. Several have told me they now avoid becoming advisors for female grad students.

Still at university, another consequence is a reduced number of male students, and thus a smaller pool of potential partners for female students. The Sexual Harassment Industry, in trying to make a safe environment for women, has made a rather dangerous one for men. One wonders why men would bother going to an arena which is so hostile to them not just in terms of 'harassment' but in its anti-male bias overall.

A lot of men are avoiding women now. The MGTOW movement - Men Going Their Own Way - is about a conscious rejection of relationships, for various reasons.

For those men who do go to university, or still want relationships with women, the going is not easy. Women have the advantage. When you're in the privileged position of being the desired and pursued gender, you can be morally in the right without having to make a move. The man, obliged to take the initiative, has to navigate the minefield of all the SHI's visible and invisible rules, and still face possible charges if he gets it wrong. As Patai said, under SHI conditions, 'Women alone should decide when "sexualizing" is appropriate and when it is not and that men are to be held legally liable if they make a wrong guess about this.' Not to mention that the woman may potentially make this decision - or change it - months or years after the event.

As a result, many young men are opting out. If the unfair divorce system wasn't risky enough in the long term, navigating the minefield of SHI and ME TOO is enough to put them off in the short term as well. In the meantime, they're still told that the systemic power structures of patriarchy are all in their favour.

Men are taking a path of least resistance. From ME TOO to MGTOW. Men Going Their Own Way - and as far away from women as possible. The SHI has successfully created a safe space for women at universities. It has also helped create an environment in which men and women can no longer stand each other. Fortunately, homosexuality has never been more in vogue.

These are some of the side effects - the unintended consequences - of the feminist crusade against sexual harassment. There's always a trade-off.

In the long run, has the SHI really succeeded in creating a better world for women? Some would say yes, but Daphne Patai isn't so sure. Looking back at her own days as a student, she notes that not all her interactions with men were ideal, but she doubts it is any better these days. We are moving towards 'an antiseptic world where human relations would be so rigidly structured that the very possibility of sexually charged encounters in school and workplace will have been eliminated.'

She herself encountered some past episodes that these days could be called harassment.

> These episodes were not pleasant, but neither were they devastating... I would feel exceedingly foolish if I were to refer to myself as a "survivor," or even a "victim" of sexual harassment. None of these experiences did me any real harm. But even if they had - and I grant that other women might react differently or have more disturbing experiences - I would have to measure the benefits of being

spared this sort of behaviour against the costs of preventing it.

In today's grim world of mistrust, we can at least end on a lighter note from the satirical website, the Babylon Bee. In the midst of Me Too mania, it published the headline 'Disney To Remove Problematic Kiss From Classic Movie: Snow White Will Now Remain Dead.'

In fact, Snow White wasn't really dead, just in a coma, after biting into the witch's poisoned apple. Male-female relations are also in a coma now, after biting into the poisoned apple of feminist ideology and Me Too panic. Is there any Prince Charming out there who still wants to wake up Snow White? These days it's not worth the risk. Let her sleep.

13

A Tale of Two Toxicities

There's been a lot of talk about toxic masculinity. I take this to mean traits of male behaviour that are either bad in themselves, or which may be good but turn sour when overdone. There has been a lot less talk about toxic femininity, at least in mainstream media - but those behaviours also exist. They've been widely discussed on YouTube.

This chapter will discuss some of these toxic traits. Most of them are not the sole possession of one gender, but tend to appear more strongly in one or the other. Naturally, writing about this topic will involve making generalisations, for which I make no apology.

It will also be clear that I spend more time discussing the female toxic traits than the male ones, but in the context of this book that's understandable.

Follow up questions are: if there were always certain toxic feminine traits, has feminism made them better or worse? Did it invent new ones? And has it tapped into some of the toxic male traits as well?

Toxic Masculinity

Here are some personality types for masculine traits which are harmful either in themselves or when overdone. This is obviously not an in depth analysis, but an overview with a few brief comments.

1) The Tyrant

Tyranny is excessive control over others, which is an abuse of power. Anyone who has power has the potential to abuse it.

This is not a masculine quality *per se*, but as ambitious men have often sought power, most tyrants in history have been male. I wouldn't say tyranny is 'toxic masculinity' but will agree that a lot of men have been guilty of tyranny.

If there are great male leaders, they are examples of power handled well. Power is not good or bad in itself. Only when it corrupts or is misused does it turn toxic.

2) The Over-Competitor

Being competitive comes naturally to most men. It's a positive quality but can turn toxic when overdone. In sport, you could cite nasty sledging (or trash talk), cheating, win-at-all-costs, or gloating. These aren't necessary parts of being competitive, but distortions of it.

In business, you might have a man who sets out not just to out-perform his competitors, but to crush them. There are also those too concerned with rank and hierarchy, which is another form of competition which can be abused - the school bullies, for example.

Competitiveness is a positive if it inspires men to improve themselves but can be toxic if it means doing unnecessary harm to others in the process.

3) The Thug and the Soy Boy

The thug and the soy boy may seem a strange combination of types, but they are both forms of unhealthy masculinity, in opposite ways.

Being a thug - that is, being overly violent and aggressive - is a distortion of the positive male qualities, strength and toughness.

In some male environments, you have to be physically tough to survive. That's just the way it is, and has been for a long time. Being tough or fearless is a highly valued male trait, inspiring respect in both men and women. Male weakness or cowardice draws the opposite response. Still, that doesn't mean you have to be a thug.

At the other extreme, the recent feminised 'soy boy' type of man is a sign masculinity has declined. There have always been gentle, sensitive men, who may still be distinctly masculine, but this modern soy boy type is different - a sort of insipid, artificially feminised man. His gender identity has been socially constructed, as the feminists say, but not in a good way. He has absorbed the message that masculinity is bad and responded by removing most of it from himself.

He is politically correct and a leftist, and supports all the GPR causes. Not all leftist men are soy boys, but all soy boys are leftist men. That doesn't mean leftist men can't be tough or masculine. Of course they can, and some certainly are. But collaborating with the Global Progressive Regime does mean compliance with a system that doesn't like you. The straight white male has the lowest social status in this system. Whiteness is bad and masculinity is suspect. The leftist male has to kowtow to his betters, be an ally to feminists, and so on. When Gillette made that man-shaming ad in 2019, he had to applaud.

During the first Trump presidency, someone remarked that the men who are the most vocal in the workplace or social settings condemning Trump are 'the ones most controlled by their wives.' It's an interesting theory.

For most of our history, being tough was a virtue, helping everyone survive. The lack of it today imperils our survival. Some leftist ideas are valid but others are absurd. Surrendering to them has made us weak. There's a place for 'diversity and inclusion' in the military, but making it a *priority* is a joke. If he could see it, the old school tough male from a century ago wouldn't believe his eyes.

The trouble with leftist ideas of gender is that masculinity is seen as bad in itself, so it's been largely removed from the men who accept that idea. At the other extreme, what counts as actual toxic masculinity can be seen in the behaviour of The Thug. Strength and toughness are positive male qualities. On the other hand, thugs abuse male strength and use violence indiscriminately, or to dominate others. These are the bully types.

What are you looking at? There are some men with a hobby of going out to start fights with strangers for no apparent reason. Maybe they just like violence. As someone once said, these guys should all just get in the ring together and punch on. That's what the football thugs used to do in England, when the rival 'firms' met up for an informal street fight. Still, if they all share the same hobby, so be it, as long as they keep it in house. Or rather, out of the house.

There's a big difference between the masculine hero and the thug. The thug practises violence for its own sake, to hurt and dominate others. This is not positive masculinity, it's toxic.

The extreme end of that is murder. While men certainly don't have a monopoly on violence, most murderers are men. If heroism expressed through strength can be called a masculine trait, violence and murder is a toxic distortion of that.

4) The Macho

The macho allows only stereotypical male traits and activities, and tries to force other men to conform. He might shame them if they pursue hobbies he considers feminine.

As mentioned, there are some male environments where you have to be tough and not show weakness, or what may be perceived as weakness. That's a reasonable part of male behaviour.

If the attitude is carried to extremes, or continues when the need is no longer there, you could say it has turned toxic.

In the past, definitions of male and female were too rigid, and ideally they should be more flexible. The Macho may be locked into old school masculinity to the exclusion of all else.

5) The Lothario and the Sleaze

Some men apparently make it their quest to seduce and have sex with as many women as possible. Whether or not this is toxic, these types can be obnoxious. Male sexual desire is natural but the need to have sex with hundreds of different women is pathological.

As a variation of the above, another type is The Sleaze, someone who is overly focused on sex, especially when it's unwanted or inappropriate. Although as some have said, possibly the main difference between the Lothario and the Sleaze is their level of attractiveness. The Lothario is desirable to women and the Sleaze isn't.

The Tyrant, mentioned above, is another with the indulgent need to screw hundreds of women. Usually a combination of the Lothario and the Sleaze, the Tyrant is able to get away with it whether his partners are willing or not. Of course, that's an abuse of power and therefore toxic.

6) The Cartoon Fascist

When feminists dressed up in red ala *The Handmaid's Tale* a few years ago in a protest, it seemed absurdly hyperbolic. *No one is trying to send women back to the 1950s*, I thought.

However, there *are* some men who want this. A while ago I had an online exchange with someone I'll call the Cartoon Fascist, because he lived up to the leftists' most paranoid ideas of what a right wing man is. He had some valid criticisms of feminism, but his proposed solution was to remove women from public life altogether and return them to the small world of the domestic sphere.

I said that I'd sooner become a leftist again than support such a policy, due to its restrictive and authoritarian nature. Also, in living up to the leftists' stereotypes, he was justifying their paranoia.

Is this toxic masculinity? Yes, this sort of arrogance fits the bill. While being a wife and mother should be a respectable option, no one should be forced into the role or stopped from having a career if they want one.

There *are* Cartoon Fascists out there, living caricatures of male control over women. Their rigid attitudes do not help the cause. They are the reason feminism began in the first place.

7) The Chauvinist or Misogynist

Related to this, there are some men who believe women are automatically stupid, irrational, and generally beneath them. They are old style chauvinists with a condescending view of women.

If this an *a priori* assumption based on gender alone, it's unfair. Of course, there *are* a lot of stupid and irrational people - male and female - but one shouldn't assume they are in advance. We must give all people benefit of the doubt, then judge them on merit.

8) The Callous

Stoicism is a worthy trait, a form of mental toughness and resilience. It means being calm in the face of turmoil, unruffled by emotions at times of stress. Both women and men can be stoic, but it's often been seen as a male quality. However, this positive trait can be taken too far, in which case a man might seem callous.

One of the mistaken feminist ideas is that men should become more emotional, including crying, for example. Supposedly in becoming more 'feminine,' men will be better and healthier people

- but in terms of relationships, there's a large gulf between theory and reality. A man who is over-emotional or cries too often is not usually one women find attractive.

I think most men are just as emotional as women, but they have to be careful how they manage and express their emotions. There has to be some control. It's not the free-for-all in which some women can indulge without fear of censure. That said, a man who denies or shuts out his feelings has gone too far the other way.

A certain stoicism, or at least self control, is a positive male trait. Still, like all traits, it can turn toxic if overdone. When stoicism turns to callousness, it has gone too far.

9) The Gynocentrist and the Male Sycophant

I described the chauvinist as a man with undue contempt for women. If that's a form of toxic masculinity, another form is the man who is overly deferential to them.

This is toxic masculinity in a different sense. In marriage, it might mean a man who is frightened of his wife, or of 'getting into trouble.' It might mean men who would never criticise women or feminism under any circumstances.

Of course, one should start by respecting women, just as one respects any individual. Automatically deferring to them is different. That so many men do this is a sign that women have cultural power and the idea that we live in a patriarchy is a myth.

This attitude is already rather 'toxic' but really comes to the fore in the Male Sycophant. This is the type of man given to ostentatious displays of praising women.

Display is the operative word. The Male Sycophant wants to demonstrate to as many women as possible what a good guy he is, how supportive, how fair, how socially just. Social media is a boon to such fellows, and if they work in the media itself, even better.

There may be some genuine goodwill there, or he might have a White Knight fantasy, but in some cases, it is pure self promotion.

Someone who wishes women well does not have to make a song and dance about it. They just do it quietly through their actions.

The Male Sycophant, on the other hand, wants to stand under a spotlight and show off. He might be sucking up to women to advance his own public standing and career. Or it might be a defensive move. Leftist straight white males realise their demographic is not highly ranked in the world of leftism, so they have to defer to their betters. In each case, it involves a recognition of the power of women and feminism.

Sycophants are usually annoying, but these male sycophants are shameless. The urge to suck up to power is never admirable, but to do it so publicly is vulgar indeed. Still, perhaps some of them think they're being noble.

10) The Male Feminist

I was going to include the Male Feminist in this list, but the topic is too large for this chapter.

As mentioned, feminism had some valid concerns: for example, freeing up gender roles, and protesting chauvinism or harassment. A male feminist is entitled to support these reforms. Buying into the whole feminist belief system is another story. Inquiring into why a man would do so will have to wait for another day.

Toxic Femininity

The next section will look at some negative behavioural traits often shown by women, but not necessarily caused by feminism itself. I'll then briefly speculate on whether feminism has made each trait better or worse. Once again, I'll associate each trait with a 'type.' These will be short and are not meant as a detailed analysis.

1) The Princess

In fairytales, the princess dreams of meeting a handsome prince who'll give her everything she wants, for no reason except she's a princess. Note the passivity implied. She'll simply be given these things, rather than earning or creating them.

There are some YouTube channels which compile interviews with young women, often taken from Tik Tok. It's striking how many of these women also seem to believe they are princesses and should be given everything by a man, again for no apparent reason. These often involve fantasies of lavish material wealth, far beyond normal affluence. It's a popular fantasy. For instance, in the bestselling novel, *Fifty Shades of Grey*, it's not enough for the male character to be a millionaire, he's a billionaire.

We would all like to be rich, but to expect to achieve it just by marrying is mostly a female trait. Apart from those who inherit it, a man who achieves wealth expects to have to earn it one way or another. This is a contrast between, as one person put it, *human beings* and *human doings*. Some people seem to think their existence alone entitles them to lavish material wealth, all to be provided by others. This is passive power in its fullest form.

A princess attitude in a woman may also include the expectation she will always get her way, which is not about wealth but the power dynamics in a relationship.

Has feminism made it better or worse?

To give credit where it's due, feminism has reduced passivity and encouraged girls to pursue active power - entering the professions and earning their own living.

The negative side remains in the idea that women should automatically be parachuted into top roles - CEOs and MPs, for example, solely because they are female and there should be 50% quotas. But at least they want to become 'princes' now rather than 'princesses.' So, feminism has helped reduce the princess trait, but has certainly not eliminated it.

2) The Parasite

Healthy human relationships are give and take. Parasitic ones are more about the take. Men can be parasitic too, but the female version takes some familiar forms.

Women tend to want to 'marry up,' that is to a man with more wealth and status than themselves. This is known as hypergamy. While, it's 'nice work if you can get it,' and many men would take it if they could, it does imply a certain parasitism. That is, latching onto a more powerful person for gain. While all relationships have to have some mutual benefit, the hypergamous one involves a weaker and a stronger person.

For a long time through history, men may have had more external power in terms of money and social status, and women had to marry to have access to it. Women no longer have to do that, but many still have the instinct for hypergamy.

Relationships are transactional, and as long as both parties understand the terms and there is some mutual benefit, it is fair. When one party marries explicitly for personal gain, or doesn't fulfil their end of the deal, we are getting towards parasitism. A woman who marries and then also divorces for gain is a parasite.

An overly 'pragmatic' approach to relationships can be parasitic if it entails negative traits like discrimination and disloyalty.

Two cases will show this. In the first, a young woman rejected a man's marriage proposal only because his salary wasn't high enough. After he later got a much higher paying job, she regretted this and wondered if she could change her decision without coming off as a gold digger (to use her own words). This woman discriminated against the man purely based on money. This may have been pragmatic, but was also rather mercenary.

In the second case, a woman was married to a plastic surgeon whose salary fell from 600K to 250K during the Covid lockdown. The wife's monthly 'allowance' dropped from 10K to 3K. She felt aggrieved and considered ditching him for another doctor who was still on over 500K, rather than settling for 'some loser with mediocre ambitions' i.e. her husband.

This woman was clearly a parasite who was ready to dump her husband as soon as he was no longer useful. This tendency to pick up and later drop a male partner when convenient is a sadly notorious form of toxic behaviour.

Another form of parasitism is when a woman begins a relationship by 'love bombing' a man, going out of her way to please him, and generally being the perfect girlfriend right up until the marriage. Then, at some point in the marriage she turns into a completely different person who, if she'd behaved that way prior, the man would never have married.

This can happen the other way around too, and feminists often depict marriage as legalised slavery with women the hapless victims of their husbands.

I'm all for equality, so let's agree that at its worst, marriage can be a tale of two toxicities. At its best, within a marriage, both parties should try to make the other one happy. So, what would we think of a man who came on like Prince Charming to seduce a woman into marriage, then turned into a complete bastard a year or so later? The woman would feel lied to, and have the feeling she'd been used. In the same way, a women who acts like the perfect match right up to the wedding, then turns into a bitch after marriage has cheated and used her man in the same dishonourable way.

Has feminism made it better or worse?
Feminism has made parasitism better in the sense that it encourages women to be more independent rather than relying on men. It has also made it worse in failing to call out the terrible behaviour of

those women who do behave like parasites, or the systems that enable them. It has failed to criticise the terrible behaviour of many women in divorce and the Family Court system which has helped destroy many a husband and father.

Feminism is also parasitic in a deeper sense in that women have benefited immensely from the advanced technological societies in which they live, largely created by men, yet feminists seem to do nothing but complain. That topic will be discussed later.

3) The Fishwife

Remember that we are looking at negative behavioural traits often displayed by women, which could be called 'toxic femininity.' These are, of course, generalisations and I had better insert the usual disclaimers.

1. Not all women are like this.
2. Some act in the quite opposite way.
3. Some men also display these negative traits.

Having said that, let's move onto the fishwife, which is the archetype of a complaining woman who is never happy.

In the Grimm's fairytale, 'The Fisherman and his Wife,' a poor man is granted magical wishes. When he shares the good news with his wife, she makes a series of increasingly demanding wishes - but she's never happy, impossible to please, and they end up back in poverty.

This type is that of the complainer who demands perfection, which is usually to be provided by somebody else.

Has feminism made it better or worse?
The answer to that is easy - it is obviously worse. Indeed feminism has been described as 'organised nagging' by Peter Wright, an Australian MRA. What is feminism but an endless series of

complaints about the misfortunes visited upon women, and demands that more should be done for them?

There's also the tendency to complain about reality itself, for example, that women are the ones who have to give birth to children.

We all complain from time to time, but that should be balanced with expressions of gratitude. Feminists complain a lot of the time, but gratitude is exceedingly rare.

Summary - It's worth noting that the first three types - the princess, the parasite, and the fishwife - are all examples of 'passive power.' The princess is simply given what she wants, the parasite takes what she wants, and the fishwife complains about not having enough of it. All three are founded on the idea of what should be done *for* women, *by* men, hence they are all examples of gynocentrism.

For a long time in history, women may have had this passive relation to power, and the expectation that power should be exercised on their behalf by men. Feminism has had a mixed influence on this trait. On the positive side, it has encouraged women to take a more active role in creating or earning what they want, rather than relying on men to provide it. At the same time, feminism has also continued the same old gynocentric traits of demanding what they want - from the government or from men - and complaining about everything that makes them unhappy.

4) The Ne'er–to-Blame

The ne'er-do-well is a male type involved in questionable pursuits. The ne'er-to-blame is a female type who is never accountable for her actions.

The ne'er-to-blame will protest her situation but rarely admit she played a part in creating it through her actions. For example, a woman might 'marry up' for her own reasons, then complain she has to give up her lower paid career when children are to be raised and one parent has to quit work. They need the money and the husband earns more. Still, that was her choice. If she had 'married down' the husband would have had to quit and she could have kept working. Why not take accountability for her choice of partner? Instead, she will blame it on male privilege.

In another case, some years ago there was a post from what you'd think was a Twitter parody account - but apparently not - in which a woman told a tale of woe about her days as a high paid escort. She said she was often taken by wealthy clients to luxury hotels, restaurants, and on shopping trips, but her enjoyment of all these was ruined by knowing she'd soon have to 'let them rape my body.' Heartbreaking, isn't it? Who would ever have thought prostituting oneself would mean having to prostitute oneself?

Has feminism made it better or worse?
In general, feminism gives the impression that women's problems are never their fault. They are always either the fault of men or of systemic injustice. What's more, feminism never seems to blame individual women for anything or call out their bad behaviour. When it comes to a lack of accountability, feminism doesn't seem to have improved the situation in the slightest.

In the above two examples, it's likely feminists could come up with a ne'er-to-blame theory of why the woman was the victim in each case. Whether or not they were victims, they were still responsible for having created their situations. Actions have consequences, and problems need solutions. Still, as Thomas Sowell has said, there are no solutions, only trade-offs.

Feminism would be a far more credible movement, and would empower women more, if they insisted on female accountability. That would be a huge improvement on the current situation.

Feminism is certainly a ne'er-to-blame movement, chiefly for its refusal to make women accountable, its tendency to deny female agency, and its insistence that almost all problems are caused by systemic unfairness. It is an Excuse Culture *par excellence*.

5) The Bitch

The word 'bitch' might seem a gendered term of abuse, but this is not to single out women. You could call a man a 'prick' or a 'bastard' and it means much the same thing. What these terms refer to is mean, nasty, or aggressive behaviour towards other people. This may be for no apparent reason, simply out of spite, or to dominate and control.

This sort of behaviour occurs in both genders, but tends to happen in different ways. Male bullies are more overtly aggressive, even to the point of violence. Female bullies can be violent too, but tend to be more covert. The aggression is not out in the open, but implied or done indirectly.

'Relational aggression' is one term for this sort of behaviour. This is non-physical aggression that operates through words, body language, or mind games. This is practiced by girls on each other through bullying, put downs, social exclusion, or reputational damage in the form of rumours and gossip. It's well known that this happens at high school - so called mean girls - but it can happen long after graduation.

In relationships with men, female relational aggression is expressed through put downs, tone of voice, body language, 'the silent treatment,' complaints, and implied threats. It can also occur through the withholding of sex, approval, or basic civility.

While physical violence *does* happen in women, as noted by domestic violence heretic Erin Pizzey, girls are brought up as social beings and express hostility through relational aggression.

Just as the feminist lobby won't admit domestic violence goes both ways, they rarely mention relational aggression either. They present 'coercive control' in relationships as something men do to women. While there are certainly men who practice coercive control over their wives, I'd wager there are far more women who do it, and more effectively, against their husbands. Most women are well versed in social and verbal skills from an early age. If a marriage goes into decline, these skills may come into play. With men faring so poorly in divorce and custody matters, a woman can hold the threat of divorce as a trump card to top all the other relational aggression.

They also practice relational aggression against each other. As someone said on Twitter, 'Women who have been bullied at school by other females know exactly what women are capable of.' Some even admit to a preference for male bosses, and a few years ago there were reports of an all-female company which formed in hope but ended in tears. Former academic, Daphne Patai, has also noted:

> I myself used to believe that women should run the world. (At the very least) they could make no worse a job of it than men had done. That was before I spent ten years in a women's studies program and saw for myself how, in practice, women dealt with large and small conflicts. It was an experience that convinced me that women are in no way superior to men in political virtue, fairness, or even plain good sense.'

Has feminism made it better or worse?

On the whole, feminism has made relational aggression worse, mainly because it fails to acknowledge it or the basic fact that women are flawed, fallible beings like everyone else. It tends to ignore or excuse bad behaviour by women, mainly because of its exclusive focus on bad behaviour by men. Feminism's need to portray women as the victims of patriarchy means it fails to hold women accountable when they do behave badly.

Relational aggression is also used by feminists themselves. Every male public figure knows that any criticism of women or feminism would inevitably lead to reputational damage, social exclusion, and likely cancellation.

6) The Hell Hath No Fury

Once again, neither gender has a monopoly on bad behaviour. Men can behave terribly and so can women.

Take the capacity to be vindictive. Men have this, as shown for example in acts of reprisal between rivals gangs or tribes.

On the other hand, men can be quite forgiving. Some men have been known to have a physical fight, then later shake hands and have a drink together with no hard feelings. If women have a dispute, however, they can sometimes hold a grudge forever. These are generalisations, but recognisable ones.

The saying 'Hell hath no fury like a woman scorned' goes back to a 17th century play (although not by Shakespeare). It alludes to some women's enormous capacity for spite and vindictiveness. In relation to men these days, it plays out most disastrously in divorce and custody battles.

Suppose a man is guilty of domestic violence or child abuse. His ex-wife or partner is entitled to leave him and take out an AVO. But suppose a man is not guilty of either offence. To falsely accuse him of those and take out an AVO - as some women do - is either pragmatically ruthless, or purely vindictive. As one male therapist said:

> I speak to dads every month and the hell some of them go through at the hands of their ex-partners who alienate their children from them, spread lies, fabricate evidence and falsely accuse them of all manner of abuse is absolutely traumatic and often influenced by misandry.

171

As feminist Marie Shear said, 'feminism is the radical notion that women are human beings.' Well, human beings can tell the truth and they can also lie. That's why #BelieveWomen was one of the sillier slogans doing the rounds a few years ago.

Believe women? Yes, but only the ones who are telling the truth.

Has feminism made it better or worse?

An enlightened feminism would encourage women to be their best selves, and that would include holding them accountable for the sort of terrible behaviour mentioned here. That would truly lead to a better world for all of us.

As today's feminism is itself vindictive at heart, it largely ignores any poor female behaviour towards men. Feminists seem to believe women are always the innocent party in any dispute, and men always the villains. This obviously false view of human nature is a poor starting point for any attempt to understand the world, let alone improve it.

As I will suggest in chapter fifteen, 'VJ Feminism' is based on the Vengeance-Justice model of 'gender equality.' It is vindictive by nature, so feminism is doing little to improve male-female relations at present. Hell hath no fury like VJ Feminism.

7) The Irrational

The idea of the irrational or unreasonable woman is a cliché going back centuries, which means there's some basis for it. Of course, there are a plenty of men like that too, especially in the clown world we live in now.

Unreasonable behaviour often comes out during arguments. One might be discussing a topic in what you think is a neutral way and it's perceived as a personal attack, which then draws a personal counter-attack. Someone on a right wing website made a comment about what it's like to discuss controversial ideas these days.

> I can have a considered conversation, even about very 'incorrect' issues, with older liberals and leftists I know (and I'm friends with a few). I have yet to meet a person under 50 except avowed rightwingers… with whom I could even broach the topics discussed here. The intellectual weakness of even the no longer so young is born of an underlying, perhaps feminist engendered, psychological weakness which manifests as an inability to be challenged argumentatively. I assert that this is likely in part a product of feminism because it reminds me of how so many women I've known responded to disagreement: by accusing me or others of "attacking" them, as opposed to challenging their position. Put another way, it's well known that women as a whole often prefer consensus, even in falsehood, to the rigorous pursuit of truth.

Has feminism made it better or worse?

Have you ever tried arguing with a feminist?

Worse.

8) The Social Conformist

The above quote alludes to another female trait, that of social conformity. Some believe this trait has evolutionary origins. There are plenty of male conformists too, but the trait seems especially common in women, for whom the fear of exclusion is more acute.

Being a conformist has value for achieving social cohesion, and is common in conservative times. Recently we have the curious situation in which leftist values are the norm, and women have mostly conformed to them too. There probably aren't many women who would fail to agree that diversity is our greatest strength.

The dark side of this trait is cancel culture which is the attempt to punish those who don't conform to current values. With the use of relational aggression - gossip, social exclusion, reputation damage - some have said that cancel culture is a manifestation of toxic feminine traits.

As many of the leftist causes are destructive, this social conformity can be used against us. A white woman virtuously holding up a 'Refugees Welcome' sign is an example.

Has feminism made it better or worse?

On the one hand, feminists have aggressively fought against social conformity in terms of family, motherhood, gender roles, and other behavioural norms.

On the other hand, they are also the most fanatical in demanding conformity to the new set of left wing doctrines, and are the most intolerant of dissenters.

Apart from that, in throwing out the baby, the bathwater, and the basin itself, they go too far. Inverting every social norm is just mindless Marxist nihilism. Some social norms are valuable and exist for a reason. Mindlessly conforming to them is not always good, but mindlessly rebelling against them may be worse.

It's a fine line.

9) The Gynocentrist

As mentioned, some believe that both men and women evolved with the urge to gynocentrism, which is the tendency to protect and prioritise women's survival over men's.

This has its uses but the drawback is when men are considered for their utility only, and as disposable. They are seen as having little value in themselves, other than in what they can do for women. One very rarely sees any empathy for men these days, a clear indication that gynocentrism has veered into the toxic end of the spectrum.

Has feminism made it better or worse?
When you start with an innate gynocentrism and add feminism, a female-centric ideology based on grievance and a selective view of history, it's a potent combination indeed. Or rather, a toxic one.
   Worse.

10) The Sexist (and Misandrist)

Sexism has long been a charge levelled against men, and no doubt there are still plenty of men who are condescending or unfairly negative towards women. However, the YouTuber, Alexander Grace, points out that many women today are also profoundly sexist, often to a much greater degree. He gives many examples of young women being interviewed in which they casually express contempt, arrogance, or aggression towards men. This is of a type and to an extent that would not be allowed against any other demographic.

   Even in educated circles, contemptuous and dismissive remarks about men are quite common. Feminists will try to excuse this with the claim that they are 'punching up,' which is a typical leftist dodge from the charge of hypocrisy.

   This is a large topic, but I will be brief and simply say I agree with Alexander Grace that the widespread indifference and hostility from women towards men should be called out for the sexism that it is.

Has feminism made it better or worse?
What do you think?

Conclusions

When it comes to toxicity, feminists have been quick to point out terrible behaviour by men, but less eager to call it out in women. Several YouTube channel have set out to fix this imbalance.

There's no doubt both men and women have the ability to act badly. Where bad behaviour does feature in one gender more than the other, it's interesting to speculate as to why, and whether this may have a biological or social origin. In the case of toxic feminine traits, one can also speculate on whether feminism has made them better or worse, or if feminism is itself partly an expression of those traits.

My discussion of toxic feminine traits in this chapter is a response to the excessive focus on toxic masculinity. At the end of the day, there is really only good or bad human behaviour. Both genders have the ability to act with honour, truth, and decency, just as they can act with selfishness, stupidity, or callousness.

We should give up the idea that bad behaviour is only done by men. If feminism wants to empower women, it should also hold them accountable when they behave badly. At the very least, we must admit that both genders can behave well or poorly. Only then can we move forward and make a better world. We cannot start from a false foundation and expect to fix anything.

14

The Buffet

You treat equality like a fucking buffet.
Jericho Green

The next two chapters will contain the book's most forthright criticisms of the feminist movement. Given feminism's hostility to the mildest criticisms, let alone strong ones, this may lead to myself being personally attacked as a result, but so be it.

Anyway, this book has so far taken a critical stance on some racial sacred cows - multiculturalism and Indigenous affairs, as well as George Floyd and Black Lives Matter. It has also explicitly stood up for white people. The book will later go on to criticise the arts world, the national broadcaster, and leftism itself. So, in terms of avoiding controversy, that ship has sailed.

My motivation in criticising all of these is not to be controversial for its own sake. It is to make the case that our thinking is not just mistaken but highly damaging, and we need to change. These causes are all part of the Global Progressive Regime. All of them superficially moral, but increasingly flawed the more you examine them. That includes feminism, which is a central pillar of the GPR, and one of the most resistant to criticism.

Giving women the false message that they're oppressed doesn't help them, and it certainly doesn't help anyone else. This chapter will explain why this false idea tends to annoy those who can see through it.

Why Do They Hate Us?

Did you know that all feminists want is gender equality? It's a modest request and a noble quest. Who would stand in the way of such a worthy goal? And yet the feminist movement arouses such anger. This is the cause of some perplexity to feminists. *Why do they hate us?* they ask.

So they come up with an answer - *misogyny*. It's a catch all, simple and succinct. Or they theorise that men resent losing the power they (allegedly) had under patriarchy. Or that men want to send them back to the kitchen like in *The Handmaid's Tale*.

There are *some* men who think like that, like the Cartoon Fascist mentioned in the last chapter. But what of the many other men who don't want a Handmaid world but still dislike feminism?

The present chapter will try to answer that question. Really, the whole answer is contained in the eloquent quote from Jericho Green at the top of this chapter. That makes any more discussion superfluous - but for those who want a little more detail, here are six reasons people don't like feminism.

1) The Buffet

Sports fans tend to have a very biased view of their team's games. They might even be called one-eyed, so partial is their perception of events. They notice umpire decisions that go against their team, but rarely those that go in their favour.

In the same way, one-eyed feminists only notice the drawbacks of being a woman but never the benefits. They're blind to both female advantage and male disadvantage.

It follows that the calls for 'equality' are rather selective. While they'll decry the small percentage of women CEOs, they're strangely less concerned by the low number of female plumbers. They'll demand an end to the gender pay gap, but say nothing about closing the gender death gap, that is those people who die as the result of dangerous jobs. They want to smash the glass ceiling but not the glass coffin.

They might complain about being seen as a sex object, but are less concerned about the incel's status as a sexless object. We'll be waiting a long time for them to demand equal swipe-rights on Tinder, or equal pay for men on Only Fans.

The buffet approach to sexual power has always led to complaints about the downside of being sexually desired, but doesn't acknowledge the benefits it can also bring. Being the more desired gender brings problems - unwanted attention and the risk of assault - but also advantages, like career help and attention from men, or the prospect of social and financial advance. Some women have lamented feeling they've become invisible after reaching their forties. In other words, they've found out what it's like to be a nineteen year old man. Being sexually desirable is a mixed blessing. You can complain about the downside, but at least acknowledge there's an upside.

How about conscription? For the sake of equality, we need women in the front line of troops. But as someone once said, the fastest way to stop conscription would be to make it gender neutral. That's not the sort of equality we want around here.

We hear a lot about women's rights in relation to men, but not much about women's responsibilities to men. The very idea is triggering, with its connotations of 'service,' but why is that? Men are expected to serve and provide for women, either individually or as a group. Men are expected to help, support, encourage, and empower women. In the name of equality, let's have a few words from the feminists about women's comparable obligations towards men.

In a video called 'What if Society Really Treated Women Like Men?' YouTuber John Griffin points out that in many key areas where men are doing worse than women, if the genders were reversed there would be a national inquiry. Feminists are strangely silent about these areas of 'gender inequality' which go in their favour.

Overall, when it comes to women and equality they'll have a little bit of this, a lot of that, not much of something else, and nothing at all of the other.

In other words: 'You treat equality like a fucking buffet.'

2) The Pretence of Powerlessness

Let's repeat the *cultural power test* from Chapter Three: Is it more socially acceptable to praise X or to criticise it? So, is it more socially acceptable to praise or criticise feminism?

The answer to that is clear. Imagine an aspiring male politician said something like: 'Feminism has achieved its aims. Girls are now free to choose their careers, and aren't forced to become wives or mothers. Feminism should take a back seat and we'll look at a few areas of male disadvantage for a while. And by the way, the patriarchy is a myth.'

The man's career would be over. His statements would be condemned by public figures, backed up by the howling mob on Twitter. Feminism is therefore mainstream, powerful, and part of the establishment.

In response to a survey pointing out how well women are doing in education, someone posed the question: 'Do we still really need 500 Women's Centres at US colleges and universities, and a disproportionate share of campus resources, scholarships, programs, awards, and fellowships going to women?'

The answer is no, but feminism's whole shtick is about women's hardships and their need for more help. We are at the stage where women are openly pandered to by governments seeking re-election, and by powerful international bodies like UNICEF and the UN. But no matter how much power women have as a result, feminists will always pretend they have none, in order to get more of it. We often get the mixed message of hearing how fantastic women are and also how downtrodden.

This sort of thing reaches its peak on the yearly International Women's Day, which should probably adopt *Poor Me, Awesome Me* as its official slogan. We get to hear about the strength and brilliance of women, but also their terrible plight and urgent need for more help. As Janice Fiamengo said, 'Do women never tire of talking about themselves, their injuries, their heroism, their unique struggles, their superiority, their leadership qualities, and especially what more needs to be done for them?'

Apparently not.

3) The Pendulum

This leads on the next point. It is almost the same point, put in a slightly different way.

In an odd way, feminism is a deeply misogynistic movement - but only half the time.

That's because feminism swings like a pendulum between its two main concepts of women. On one side, it says women are the equal of men and can do anything they aspire to. On the other side, it says women are fragile creatures who need constant help, support, and special treatment.

You can't have both. Either women are the equal of men and don't need help, or they aren't equal and need special assistance to achieve the same result.

Feminists tend to resolve this paradox is by saying women are indeed the equal of men, but are only prevented by 'systemic unfairness.' Hence the need for all the special programs and help.

One of the few areas there may be real disadvantage is the time lost from careers for parenting. In that case, there should be some help with childcare, and fathers should have the option of taking on the stay-at-home parenting role. If there are other examples of systemic unfairness they can be taken on a case by case basis.

We hear demands for 50-50 gender quotas for CEOS or politicians. Underlying such demands is the misogynistic belief women can't achieve that 50 percent on their own, without special help. What's more, to expect a 50 percent end result is to focus on equality of outcome. To ask for that rather than equality of opportunity is insulting to women. If feminists really think women are as good as men, they don't need it.

Overall, feminists should stop swinging that pendulum and make up their minds. Are women strong, capable, and empowered people, or weak and disabled ones who always need the playing field adjusted in their favour? Choose one. You can't have both.

4) Dirty Tricks

One would hope a social justice movement like feminism would be an ethical one - but it's not ethical to bully and to lie.

Feminists bully anyone who fails to support their agenda. They bully politicians who aren't sufficiently gynocentric. They bully activists who dare speak up about men's issues. They bully conservative women who don't fully accept their leftist ideas. And they bully those who point out that women are just as capable of terrible behaviour as men.

This is an extension of the 'relational aggression' of the schoolyard - the reputational damage, social exclusion, and so on. It's been said that cancel culture itself is part of that same behaviour.

It's been interesting to see the recent bullying of feminists by trans activists. They have learned what it's like to be attacked by a fanatical, agenda driven movement like themselves.

Lying is another dirty trick, so ingrained it's taken for granted. There are many ways to lie: lies of omission, the skewed interpretation of statistics, rhetorical sleight of hand. When it comes to ideas about female power and 'gender equality,' or volatile topics like sexual assault and domestic violence, feminists have a partial relationship with the truth. Or perhaps the ideological lens is so strong they don't think they're lying at all. It's not a lie if you believe it.

Then there are the other dirty tricks, typically used by leftists, to be covered in part five of this book. Do you fail to accept every aspect of a feminist woman's theories, and even question them? You're not arguing, you're 'gaslighting' her. Call women out on their sexism against men? That's not allowed. Just as blacks can't be racist towards whites, women can't be sexist towards men.

Bullying, lying, and dirty tricks… when 'gender equality' is at stake, anything goes.

5) Ridiculous Demands and Gestalt Theory

At an Australian high school in 2023, all the male students were asked to stand up and apologise to all to the female students, on behalf of their gender, for all the crimes of sexual assault against women. This was not for specific acts between the boys and girls at that school, but for the crimes of men against women everywhere.

This apology may seem ridiculous, but this sort of public shaming and the demand that men 'stop raping women' is from time to time made by feminists, including one who I'll call 'Jackie.'

Like many feminists, Jackie has the strange idea men make up some kind of collective, gestalt entity. She seems to think individual men have the ability not only to see what millions of other men around the world are doing, but to precognitively detect assaults against women and stop them happening.

While it may be convenient for feminists to treat men as a collective and berate them as such, it is pointless to do so. Each man is accountable only for his own behaviour, and has no control of what others think or do. Much as one would like to stop a random act of sexual assault being carried out right now somewhere around the world, it isn't possible to do so.

Another demand is for politicians to do something about the problem of the 'gender pay gap.' Apparently it's a problem if the total amount of wages earned by all men and all women doesn't average out to exactly 50-50. Despite the many variables in such a complex issue, if it doesn't come out 50-50 it's a crisis.

I've discussed this issue in more detail in another book, but for one pointer as to why this pseudo-problem exists, consider the case of a recent high school graduate who I'll call Rebecca. This is an actual case that made the newspapers. This talented girl achieved a near perfect school leaving score and would have been accepted into any course of study she wanted. However, for reasons best known to herself, she chose to study to become a high school Maths and English teacher.

While you can admire her commitment, it's easy to see this choice is going to make the gender pay gap worse, because high school teachers aren't very well paid. We should applaud Rebecca for following her passion rather than chasing a high salary, but if we want to solve the gender pay gap, we could make some more ridiculous demands. We could demand Rebecca give up her teaching dream and start training to become an investment banker, stock broker, or mining tycoon. Or we could insist that the government increase teachers' salaries by ten, taking them from, say, $100,000 to $1,000, 000. No doubt all the other high school teachers would appreciate a million dollar salary too, so it seems like a terrific solution all round.

Or we could realise the 'gender pay gap' doesn't matter. If you see the entire male gender as one gestalt entity and the whole female gender as another, with the many complex variables in their working conditions, their collective pay will never even out to 50-50.

As well as that, we might consider some basic differences in the way men and women are treated, in understanding why such a gap might exist in the first place. The female MRA group, Honey Badger Radio posted the following comment on Twitter.

> Society to men: You're only worth anything if you win races. Society to women: You're lovely the way you are. Change nothing. Feminism: Why do so many more men win races? Women should win their fair share!

As this is essentially true, in that men are seen as 'human doings' rather than 'human beings,' the only surprise is that the gender pay gap isn't wider. So, in terms of treating men like a collective, if one is going to complain about different average results, one might at least consider the causes of those results.

In general though, most men would like to be seen as individuals rather than as part of a collective, and judged on their own merits.

(6) Anger: Women's and Men's

(6a) Women's Anger

Women are angry. Have you heard? Well, how could you not? Female anger is everywhere.

As mentioned, in 2021 ABC Australia made a four part documentary called *Why Women Are Angry*. Its four episodes covered domestic violence, 'unpaid work,' sexual harassment, and the gender pay gap. To briefly comment, there is some cause for women's anger in these areas, but feminists never give us the full story on any of them. We certainly didn't get it from this documentary. Let's consider them in turn.

Domestic Violence - There's no justification for violence, and male on female domestic violence is a genuine problem - but there's far more to the story than we are usually told.

Erin Pizzey started one of the first domestic violence shelters in England in the 1970s, but then made the mistake of saying a lot of male / female violence in marriages was reciprocal. She was acknowledging women's capacity for violence. Some feminists were upset by this claim and set out to refute it, ironically by targeting Pizzey with 'death threats, and bomb threats' and other forms of harassment.

Ever since, feminists have continued pushing the lie that domestic violence only goes one way - male to female. The DV posters on buses, for example, always show a female victim.

Once again, it's not a lie if you believe it, and it's possible feminists aren't aware that violence goes both ways. Even if was the case that most domestic violence was done by men, that's not the full story, and there do seem to be lies of omission and various forms of bias in discussing it.

In *Why Women Are Angry*, the episode on domestic violence framed it as a problem inflicted only by men upon women. There was no mention of female on male violence, female murders of a male partner or children, violence in lesbian relationships, or of non-physical 'relational aggression' as a toxic behaviour in itself or a possible factor in DV cases.

There have been studies suggesting there's more domestic violence in lesbian relationships than in male homosexual ones. If true, the implications are clear.

In the program, the issue of 'coercive control' was presented as something done by men. As if many women don't practice coercive control. Please. They are the masters of it. There was also no mention of the false accusations of domestic violence and child abuse some women make in divorce and custody battles.

Violence against Indigenous women was also mentioned. While the rates of violence *are* much higher for this group, it was implied that this had an external racial cause. It seems the Edenist view of Aboriginal society got dragged into the mix, but that's another story.

Overall, while male on female domestic violence is a genuine problem, to portray it as the whole issue is simply false.

The Buffet

'Unpaid Work' - This episode was largely on the familiar bugbear about housework in marriage, along with caring for elderly relatives.

In many traditional marriages of the past, wives without jobs did most of the housework. This may have been seen as a fair division of labour if the man was the one earning a living. In such cases, the housework although technically 'unpaid' wasn't really, as the wife had an equal stake in the family, the home, and so on.

More recently, most wives have had to work. For the sake of argument, let's suppose the husband and wife are working the same number of hours. If that's true and the wife is still doing most of the housework, that is cause for complaint.

In one of my previous share houses, I had a male flatmate who did very little housework, and it is certainly annoying. As it was only a short term arrangement, it didn't matter. If it was longer term, we would have had to address the problem.

A poor way to handle the situation is to do the housework anyway, grumble under your breath, be passive aggressive, then eventually explode in rage. You have to be upfront about it - but some feminists speak as if the institution of marriage is exerting a mysterious force compelling women to do all the housework. It isn't, and it's silly to pretend otherwise.

Instead of feminists publishing articles, or entire books, about the unfairness of having to do most of the housework, all women have to do is follow this simple plan:

1. Before you get married, negotiate a fair agreement with the man on how the housework will be done and who will do it. Make sure both parties agree.
2. If you can't do that, don't get married.
3. Maintain the agreement during the marriage.
4. If the agreement isn't kept, get divorced.

If that's not worthy of a Nobel Prize in rocket science, I don't know what is.

When it comes to parenting, and even 'caring for elderly relatives,' it's not as simple, but even so, the same sort of negotiation can apply as to what are reasonable expectations.

These days there is no actual law compelling women to do so called 'unpaid work' in marriage. There may be some 'social expectations,' but if a prospective husband has such expectations that one doesn't like, don't marry him.

It is up the husband and wife to negotiate a fair deal on how work is to be done - before the marriage takes place. If the husband-to-be refuses to do that and she marries him anyway, that is a problem of her own making. If a woman chooses to marry an arrogant, selfish man, or just a man with traditional ideas of gender roles, she must take accountability for that choice rather than pretending the situation simply happened without her knowledge.

Sexual Harassment - This topic was covered in Chapter Twelve. It's also covered at length in Daphne Patai's book *Heterophobia*, and some episodes of *The Fiamengo Files* YouTube series.

While blatant harassment should be banned, the over-zealous policing of male-female interactions by the Sexual Harassment Industry has been bad for both genders.

Being sexually attractive brings both good and bad results for women, but in the usual 'buffet style' they only mention the bad. To repeat Thomas Sowell, when it comes to solving complex problems there are no solutions, only trade-offs. Can all hint of sexuality really be removed from the workplace and other public spheres? Should it? At what cost?

The Gender Pay Gap - The Gender Pay Gap is the zombie that will not die. The idea has been debunked hundreds of times but no matter how many times it is slain, it comes back to life once again. There is a 'gender pay gap' but it's not an injustice, once you consider the many factors that cause it.

In *Why Women Are Angry*, the gender pay gap gets yet another airing. As expected, it's a one sided discussion with little mention of the many factors that create such a gap.

The episode in question is called 'Economic Insecurity' which was presented as a women's problem - as if many men don't suffer from economic insecurity too. There were the usual omissions. They featured a woman who suffered financially when her husband of thirty-four years left her, but made no mention of the many men destroyed after divorce and family court nightmares. They mentioned the rise of female homelessness, while failing to say that the majority of homeless have always been men. The whole thrust of the program was to paint women as hard done by, and implied that men - especially white men - were privileged people with easy lives. This false picture showed no understanding of men's experiences, let alone empathy for them.

So, those are the four causes of women's anger listed in this ABC documentary. Domestic violence, 'unpaid' work, sexual harassment, and the gender pay gap. While there is *some* justification for the anger, all four areas are problematic when closely examined.

The documentary was based on the idea of male privilege and the lack of female power. This premise is undone by the existence of the program itself, for while our *national broadcaster*, no less, will employ activists to lobby on behalf of women, it won't extend that privilege to men, who have at least as much to be angry about.

(6b) Men's Anger

Let consider a few reasons why men might be angry.

One might mention the way men are valued for their utility rather than for themselves, that is, for what value they provide to women, children, and society. Then their disposability if they can no longer perform this role.

You might cite the way men often suffer in divorce, falling foul of the family law court system, being victimised by their ex-wives, or having their children used against them.

Then there's the denigration of men as a class, the contempt and anger aimed at them in feminist influenced university courses, and as depicted on TV shows.

Men have the dubious privilege of their entire gender being assumed, under the apex fallacy, to possess the power of the top 5% of men, and are at the same time tarred as being guilty of the atrocious crimes of what you might call the bottom 5% of men in terms of morality.

Meanwhile there is a general indifference to their problems. This is not so bad, as they do not grow up with the expectation they will be pandered to. In the meantime, they have to hear an endless list of gynocentric demands for what more needs to be done for the poor downtrodden women of the West.

Women are doing pretty well in some regards. They are certainly ahead in education. Boys are falling behind in school, and are less and less inclined to enter a university system that is hostile to them. Yet the struggles of boys are not a concern for feminists, but for some a matter of vindictive glee. One feminist responded to the issue with an off the cuff *let's give it another two thousand years and then take a look at it.* This was apparently meant as a joke, yet many of them actually think like that.

This vindictiveness is part of an ideology that takes a very partial - or false - view of history. Furthermore, while they are quick to blame and complain, there's little in the way of gratitude. Camille Paglia, an outspoken critic of feminism, says:

> Men have crippled themselves physically and emotionally to feed, house, and protect women and children. None of their pain and achievement is

registered in feminist rhetoric, which portrays men as oppressive and callous exploiters.

There seems to be a lack of awareness of the harshness of life, and it's been forgotten that our civilisation has been achieved against the odds and with a lot of effort. Another critic, Steve Brule, has said:

> What kind of mentality looks at our modern world and, despite knowing that humanity rose above the chaos of nature into prosperity and incredible luxury almost 100% by the labor of men, still hates men and insists they are evil?

Despite the benefits of civilisation, life is still unfair at times for a lot of people, but feminists make the mistake of seeing this as going specifically against them and *because* they are women. For a third quote in the series, an anti-feminist named Judith said:

> One of the main reason feminists believe in the patriarchy is because they erroneously believe that men are free to do whatever they want, whenever they want. So when a feminist faces an obstacle, or is told no, they think society is trying to control them because they are women.

Many men have difficult lives and feel powerless, yet they're assumed by feminists to have it easy. This false belief, and the general negativity aimed at men, is further cause for resentment.

Let's return to 'Jackie' mentioned earlier, and a recent published rant where she admits women do sometimes hate men, and claims it is justified. She believes society is full of misogyny and is inherently anti-women, so she is entitled to hate men in return.

As part of her argument, she mentions some recent high profile crimes against women.

If Jackie thinks men are the problem, and systematically so, she and her colleagues could try forming an all female society. Of course, this will never happen, because it would mean giving up the enormous benefits of a civilisation largely created by men. Jackie will never acknowledge this. She has the gynocentric need to accept such a society without gratitude, and also demand it is perfectly safe for her benefit. She does not see or understand the good that men have given her and countless other women through history. She is determined to selectively view only the crimes, suffering, and misfortunes visited upon women.

Jackie also mentions pornography, which she thinks is 'based on nothing but an absolute hatred of women.' Whatever one thinks of pornography, that is an odd statement. There are many types of pornography and it is 'based on' various causes, one of which is men being sexually attracted to women. 'Being sexually attracted to women' is hardly a synonym for 'absolute hatred' for them, although for some of the radical feminists, perhaps it is.

In denouncing pornography, Jackie has some 'strange bedfellows' who are there for different reasons. Some Christian groups see porn as the work of Satan, while some right wing types believe porn is a leftist plot to degrade and attack white societies and their values.

In a world as troubled as ours, there will always be someone to blame. It's only a question of which villain fits into your own belief system. As the pithy commentator Mr. Eccentric Hat has said:

> If you blame society's problems on blacks, you're a racist. If you blame society's problems on Jews, you're an anti-Semite. If you blame society's problems on gays, you're a homophobe. If you blame society's problems on men, you're a feminist.

15
VJ Feminism

There's a t-shirt for sale with the slogan *You're lucky women want equality and not revenge.* As many feminists don't want equality and do want revenge, this is a lie. The idea we're in any way lucky they think like this makes the dishonesty complete.

When it comes to equality, most women take the 'buffet approach.' That is, they're selective about which kinds of equality appeal to them, and ignore the ways in which they're better off.

Feminists say they want to make a better world through gender equality but they help women only. This is based on the false idea that women are disadvantaged under a patriarchy and men are privileged. As that isn't true, the campaign for gender equality is really about something else.

Western women aren't oppressed. They may have had limited life choices in 1950, but that's not the case today. On the whole, they're free to pursue almost any education or career they want. They are not forced to marry or have children, or even to be heterosexual. They have a voice, support groups, and are pandered to by governments. Yes, woman may still face some sexism and the threat of violence, but men probably face more of both. In other words, Western women have got it pretty good on the whole, compared to men, and compared to women of the past or the third world today. Yet still the complaints never end.

The idea women are oppressed today is false - but what about in the past? Most feminists believe women have been the eternal underclass of human history. Not everyone agrees. A female MRA named Hannah Wallen says:

> One of the most disturbing things to me is how common it is to believe that throughout history, the male population designed and controlled civilisation

to oppress women for men's benefit, and compassion
for women was spontaneously invented by feminists
during the 20th century.

Women had more limited opportunities in the past, but this
wasn't always 'oppression' in the manner supposed. In some ways,
they led more protected lives, which was their good fortune. Men
having to go out into the world wasn't always a privilege but a
duty, and often an irksome one. It wasn't necessarily 'power.'

One woman prepared to call this out was Nancy, an 80 year old
British woman interviewed by another female MRA, who calls
herself F. Housebunny. Nancy offered the following view:

> Women have never been oppressed, not in my
> lifetime have I seen it. It's fictional and is poppy cock.
> All the women certainly in my family, friends circle,
> etc were spoilt rotten compared to the men. My
> father went to war but was ordered by my mother to
> return home immediately because she couldn't cope
> not having him working and giving her money, the
> financial stress she put him under eventually killed
> my poor father and he died of a stroke. Growing
> up my sisters and I knew we could get anything we
> wanted in life.
>
> We all went to university, they studied medicine,
> I became a teacher. I have never been oppressed
> and nor anyone I have known who is female. Our
> generation were go getters. Men did the hard work
> and put their lives at risk, not us. I was well kept as
> were most of my friends.

Feminism is a myth. I think the whole thing is ridiculous, I have no more to say on the matter - Nancy, 80 years, Hertfordshire.

As the interviewer added, 'Nancy's mother was already financially secure and the extra money was for lavish clothes for all the children and her habitual buying of clothes. She wasn't ever happy. According to Nancy, her father couldn't ever fulfil what her mother wanted, no matter how hard he tried.'

VJ Feminism

Those two skeptical quotes express doubt about the notion of women's eternal oppression. We now come to the feminist view of history, and how they think it should be used as a guide to current action.

> Girls today are far beyond needing equality. They need compensation for two thousand years of being repressed, mutilated, enslaved, raped, and treated as inferior.

This may seem extreme, but most feminists believe in some version of this idea. Many assume that under 'patriarchy' men have always been powerful and women their victims. Yet history was far from the oppressor-oppressed dynamic implied here. While it's true women suffered, so did men, and in some ways worse given their sacrifices in war, hazardous jobs, and the rest of their duties. Once again, the apex fallacy, leads feminists to see only the most visibly powerful men in history, and falsely attribute their power to the rest of the male gender.

This idea is behind gender activism today. It's the foundation of what we might call VJ Feminism - the Vengeance-Justice model of progress. The VJ model has two key traits: a crusading zeal to 'compensate' women, and a vindictiveness towards men. In a practical sense, it means women's 'empowerment' being given priority at all times and men's issues being ignored.

What are the ethics of this? First, let's pretend for a moment the feminists' false view of history was actually true. It still wouldn't justify action in the present. Leftists always think in terms of classes, but the truth is there is no connection at all between the women living today and those in the past, just as there is zero connection between past and present men.

It is typical leftism to use this sort of vindictive class based thinking for their own gain. In this case, all the men who ever lived are seen as some kind of gestalt entity, and all the women who ever lived are another, so today's boys are to be punished and today's girls rewarded. Well, this is a scam. Today's boys should not be punished for crimes they never committed, and girls should not be compensated for crimes they never suffered. Each child, of any gender, enters this world with a moral blank slate, and it is pure opportunism for anyone to run this racket against them.

Forcing class identification on people is one of the left's dirtiest tricks, and they run the same racket on race. It's an attempt for one group to give itself unearned rewards at the expense of another, based on spurious reasoning. It also requires the men of today to accept a status of moral inferiority in the name of social justice.

This would be unfair even if the oppression version of history was true, but as it isn't true in the first place, it's even less 'justified.'

As a result of these false ideas about history, and the pretence Western women are oppressed in the present, we still hear about the need for gender equality. In their pursuit of this goal feminists claim they are trying to make a better world for women, for society as a whole, and also for men because 'patriarchy hurts men too.' Based on current results, they will not succeed because as it stands feminism seems to be making the world worse for men, *and* for women, *and* for society as a whole. Let's look at some of the consequences of feminism for each of these.

For Men

There are some positive consequences of feminism for men. If women are more educated, have careers, and can develop their full potential, that should in theory make them happier. Generally, men would like to be surrounded by happy women, rather than angry ones, but for various reasons that hasn't worked out.

If 'gender equality' helps relieve men of the pressure of being the sole wage earners, and frees them from too strict gender roles, there are benefits in that too.

A common feminist idea is that men dislike 'strong women' but plenty of men would rather be with a competent, educated woman than otherwise. The problem is most education now is riddled with leftist ideology, especially feminism with its hostility to men. Girls are taught that they're oppressed in the present, and that 'they' were also oppressed in the past. Many acquire a sense of grievance, a belief they're owed special treatment, and a sense of moral superiority. Women who think like this can be hard to get along with, to say the least.

Yet feminism is not just academic, it's an activist movement that tries to reshape society in line with its beliefs. Far from advocating for gender equality it cares for one gender only. Its false premise that women are the eternal victims of history justifies discrimination in favour of women and against men. This manifests in the world of work ('affirmative action'), family life (divorce and custody battles in the family law court system), education (special programs and women-only scholarships), and other areas.

Pro-male activist, Bettina Arndt, has noted the heavy gender-bias in the key areas of health, family, and education. For example, the male suicide epidemic has been largely ignored. Many suicides can be linked to family breakdown, yet the idea of family has itself become politicised, and the man assumed to be at fault in any marriage. In education, it's still all about empowering girls, regardless of how poorly boys are doing.

Such is the power of the feminist lobby and the weakness of gynocentric governments that all this has been uncritically accepted, its harm to men and boys ignored. This is based on a vindictive concept of gender relations through history. Feminists want to empower girls, but men's issues are treated with indifference or hostility.

Some feminists have such a one sided view of gender relations you would not put them in charge of anything. There's a story of a female teacher who gave a male student 2/10 because he wrote about men's issues in a class assignment. 'Men have no issues,' she said angrily. 'They are the creator of issues.'

As feminist ideas are dominant at university, men are less likely to study there. An article on 'quiet quitting' noted the lack of appeal of higher education for the male gender. As one person commented, 'Education is a joke. Men aren't "underachieving." Men are simply refusing to participate in the rigged institutions that are saturated with hatred of men.'

There has been a conceptual 'war on masculinity' for some decades, and especially on regime enemy, the straight white male. One possible side effect is the increase of homosexuality and transgenderism. This is partly because it's more socially acceptable now to be gay or trans, but the hostility to masculinity may also be a factor, as some men unconsciously try to escape their classification as a regime enemy.

Ironically, one might suppose that with less competition, heterosexual men would find it easier to get female partners now, but that's not the case, for the pool of possible partners is ever shrinking. It's a choice between the vapid and the rabid. You've either got the greedy materialist princess types, or the hair trigger feminists with their rage and moral superiority.

More importantly, thanks to vindictiveness in divorce and anti-male family court systems, the risk of marriage being a life-destroying mistake is higher than ever. As a result of these factors, many heterosexual men are rejecting marriage altogether.

The 'no fault divorce' policy, passed in the late 1960s, made divorce much easier to attain. This was a mixed blessing. While it helped some abused women, it also gave some other women the chance to abuse their husbands within, and especially after, marriage. As Janice Fiamengo has said:

> A large number of pathologically narcissistic and
> dishonest women in our society abuse their men and
> then seek to destroy them with claims of victimhood.
> A massive legal and social industry enables them to
> do so.

This has been made possible by feminist attitudes, first, in the form of a deep bias towards women and against men, second, by the false belief that abuse within marriage is always husband on wife, third, by a refusal to admit women can be evil and fourth, through a deeply negative view of the institution of marriage itself. On top of all this, VJ Feminism sees any suffering of men in such disputes as a form of payback for the alleged historical oppression of women. This is in turn enabled by governments and the legal industry.

These are among the real world effects of VJ feminism, an activist movement with a will to power. It lobbies government towards fem-friendly reforms. Far from being a patriarchy favouring men, most of the weak gynocentric governments of our time cave to the demands of these activists. There are real world consequences for men, very few of them favourable.

Overall, the positive consequences of feminism for men are heavily outweighed by the negative ones.

Consequences for Women

There have been many positive consequences for women, with the main one being the expanded life choices in terms of education and careers, as well as freedom from limited gender roles. Feminism has probably also helped some women stand up for themselves against those men who were bullies, or against some chauvinist attitudes that existed a few decades ago.

While there *are* some clear benefits of feminism for women, my main focus will be the negative consequences. Other people can discuss the positives. I'll point out some of the unexpected side effects that are less so. Ideally, if sense prevails, we could keep the benefits but get rid of the negatives.

Most of the negative consequences are unintended. One is that *some* women have taken up jobs or careers and learned that work isn't the privilege they may have imagined. Those with satisfying jobs will be happy. Others with dull or difficult jobs might be glad to give them up.

It should be understood that some feminists have explicitly made war on the family, because they see it as the centre of patriarchal oppression. Many women have bought into this anti-family rhetoric and avoided marriage and motherhood for a career. Some are glad to have done so, but others have later regretted that choice and may have been happier in the traditional roles despised by ideologues.

Women who do want marriage have often found it harder to find a husband. The campaign against masculinity has had many side effects. Some men have become hyper-masculine in a reactionary sense. On the other hand, as mentioned, turning gay or transgender may be a way for some other men to escape being a class enemy. However, even heterosexual men seem to have become less masculine. Progressive women may not find that quite as attractive as promised. Some years ago, an article was published with the title, 'The Terrible Price of Being in a Relationship With a Modern Man Who has lost his Manly Ways.'

On top of this, men's reluctance to go to university removes another traditional way of finding partners, and the hypergamous nature of women makes them reluctant to pair with a man of lower status.

Another consequence - unintended - is that waging ideological war on men has brought more scrutiny on women's behaviour than ever before. Feminism has held an antagonistic and highly critical view of men, and also the gynocentric expectation this won't bring any bad consequences, but only men falling into line with what women want.

That was a mistake. One of the consequences of war is a backlash from men in the form of close scrutiny of negative female traits: hypergamy, selfishness, hypocrisy, sexism, materialism, disloyalty, and other toxic behaviour. Such scrutiny has brought forth cries of *Misogyny!* Too bad. Make war, get war.

Another consequence for women is that feminist theory tends to create a deep sense of grievance, including other states of mind like envy, resentment, and paranoia. In the worst cases, it can lead to what is almost mental illness. One recent diatribe I read contained all the worst feminist ideas. The author was seething with resentment at men's alleged privilege and women's persecution. She was oblivious to the idea men might have problems or deserve any compassion. Her rage was aimed only at white men, as her article contained the usual deference to minorities. This woman's mind was so parasitised by leftist ideas that being around her would be almost impossible for a man. To stay as far away as possible from such types must be seen as a win-win.

If such a woman wants to buy into that whole belief system, that's her affair, but as her interpretation of reality is partial at best, she's not even martyring herself for truth. You wonder what benefit she gets from it.

Apart from anger, encouraging a victim mindset can lead to weakness. In one case, a male astronomer was accused of sexual harassment and later sacked, although it did not sound like a very severe case. Later, a female astronomy student said that even seeing mentions of the man's name, or his research and discoveries, made her feel 'unsafe.' When the student posted this comment on social media, it received hundreds of likes. But if feminists really want to empower women, these sort of comments should be met with derision rather than sympathy. Such fragile displays aren't admirable, and it's a bad look for feminism if their movement creates such insipid weakness.

Another female scientist was much mentally tougher. A biologist named Rachel Bok published a piece in 2020 on why she left feminism. Bok slowly came to realise she no longer believed some of the core feminist ideas, and that the general hostility to men was misplaced. Her feminist beliefs had actually tainted her interactions with men. She realised that most of the men in her life had been highly supportive of her, rather than hostile, and more basically, that women weren't oppressed.

Bok also came to a more disturbing realisation about the Marxist nature of feminism. Marxism divides people into an oppressor and oppressed class, with the aim of creating conflict as a means to revolution.

That is a rather large topic, and brings us to see the consequences of feminism for society overall.

Consequences for Society

If there was an enemy power set on undermining and destroying a nation, a good strategy would include the following three steps. First, contrive a gender war that set men and women at each other's throats. Second, weaken men and masculinity. Third, attack the concept of the family. Coincidentally, feminism has been heavily involved in all three.

To take these in turn, there's a great deal of antagonism between men and women these days. This isn't necessary, as the main feminist battles were won decades ago in terms of education and careers, expanded gender roles, and the choice about whether to marry and have children. But that wasn't enough and feminists have continued waging their phony and vindictive gender war to this day.

Part of this has been a sustained attack on men and boys, and the idea of masculinity itself, which has created all sorts of problems. A systematic undermining of masculinity makes our society weaker, less functional, and easier to control.

As for the family, one commentator has said 'Family is the most fundamental aspect of life; the wellspring from which all other endeavours and aspirations flourish. If feminism is responsible for the breakdown of something as important as that, how can feminism be anything other than evil?'

But that's not how they see it. As mentioned, many feminists see the family as the smallest unit of patriarchy and the main method of women's oppression. The family itself becomes evil in their belief system, so resisting it seems a noble act.

Feminists often think there's a *Handmaid's Tale* agenda to force women back into the home, but that need not be the case. Protecting the concept of the family doesn't have to mean a return to traditional gender roles. Women could still be free to have their choice of careers and enabled to combine that with family life. To be fair, and for the greater good, men should help them do it.

It's not that feminism is necessarily 'evil' but so myopically focused on its own concerns as to lose sight of the bigger picture. In a way, the feminist movement has been used by hostile forces to help carry out their civilisation-harming agenda.

There's a tie-in with racial politics. Feminism has largely been a war on white men. Through the notion of intersectional oppression, non-white men were seen as an oppressed class, so feminists reserved most of their vitriol for white males. Attacking them became a destructive obsession, and they were oblivious to the wider damage done. In various ways, white feminists were fooled into collaborating in the destruction of their own society, which had given them health and succour, and which they so ill appreciated.

You can just see the feminists fuming at that last sentence, for they believe society has done nothing but harm and oppress women. Well, it hasn't.

As part of their 'struggle,' it has not been enough for feminists to just attack masculinity and the family. In their petty war against white males and patriarchy, there are any number of other destructive causes to which they have enthusiastically aligned, many of them race-related - multiculturalism, DEI, BLM, 'anti-racism,' censorship, and the general anti-white, anti-Western mindset.

It's conceivable that a sane form of feminism could have behaved quite differently. It would have taken a more balanced look at the state of gender relations past and present. It would not have seen women's rights as some sort of package deal in which destruction of the Western world was a necessary part. Having achieved freedoms for women, a sane feminism might have looked at Western civilisation with appreciation and helped protect it.

Rather than do this, they have allied their own revolution with every other kind, seemingly out of spite, and in the vague and ill conceived hope this would benefit them.

There's a certain irony in this. For a long time, women were kept out of influential public positions due to the misogynistic belief that their thinking would be tainted by emotion and poor judgment. It was decided this was unfair and women had the right to take influential positions after all. Feminist women could have repaid this faith by protecting the civilisation that had given them these rights. But most feminists are leftists and ally with other left wing causes. Their willingness to collaborate with civilisation-destroying causes like mass immigration shows that perhaps those old 'misogynists' were right after all. What a wasted opportunity for feminists to prove their worth.

There are also plenty of terrible male leaders who have collaborated, so this is not to single out women. But is there even *one* left wing cause feminists have had the sense to oppose? The only one that comes to mind is the transgender issue, and that only because feminists felt themselves under attack by trans activists. Apart from that, the willingness of left wing women to betray their own people is testimony to their selfish and myopic thinking.

It should be an embarrassment to feminists that they turned a blind eye to ethnic grooming gangs in Britain, or to the abuse of women in Indigenous towns in Australia simply because the male perpetrators weren't white. It should be even more of an embarrassment to them that they've been duped into supporting every civilisation harming measure of the last few years and largely, it would seem, out of a spiteful rebellion against the so called patriarchy.

So, well done feminism for helping destroy the Western nations to which they might have shown greater loyalty. This helps explain why feminism is such a crucial part of the Global Progressive Regime. Not content with merely undermining the family and making men and women hate each other, feminism has allowed itself to be used as a tool by Marxist revolutionaries trying to bring the whole thing down, leaving the usual collateral damage in their wake.

Feminism as a Scam, and What Real Female Empowerment Might Look Like

During the Me Too craze in Australia, a couple of high profile rape cases were used for political purposes. One of them, though unproven at the time, was used to help bring down the government. The cases were also used as an attempt to smuggle in the wider feminist agenda. During the so called 'March on Parliament' some activists presented a list of demands, conspicuous among them the demand for 50% female MPs.

The reasoning behind this was the claim that rape is caused by gender equality, that having less than 50% female MPs was also gender inequality, and therefore if we mandated 50% female MPs that would help end rape and sexual harassment. This dubious claim was part of feminist efforts to sell us a job lot of beliefs. Their use of the emotive issue of rape to advance the rest of their agenda was questionable to say the least - but it worked. It helped elect a Labor government that has been the most gynocentric in Australia's history

The agenda was barely even disguised. One newspaper article of the time boasted that in these protests, we were seeing the birth of a new power. The article implied it was a moment in history when 'powerless' women were throwing off the shackles of male dominance and ushering in a new era. It wasn't just happening in Australia, but around the world. To support this claim, the author mentioned Black Lives Matter founder, Patrisse Cullors, the Democrat politician known as AOC, and climate change warrior, Greta Thunberg. To some readers, each of these names would provoke sniggering behind the hands rather than inspiration, but that's another story.

It's not so much that we were seeing the rise of a new power, but the opportunistic grab for power based on contrived panic and outrage, and a very partial interpretation of gender relations.

If this social justice movement is driven by gender equality, it has an odd way of going about it. What should we think of a movement that claims gender equality as its goal but only ever advocates for one gender? What should we think of a movement which ignores, trivialises, or denies male concerns and focuses only on female problems?

A movement concerned with gender equality would admit that men too deserve fair treatment, and that women are equally capable of terrible behaviour. Yet feminists present domestic abuse, for example, as a purely male on female issue. If they really cared about gender equality, they would help men and hold women to account. They do neither.

Feminism certainly gives women some mixed messages. As mentioned, *Poor Me, Awesome Me* would be a good slogan for International Women's Day. On the one hand, girls are told about their innate awesomeness, but also their constant disadvantages. They're told how wonderful they are, and also how downtrodden and in need of more help.

If feminism really wanted to empower girls it wouldn't tell them they're oppressed. While feminism is largely selling them a false belief system, many girls and women don't see anything wrong with it. Gynocentrism, years of immersion in the fem-friendly education system, confirmation bias, and a lack of empathy for the class enemy - straight white men - and they have no idea there could be anything less than righteous about their cause.

If they were given a counter perspective they might think differently, for the benefit of all. Girls in Western nations should be given some straight talk, with a couple of points for starters. First, that while some other women around the world may be genuinely oppressed, *they* are not. They are free to pursue any education or career they want. They're not obligated to marry or have children, and if they do marry, the roles within marriage are not set but are open to negotiation. They are not victims.

Second, when it comes to history, the past is complicated - but whatever it may have been like, there's no actual connection between them and the past. Class identification is a scam, and should not be used to gain special privileges for their own class (women), or to punish another class (men).

Although such changes would be for the better, they are unlikely to happen because VJ feminism is going to pursue its Vengeance-Justice model to the bitter end.

In a parallel universe, a sane feminism could have existed and helped make a better world. Sane feminists could have showed gratitude at the rights they had achieved, the men who had helped them, and the civilisation that had evolved to that point.

Instead, like in 'The Fisherman and his Wife,' nothing was ever enough for feminists, who were never satisfied, always complaining, always demanding more. Such is VJ Feminism, based on the Vengeance-Justice view of life. Even if it was once about ideals, this selfish movement has caused untold collateral damage to men, women, and society. In its willingness to ally with every other kind of intersectional left wing folly, feminism has betrayed the society which gave it birth, thus justifying the misogynists who thought women should have been kept out of public life.

It would help if male leaders would stand up to this movement, but they lack the courage. Despite endless claims to women's powerlessness at the hands of the patriarchy, it is men who are too cowed to speak out. Woe betide any male public figure who fails to kiss the arse of the Australian feminist lobby. Like a gang of teenage mean girls, feminists are prepared to hound, exclude, and destroy the social standing of anyone who doesn't kowtow to them.

Recent Australian leaders, timid and gynocentric, have been unwilling to stand up to them. If a male politician served up even a tenth of the 'truth-telling' they deserve - we would never hear the end of it. The cries of outrage would be deafening.

Instead, governments pander to women and false ideas about their position. In the 2024 US election, the Democrat party ran an absurd scare campaign about the *Handmaid's Tale* that would result if Trump won. One ad about how to vote contained the line, 'In the one place in America where women still have a right to choose, you can vote any way you want, and no one will ever know.' This was an astonishingly false statement. To suggest that American women do not have any choices these days was surely an attempt to set a new world record for dishonesty.

Feminism may originally have been driven by two main factors, one worthy, the other ignoble. The first was the desire for justice, the second was about self interest. One would hope the realisation that today's VJ feminism has very little to do with justice would make them abandon the crusade. The inability to be self critical or see the bigger picture makes that unlikely.

Unfortunately, it will only be the second cause - self interest - that may finally bring an end to this contrived gender war. When feminists finally understand that waging war on half the population isn't that great - for themselves - there might be changes. When they realise half the men have become weak, feminised wimps, and the other half want nothing to do with them, the penny might drop that the relentless self bias of the feminist movement may not be such a great idea after all. Or it may be that the racial tensions of a diverse society, which they have helped create, will lead to an unforeseen dystopia. We will see.

Still, that is a long way off, and we may never get there. Perhaps it's all a lost cause - but when society finally grinds to a halt thanks to the unintended consequences of feminism, one thing's for sure. There'll be a government study into what went wrong, and it will inevitably conclude that the only problem was we just didn't have enough feminism!

Race and Gender Struggles - Common Factors

Having come to the end of the two Sacred Cows sections, it's interesting to see the connections between race and gender activism.

We can see that both race and gender struggles are 'revolutionary movements' in which an oppressed class (non-whites, women) rises up against an oppressor (white people, Western society, men, and patriarchy).

The 'oppressed groups' then create a parasitic relationship with the 'oppressor' using guilt and grievance to manipulate and make demands. The oppressor is supposed to make amends by giving money, social power, resources, and other help to the oppressed groups, while receiving nothing in return.

All this is based on a class based conception of human beings. One's membership of a class (white or non-white, male or female) automatically determines your moral status, making you either a villain or a victim.

If your class status makes you a villain, you are expected to submit and give your allegiance to the victim groups. If you refuse, you may be subjected to hostility and intimidation.

From the characteristics of these groups, it's clear they are Marxist in nature, not just in waging class struggle, but in the manner in which they go about it.

That this is a dysfunctional, un-harmonious way for society to function should come as no surprise, for the purpose of Marxist struggle is to stir up so much turmoil that society breaks down. It can then be rebuilt by the revolutionaries as they see fit.

This struggle has been going on for decades now, and the race and gender activists have gained major influence. After a successful 'long march through the institutions,' leftist ideas have penetrated, like termites, deep into the woodwork.

The next part of the book will look at how these ideas have gained control of a couple of key institutions, first the arts world and second, the national broadcasters of Australia and Great Britain.

Part Four

Captured Institutions

16

The Leftist Cartel in the Arts

A long time ago, in the late 1990s, I entered a competition for new authors trying to get a novel published. My entry didn't make the short list, but I saw that the winning book was about immigrants and the runner up was about Aboriginals. They were tales of struggle.

I began to notice a lot of the books published in Australia at the time had similar themes. There was a focus on what were seen as oppressed groups - women, immigrants, gays, Aboriginals - and an odd fixation on tales of trauma. All those who had been 'marginalised' were to be 'empowered' whether or not their stories were well written or interesting.

It dawned on me that the literary world was not simply a purveyor of stories, of whatever type, but an arena of political activism. There seemed to be a sense of revolutionary mission. The old world of straight white men would be usurped by an alliance of the downtrodden. It was - as Bruce Bawer has said - a *victims' revolution*.

In hindsight, it's clear the literary world, and the arts world overall, was part of the GPR. That is, the Global Progressive Regime. Now, nearly three decades later, the arts world has become even more global, more progressive, and more like a regime. These days we have cancel culture which can harm even someone as powerful as JK Rowling for saying the wrong thing about trans-women.

It's understandable that politics finds expression through art. The trouble is only a small range of ideas are acceptable - those of the GPR. This narrow range of leftist causes has a stranglehold on the artistic world. I call it the leftist cartel in the arts, and the current chapter will discuss why it is discreditable for the arts to operate like this.

The chapter after that will discuss how artists themselves have become cowardly and conformist under the present regime.

Chapter Three mentioned Alan James' theory of the elites in which a small group of people at the top of a society set the range and limits of acceptable ideas. These 'rules' are then enforced at the various levels lower down the hierarchy.

The same thing operates in the arts world. Remember, these rules need not be explicitly stated. They may be assumed, implied, or unconsciously absorbed.

In speaking of the arts world, I mean the creative arts overall including music, literature, and the visual arts, as well as theatre, film, and TV. Entry to the arts world is highly coveted, and there are always less spots available than the number of people who want them. Progress within this world is not down to talent alone. It also depends on cliques, networking, and the help of those higher up. There are various gatekeepers preventing entry and policing who gets to rise up the ranks.

The arts world has been like this for a long time. Because progress within this world was rather haphazard and subject to gatekeepers, there was plenty of power abuse going on, but that's another story.

On top of that, there's this new element now which is the political fanaticism. The arts world is dominated by leftist politics, and especially the causes of the GPR - feminism, 'anti-racism,' diversity, and the rest of it. You can add in new ones like the transgender issue, which is part of gender politics. Support for these causes is mandatory. You aren't allowed to question any of these causes, let alone criticise them.

To show how much of a stranglehold the GPR has on the arts world, consider that it's not enough to support, say, 90% of the GPR's causes. It has to be 100%. One might support almost all of it, but a single instance of wrong-think about any of the sacred cows could be fatal. JK Rowling seems to be an all out leftie, but one misstep on the trans issue was enough to have her not quite cancelled, but under heavy attack and her stocks falling considerably.

If someone as successful as Rowling can be harmed, imagine how hard it is for aspiring artists trying to enter the arts world or rise up the ranks. They are forced to adhere strictly to GPR values. Of course, plenty of artists do this willingly, but there are some who do it mainly because they have to.

The authoritarianism this implies is clear. Not only is the arts world dominated by leftism, it operates as a sort of cartel to ensure this dominance is maintained. The arts cartel is not about price fixing, it's about idea fixing. The 'cartel' is a group of parties and factions united in a common cause. Cartel members decide who gains entry to the artistic world, the kind of art they're allowed to make, and the views they're allowed to express.

In other words they act as gatekeepers, police thought and evict dissenters, and ensure that the arts are used to help sell GPR values to the public.

This can operate in various ways and at all levels. At a high commercial level it can operate through progressive values being imposed on films, or the parasitic takeover of science fiction franchises. In literature, it can show in the sort of people who are invited to writers festivals, or who get published in the first place, and the type of books that are made and promoted.

This need not be an organised conspiracy, in that it is all done consciously. Certain ideas are absorbed simply by repeated exposure to them. After a while, it becomes automatic. Mind you, this state of affairs has not spontaneously emerged on its own. It took some effort to push the cultural world in this direction.

After so much repetition, the leftist dominance of the arts seems natural. The illusion is self sustaining. It's only when an anomalous event draws attention to this do we even notice. For example, a brief scandal erupted when an Australian bookshop owner made online comments about the type of books being published. These included the following:

> What's missing from our bookshelves in store? Positive male lead characters of any age, any traditional white family stories, kids picture books with just white kids on the cover, and no wheelchair, rainbow or Indigenous art, non indig Aus history.

Also:

> Books we don't need: hate against white Australians, socialist agenda, equity over equality, diversity and inclusion (READ AS anti-white exclusion), left wing govt propaganda. Basically the woke agenda that divides people. Not stocking any of these in 2024.

These comments were surprisingly frank. No one involved in the arts world would normally dare make such remarks. However, the bookshop owner was correct in noticing the arts world's domination by GPR values and the anti-white, anti-male zeitgeist, along with its slavish embrace of the allegedly oppressed. It's hard to know which of the remarks offended leftists more: calling for positive books about men or white families, expressing fatigue about gay or Indigenous themes, or skepticism towards diversity and equity.

The comments were from a small Twitter account, and only came to light when some vigilante outed them. Outrage soon followed. Unfortunately, rather than standing firm, the bookshop owner seems to have caved - apologising and deleting the Twitter account.

The thuggish leftist cartel in the arts had intimidated another victim into silence.

Hard and Soft Leftism

Given the stranglehold leftism has on the arts, this leads me to ponder a few questions: What actually *are* left wing values? Should artists be automatically on the left? As an artist myself, should I be leftist too? Am I a fairly tolerant person, as I've always believed, or a raging fascist, as some other people may believe? And if the arts world is on the side of the angels, why is it so hideously authoritarian?

In trying to understand what leftism is, let's consider two sets of ideas. Group A contains some simple values that make up an old fashioned form of leftism. Let's call this 'soft leftism.' Here are its values.

Group A: Gay rights, equal opportunity for women, respect for all racial groups, free speech for all.

Now we come to Group B, which is made up of specific political causes or ways of thinking. I'll call this 'hard leftism.'

Group B: Identity politics, feminism, 'anti-racism,' Black Lives Matter, multiculturalism, DIE principles, cancel culture.

I support everything in Group A, but query or criticise everything in Group B. In my view, support for everything in Group A should be more than enough to qualify someone as a decent person. It would actually make me as a leftist, in the basic sense as used to be understood a few decades ago.

In the Global Progressive Regime, that is not enough. Artists are expected to support everything in Group B as well. This is not optional. Even a mild criticism of anything in Group B would be enough to raise eyebrows. Openly criticising one or more of them would get you cancelled.

This is absurd. Artists should not be *forced* to support anything, and they should be free to criticise anything.

The next question is, should artists be automatically on the left of politics, for moral reasons? Again, artists should not be *automatically* anything. They should be critical thinkers. The question also contains some undue assumptions: first, that artists are paragons of morality, which is laughable, and second, that left wing values are intrinsically the more moral ones, an idea I have come to doubt.

In saying this, it bears repeating that there are two kinds of leftism. There's the 'soft leftism' of Group A, which I go along with. These stances - gay rights, equal opportunity for women, racial respect, and free speech - are examples of basic fairness and tolerance. Then there's the 'hard leftism' of Group B, which I mostly oppose. Most of the time when I mention leftism in this book, it is the hard leftism of Group B - the series of causes which make up the Global Progressive Regime.

The Left as the Establishment

Another key point is that the leftists are now in power, which they weren't before 1960. In the 1960s, being a leftist was being a rebel against the establishment. Today, leftism *is* the establishment. Government, corporations, media, and universities all support GPR values. Leftists who thinks they're still being rebellious today are having themselves on.

Whether a view is orthodox or rebellious changes over time. In 1920 it was risky to be pro-gay. In 2020 it was mandatory. In 1970 it was edgy to support feminism or black civil rights. Today, the failure to do so will get you cancelled.

In the arts world, the victims' revolution has succeeded and set up a new regime. Having done so, they want to retain their underdog status. Well, no, they are no longer the underdogs. In a similar way, artists may think they are rebels for supporting anti-racism, trans rights, feminism, or anti-Western ideas. They are not. Supporting such ideas is expected and there's nothing remotely rebellious about doing so.

As given in Chapter Three, the test of whether an idea is 'in power' is to ask: *Is it more socially acceptable to praise or to criticise X?* Ask that question in the artistic world about any GPR cause and the answer will be obvious. Conformity is not just expected but required.

Art doesn't have to be rebellious. It can be used as Renaissance artists did to celebrate the 'glory of God,' or by the Aboriginals, whose culture barely changed in 60,000 years, to interpret Dreamtime stories.

Artists did play the role of rebels in the 1960s. Now, with leftist ideas as the establishment, this puts artists in an odd position. Those with rebellious instincts may be inclined to question the GPR causes to which they're forced to kowtow. Yet that is not permitted.

The main reason to criticise those causes, however, is not for the sake of being a rebel, but because they are flawed and deserve to be criticised. If they weren't, there'd be no need to do so.

As mentioned, the leftist cartel in the arts means that compliance with GPR values is enforced. This suggests the alliance between the arts and leftism is not automatic, it has been contrived. Many of the beliefs held today are absurd.

While it may be fairly natural for artists to ally with the soft leftism of granting basic rights and respect to women, gays, and non-whites, it is not natural to equate 'whiteness' with oppression, see masculinity as toxic, believe diversity is our strength, or pretend Western culture is inferior to others. There's nothing natural about believing such ideas. These beliefs have been induced, then reinforced through repetition.

What is the real role of artists? It is simply to create. To express concepts, stories, and musical or visual patterns. There should be no political obligation. The creative arts should be free to express a wide variety of concepts, rather than forced to service a narrow range of beliefs or causes.

The role of the arts world is to operate as a fairly neutral arena in which almost all sorts of ideas can find expression. It should tolerate criticism and those with dissident views, and should not discriminate against particular types of people.

Of course, the arts world doesn't operate like that these days. It is a cartel pushing the causes of the Global Progressive Regime.

Discrimination Against Regime Enemies

We've all heard how wonderfully inclusive life is in the GPR. That is, unless you're a regime enemy. The two main regime enemies are first, the straight white male, and second, anyone who criticises the causes of the GPR. These two categories may, of course, overlap.

As mentioned in Chapter Two, the system of identity politics sees the straight white male as the class enemy of all others. In terms of social power, he is seen as the privileged 'oppressor' of gays, non-whites, or women.

Some leftists are quite open about their hostility to straight white males. Some are passive-aggressive, which is handy as they can then deny it. The simplest way to show passive-aggression to straight white males is to exclude them. One academic said she worked in the English department of a Canadian university for several years, and saw them routinely discriminate against men in hiring. This played a part in her decision to stop being a feminist.

In the arts world, there's little doubt the same thing goes on. You can infer it simply because they're so proud of hiring someone from a victim demographic, as if it's one small step for a non-straight white man, one giant leap for progress. While writing this chapter, for example, a high profile artistic body in Sydney announced two appointments to its board: an Indigenous man and a Muslim woman. A white woman mentioned in the same report was the head of a major writers festival. This is how the various 'oppressed' groups collude with one another.

You wouldn't mind if it was based on merit rather than high school cliques and petty alliances in the victims' revolution. When 'diversity' is promoted as a virtue, it gives license to discriminate against straight white males, and to do so under a façade of morality. The rationale, in the arts, for example, may go like this:

1. In the past most writers, musicians, etc, were straight white men.
2. This was unfair.
3. It will only be fair when the number of artists is divided up equally between all the demographic groups.
4. Therefore we are going to discriminate against straight white men until this is achieved.

There is a lot wrong with this reasoning. Let's apply it to Britain, for example.

It is true that most British writers, artists, and musicians were white men (although not necessarily straight). Whether that was right or wrong, let's grant the leftists' premise that this was due to discrimination against women in the past, who didn't have the chance to become artists. If you want to fix that, all you have to do is grant women an equal chance to become artists now, which they do indeed have. Problem solved.

But for leftists, it's not enough to grant women equal opportunity to become artists, you have to ensure equal numbers actually *do* become artists, or preferably more, which will right the historical wrongs. This justifies discrimination for women and against men to vindictively reach 'justice' today.

Moving on from this dubious practice, diversity advocates also demand representation in Britain today for, say, black, Asian, or Middle Eastern artists.

This is different. You can't point to the high numbers of white male artists in the past as proof of racial discrimination because Britain was almost entirely white. As there were very few black, Asian, or Middle Eastern people living in Britain then, you can't make a claim about righting historical wrongs.

But those people are in Britain now, says the leftist, *so they should be represented.* This is debatable. Britain was transformed into a multi-ethnic society without the consent of the people. It is not up to the former majority populations to fix the mess that's been created. At this point, the only real solution is to get rid of identity politics completely and treat everyone as an individual.

The Leftist Cartel Holds a Literary Festival

While the arts world is dominated by left wing artists and ideas, some people make the mistake of assuming this is natural rather than the result of decades of indoctrination, bullying, and gate keeping.

In 2022 *The Guardian* published a short article with a long heading, 'I'm sure rightwingers read books. But you'll never meet one at a literary festival.' This piece, by Zoe Williams, described her attendance at the Bath festival of books in Britain.

According to the article, there's some kind of convention at these events where you begin a session by pretending the audience is politically neutral. But the audience is all lefties, and they spend the first ten minutes 'desperately signalling' this with applause and foot stamping at key points. Williams is sure everyone there voted No to Brexit, hates the Tory government, and thinks as one on all the key issues. Williams loves this consistency of beliefs, and finds the atmosphere 'electrifying.' She concedes there could in theory be right wing book festivals, but thinks it highly unlikely.

What to say about this odd article? First, let's agree Williams is correct that literary festivals are dominated by leftism. Rather than being cause for smug celebration, this shows the rottenness of the whole scene.

Leftists tend to think their views are the correct ones, and that they are themselves morally and intellectually superior to non-leftists. But a healthy arts scene would allow the expression of many viewpoints, including some Williams would consider right wing. If the whole book festival audience does think as one, as Williams implies, it's not really an intellectual event, but an evangelical celebration of right-think (or rather, left-think).

What would Williams say about someone like myself who supports the 'soft leftism' of equal rights for women and gays, racial respect, and free speech, but opposes the 'hard leftism' of DEI, Black Lives Matter, feminism, and cancel culture? Would Williams classify me as a 'right winger?' That would seem to make literary festivals not just left but hard-left, which indeed they are.

If that whole festival audience is united in thought, there are a few possible explanations. First, there's a true way to perceive the world and they've found it. Second, they've been brainwashed into the same views, which aren't necessarily true at all. Third, they've been intimidated into those views and are now scared to express any others. Or fourth, those who do dissent from left wing views have been excluded from the event in the first place.

Williams' reasoning seems rather circular. She says you'll never meet a right winger at a book festival, but notes approvingly that the entire audience is made up of leftists who think alike. Perhaps that's why right wingers don't show up.

Why would a right winger (or a soft leftist) go to a book festival? They'd know they were unwelcome. Then they'd have to listen to almost exclusively leftwing viewpoints, and be surrounded by evangelical leftists booing and foot-stamping every time Brexit or cartoon villain Trump was mentioned.

A basic value associated with intellectual work is the humble acknowledgement that *you could be wrong*. The impression given by many leftists is that they think it's *impossible* they could be wrong.

If they were serious about truth rather than just power, they'd allow critics to speak. Yet barely the mildest criticisms are allowed, and critics are excluded. When it comes to the uniformity of thought at book festivals, therefore, it's not due to the triumph of reason, but the power of the leftist cartel in the arts.

In an article called 'Heroines of the Hive Mind,' Tobias Langdon criticised Williams' piece. He wondered how Williams could be so sure everyone in that audience really did think alike.

> Although Western leftists long to realize Orwell's dystopian nightmares and directly monitor the brain for crime-think, they can't actually do that yet. Like the securicrat goons of North Korea, all they can go on is outward behaviour.

> But Williams didn't consider any possible mismatch between outward behaviour and inward opinion at the literary festival. She never asked herself if there might be crime-thinkers in that 'desperately signalling' clapping and foot stamping crowd. She never saw an uncomfortable parallel with the torrential applause that greets the speeches of tyrants like Stalin, with every member of the audience fearful to be the first to stop clapping.

> But just ask yourself what would happen if someone at such a festival admitted to voting for Brexit. Or if someone pointed out, with full facts and figures, that Black Lives Matter is a cretinous protection-racket that has brought about a massive increase in

the murder of Blacks by other Blacks. Obviously, that crime-thinker would be punished with immediate loss of reputation and livelihood. If you hum with the Hive-Mind, all's well. If you break from the Hive-Mind, you'll be severely stung. But Zoe Williams finds it 'electrifying' to attend a lit-festival where any possible dissidents would be frightened, with very good reason, to express a heterodox opinion.

In other words, the apparent unity of thought in the book festival crowd is a fake consensus which has been cultivated over a long period of time. It's done through the creation of a system in which some ideas are allowed and others are taboo. Through education, social reinforcement, gate keeping, and occasional cancellations, we all end up thinking alike.

Eventually you end up with a book festival of evangelical leftists hollering and foot stamping in a magnificent unity of thought. The leftist cartel in the arts has achieved another triumph.

17

A New Reason to Despise Artists

I never thought I'd live to see the day when the right wing would be the cool ones giving the middle finger to the establishment, and the left wing becoming the snivelling self righteous twatty ones going round shaming everyone.

John Lydon (Sex Pistols, PIL)

'Cancel culture' is a key tool of purification in our Cultural Revolution. It means anyone who offends against GPR values can be removed from public life.

In the arts, it also means the removal of any art that's not politically correct, or that's made by artists with less than impeccable character. But as most artists are terrible people, it's surprising there's any art left at all.

I'm joking, of course... or at least exaggerating. Plenty of artists are decent people, and are loved for what they create. Still, there are lots of traditional reasons to despise them. These are well known and need be mentioned only in passing. Recent years have given us a new reason, which will be the topic of this chapter.

Once again, I mean artists in the general sense to include writers, musicians, actors, and so on, as well as the visual artists.

The traditional reasons to despise artists are for their terrible character traits. There are the terminal womanisers like Picasso or Diego Rivera (Frida Kahlo's husband). The self absorption of rock star Axl Rose, who often made his audience wait hours for the band's shows to start. There's the vanity and megalomania of the divas. The hedonistic self indulgence of the drug addicts. The mental instability of many artists, and the belief that normal standards of politeness and reliability don't apply to them.

Of course, these are generalisations, and such flaws apply to many other people besides. Still, you can always rely on plenty of artists to possess them.

These were some of the traditional reasons to despise artists. We now have a new one, and that is artists' political posturing over the last few years. This was most noticeable after Trump became US president in 2016, for reasons that will soon be discussed. I'm not saying artists should necessarily have liked or supported Trump, but their hysterical reactions to him were quite revealing.

Artists were once seen as rebels. Not anymore. In recent years, we have seen an amazing conformity of belief, and obedience to the values of the Global Progressive Regime. Many artists seem to have taken the superficially moral ideas of the GPR at face value. Any who might disagree with them are too scared to speak out.

While many artists have been cowardly in not speaking out against the GPR or cancel culture, I must admit that in their position, perhaps I would be just as weak. If I were a young aspiring artist, or an older well established one, I would probably be too scared to speak out myself. After all, who wants to be cancelled or have your life ruined?

As I'm relatively old and obscure, I can speak more freely, and will take this chance to do so on behalf of those who don't feel that they can.

My honest opinion is that most artists these days are not rebels against an authoritarian regime. They are collaborators in one, and their political posturing sounds like the bleating of a herd of self righteous and rather dim witted sheep.

The Global Progressive Regime was well established long before Donald Trump was elected US president in 2016. When Trump appeared as a sort of cartoon super villain, it triggered a lot of moral posing from artists who were already in thrall to the regime. I'll try to explain what this means and why it was discreditable.

This will be in relation to four main traits: 1. Hysteria, 2. Cowardice, conformity, and bullying, 3. Elitism, and 4. Superficiality.

1. Hysteria

An American singer touring Australia in 2017 was interviewed by a major newspaper and described her reaction to Trump's election win in 2016. She said that on election night she went to bed crying, then peed the bed in fear like a small child. When she woke up, her mother had phoned her, also crying, and left a message.

Rather than being embarrassed by this hysterical reaction, the singer boasted about it in the press.

Now, compare this to the reaction to Obama's win in 2008. Another woman, an author, described being in a crowded bar in Brooklyn, and they were crying then too, but tears of joy. At one point, the entire bar went to the street and formed dance circles, with people holding hands and singing. Some people were apparently having sex in the street with strangers out of sheer joy.

Both of these reactions were way over the top, and showed a simple minded perception of the world as a battle between good and evil, which had little to do with reality. Just as Obama triggered wildly inflated hopes of a new age of love, which never happened, Trump triggered wildly inflated fears of a new age of fascism, which also never happened.

So, were these sort of responses unusual from artists? Not really. Simple minded and hysterical behaviour became the norm in the Trump era.

2. Cowardice, Conformity, and Bullying

As a fan of rock music, I often read music websites. During the Trump era, it was remarkable how many rock stars departed from their usual spiel of discussing a new album or tour to issue a dire warning of the threat posed by Trump, a denunciation of his terrible moral character, and how appalled they were by him being president. Almost every day, as I read yet another expletive-filled, semi-coherent rant, it became clear that most rock stars were much dumber than I had thought, and remarkably conformist. They all seemed to be of one mind on the topic. Only a tiny minority went against the orthodox view, and they were probably right-leaning prior to Trump anyway.

Meanwhile, the same sort of 'performance' was coming from actors and celebrities. Multi-millionaire actors stepped out of their palatial mansions to denounce Trump and warn everyone about his white supremacy and imminent *Handmaid's Tale* regime.

One can only speculate about the reasons for all this. Most likely, artists of all types had for decades been conditioned to believe in GPR values. When Trump emerged, he was seen as an arch enemy of those values, especially in offending against race and gender pieties. His surface vulgarity and refusal to kowtow triggered a kind of hysteria in artists. Having been so clearly framed as a regime enemy - an 'existential threat,' as some said - artists also saw public denouncement of Trump as a great chance to show allegiance to the regime. Hence the endless line of artists and celebrities doing exactly that.

Perhaps some of these people thought they were being brave criticising Trump, 'speaking truth to power,' or some such nonsense. But not a single artist was ever at risk of being cancelled for slamming Trump. On the contrary, any artist who spoke in *favour* of Trump would have been denounced by the hideous Red Guards of cancel culture.

The power of cancel culture ensured that being rabidly anti-Trump was the only acceptable option for artists. Dissenters would have gone straight into the gulag of social oblivion. In short, there was no moral courage shown in 'defying Trump.' It was the most timid, conformist thing any artist could have done.

3. Elitist

When Trump first ran for president, several famous actors and celebrities said they would leave the country if he won office. It's possible these types are so sheltered they don't know that for most people, leaving the country isn't an option if an election doesn't go their way.

Most of the rich Trump-hating celebs exist in an elite bubble where everyone shares the same political views. They are also sheltered by their wealth from any bad consequences of leftist policies.

Those who *are* affected by them are the poorer or middle class Americans, including those Hillary Clinton called the 'deplorables' in 2016. These are the people actually affected by leftist policies. They didn't take well to being lectured by pompous, affluent Hollywood actors. In general, it's likely these sort of celebrities have never been more despised than they are now. They are seen as arrogant, sheltered, and pretentious.

When Ricky Gervais insulted Hollywood's elite at the 2020 Golden Globe Awards, millions of people around the world cheered.

4. Superficial

I'm not saying artists should have been pro-Trump, but in a sane world, some would be anti-Trump, some pro-Trump, and some neutral and open minded. The frenzy of denunciation indicates something odd was going on.

Remember also all the fawning over Obama. He was superficially charming, but by the end of this chapter I'll give reasons why it was at least as rational to support Trump as the supposedly more moral alternatives of Obama or Joe Biden.

For now, suffice to say that most commentary from artists seemed very superficial. It's easy to denounce racism. A child of ten can do that. It's harder to look at the racial issues and actually think about them. *Is multiculturalism a good system? Is major demographic change good for America and other countries? Why do we only discuss slavery in terms of the transatlantic slave trade? Is 'diversity is our strength' really true, or just a mindless platitude?*

We never seemed to get much detail on these topics from artists. Simple minded posturing is easy. Detailed argument is hard.

Reprise: What is Leftism and Why Support it?

We now return to the questions asked in the last chapter: what is leftism, and should artists automatically support it? First I made the distinction between two types of leftism, using the term 'soft leftism' to describe a set of basic values like support for gay rights, equal opportunity for women, respect for all racial groups, and free speech. If that was all it took, I would qualify as a leftist.

Then there is the 'hard leftism' of the Global Progressive Regime. This includes identity politics and the DIE principles diversity, inclusion, and equity. It means Critical Race Theory, BLM, and multiculturalism. It means the permanent revolution of modern feminism. It means the anti-white, anti-Western, or anti-male slant of most of these movements. It means cancel culture for those who fail to fall in line.

A key mistake made by many leftists, including artists, is confusing this soft and hard leftism. They think that because they support soft leftist values, they also have to accept hard leftism. Well, no, they do not. There is good reason to oppose, or at least question, almost everything I've listed as being part of hard leftism.

How does this relate to US politics and the 2016 election of Trump?

The first point to make is that neither of the mainstream parties in America are very admirable. As in Britain and Australia, neither party has done much to stop Western nations becoming divided and going into general decline. Many people have come to believe left and right wing parties are really just two sides of the same one - a so called uni-party. While each side stages mock battles over fairly trivial issues, the main agenda slips through unopposed.

Having said that, in America it's the Democrat party that's easily the closest to the values of the Global Progressive Regime. While the Republicans have passively accepted GPR values, the Democrats have actively pushed them.

Remember that the regime has a façade of morality. All its main causes have a veneer of social justice. They certainly look good on the surface, and the perfect front man for the regime was Barack Obama. Handsome and articulate, he was the first black president, and a victory for 'the lazy politics of symbolism.' In his speeches, he seemed to observe all the required GPR pieties.

Then there was Trump, who didn't present so well. This straight white male who made money from selling real estate, hosted a reality TV show, an apparent womaniser, a fairly uncultured man who didn't seem to read or partake in the arts, who came across as rude and combative in debates. Trump became a cartoon super villain for the GPR, just as Obama was a cartoon hero.

Just as people accepted the charming, smooth talking Obama at face value, they also took the rude, combative Trump at face value - but Trump's offensiveness was actually part of his appeal. We had become used to inoffensive but weak globalist leaders. These feeble figureheads looked good while pathetically toeing the line on every civilisation-harming issue.

Then, for once, here was a straight shooter, not politically correct, who didn't kowtow or offer the usual empty platitudes. He didn't cry over alleged racial guilt or historical sins. He didn't pander to women the way Obama did. He was openly patriotic.

Trump was elected as an instinctive rejection of the GPR and its hard leftism. The people who voted for him then got to witness the four years after 2016. Whatever the merits or flaws of the presidency itself, the real revelation was the behaviour of leftists.

Leftism showed its true ugly face - the smug superiority of the white middle class, the endless rage from the 'party of love' Democrats and a parade of screeching revolutionaries, and a media so biased some would never trust it again. Many people became 'red-pilled' during this time, from their disgust at what leftism had become. The Walkaway movement, for example, featured testimonies from many former lefties who could no longer stand the cultishness of it all.

Fossilised Hippies

Getting back to artists, many of them expressed their hyperbolic horror of Trump during those four years. It would be unkind to mention some of the dumber artists by name, so I'll mention three of the more intelligent ones - two musicians and an actor - because some general points emerge from what they had to say.

The main point is there seems to be a mindless assumption that artists have to automatically align with the left. For the younger ones, this idea has been hammered into them from an early age. For a lot of the older ones, it comes down to what you might call 'fossilised hippy syndrome.' These people were young in the 1960s and 70s when the leftist counter culture was actually rebellious. Listening to these people now, you sense they don't realise the rebellious soft leftism of their youth has evolved into the hideous hard leftism we have today, which has become the GPR establishment.

John Cleese is one example. I followed this brilliant comedian on Twitter for a while, but he seemed to be also in the grip of another syndrome - Trump Derangement Syndrome - and his daily not-very-witty pot shots at Trump soon wore thin.

One can only infer Cleese still supported the Democrats and was a leftist. It's hard to know why. Cleese had plenty of good reasons to abandon leftism. For example, the ludicrously large divorce settlement for his ex-wife should have been enough to turn him into a Men's Rights Activist. Apart from that, his classic 70s TV show, *Fawlty Towers*, had an unpleasant brush with cancel culture, and let's not forget that his other gem, *Monty Python*, would never be made today for the lack of diversity in the cast.

However, Cleese's real 'right wing' claim to fame was his remark that London is 'no longer an English city,' a clear reference to the changing demographics of the place. What you have then, are several good reasons for Cleese to see the consequences of leftism and abandon his fossilised allegiance to it. In some of his interviews, you sense he was leaning that way. Yet he still did all that silly Trump Derangement Syndrome tweeting.

It's a generational thing. Cleese's Python colleague, Eric Idle, labouring under delusions of rebelliousness, made similar snooty remarks about both Trump and Brexit in his autobiography. However, the views of these two aging 1960s leftists have little to do with actual rebellion today.

The next artist is Johnny Marr, brilliant guitarist from the Smiths, who someone once dubbed 'the Mozart of alternative rock guitar.' This does not pertain to the Trump era, but back in 2010, Marr was not impressed when he found out David Cameron, a Tory prime minister, was a Smiths fan. Marr responded in a jokey manner, *No, I forbid you to like us,* or some such remark, but reading Marr's autobiography, it seems he wasn't really joking. He found it inconceivable Cameron could ever have owned a copy of *The Queen is Dead,* the Smiths' famous third album.

Marr grew up during the Thatcher years so he may harbour a lifelong animosity to Tories, but he's being a bit precious here. Imagine an artist, in effect, *granting permission* for someone to like their music.

More to the point is this childish elitism of assuming only someone with the right political views could possibly like your music. I've only ever known one CEO type in my life. He was a multi-millionaire banker, and certainly no leftist, and Marr may be surprised to know he was also a huge fan of the Smiths. When ex-Smiths singer Morrissey toured Australia in 2018, this guy went to all four of his Sydney concerts, and later in the year went to Marr's gig as well.

Probably the strangest aspect of Marr's belief that a right wing person couldn't like the Smiths, is that Morrissey himself - the Smiths singer - is also rumoured to be right wing. Although a Thatcher and royal hater back in the day, Morrissey has fallen foul of the cancel culture purge in recent years, due to various suspect remarks. Morrissey was as central to the Smith's success as Marr ever was. So, even someone in Marr's own band was a suspected right winger but Marr still seemed to think only people with the correct political views could like his music.

Artists really need to start showing some of the famed 'tolerance, diversity, and inclusion' which are supposed, but rarely seen, leftist virtues.

The third artist is another old rocker, Brian May, the guitarist from Queen. May is in some ways highly intelligent. He's not just an outstanding guitarist, he actually has a PhD in astronomy - which just goes to show you can be almost literally a 'rocket scientist' and still have not much idea about politics. Or perhaps it's the case, as Thomas Sowell has said, that experts in one field often overestimate their understanding of matters outside it.

When Joe Biden beat Trump in the 2020 US election, Brian May made a series of tweets. To summarise, May said he was overjoyed at Biden's win, and that while America itself had been divided over the Trump-Biden contest, the rest of world was not divided. Indeed the whole world was 'rejoicing' at the result, and happy to have America back where it should be.

May said he had looked on from afar seeing America's 'freedoms and decency being eroded.' Now America could begin to heal from the awful damage it had suffered and reclaim truth, dignity, compassion, and so on. May congratulated President Biden and 'trailblazer' Kamala Harris. His remarks were punctuated by exuberant exclamation marks!!!

Much as I respect Brian May's guitar playing and PhD in astronomy, his comments here were amazingly out of touch.

For a start, May had some nerve claiming to speak for the whole rest of the world. In my view, Trump's 2016 election win was an instinctive protest in America against the Global Progressive Regime, most closely linked there with the Democrats. Similar hatred for the GPR was felt in other Western nations - Britain, Australia, and various others, so it's hard to know where Brian got the idea the whole world agreed with him. Most likely, it was from living in an echo chamber with other aging millionaire rock stars who were young in the 1970s, and confusing this with 'the whole world.'

It's not as if he had to look very far to see the same thing in his own country. The Brexit dispute had divided Britain and, like the Trump win, Brexit was a protest against globalism. Both had been pejoratively called victories for 'populism' which rather contradicts May's view that Biden's 2020 win was a victory by and for the people.

Now we come to May's claim that America had suffered 'awful damage' under Trump, and Biden's win would see the return of truth, dignity, and compassion.

It's true America has suffered awful damage, but much of it had happened long before 2016. During the Trump era, a lot of it was due to the Democrats. Despite their later feigned reverence for Our Democracy, they never really accepted the 2016 election result and spent the next four years encouraging their supporters to 'resist' as much as possible, a trend which finished with three months of Antifa and Black Lives Matter rioting in 2020. It's true America was in a fairly chaotic state by then, but it would be absurd to blame it all on Trump.

As for compassion, there is real compassion, then there is fake compassion which ranges all the way from identity politics narcissism to open borders lunacy. Let's not even discuss 'freedoms… being eroded,' for surely we all know which side of politics was most active in censorship at this time.

So, no, the entire rest of the world wasn't rejoicing in 2020 at the noble Democrats' heroic victory over evil fascist Donald Trump.

What They Think They're For vs. What They're Really Fighting For

After the Democrats' win in 2020, the columnist Tim Blair summed it up in the headline, 'Fake Tyranny Gone, Real Tyranny Takes Over.'

To repeat, neither party in the USA is very impressive - but to equate the Democrats with good and the Trump-led Republicans with evil was far-fetched at best. Still, many heroes of The Resistance did seem to think they were fighting for freedom, justice, gender and racial equality, and the rest of it.

In reality, they were just fighting for the Global Progressive Regime. Therefore they were fighting for DIE principles and identity politics. For BLM, CRT, and reparations. For mass immigration and multiculturalism. For feminism and gender politics. For cancel culture and censorship. For the statue-smashing, rioting, anti-white, anti-Western state of mind. For the erosion of borders and eventually of nations.

It's amazing how many people have been conned into supporting all these pseudo-moral causes. They do all have that thin veneer of morality but are mostly rotten underneath. It's time people realised that.

That includes artists, who should rethink their blind and automatic allegiance to leftism. They should stop reacting like Pavlov's dogs and start actually thinking. Stop the groupthink and the weak conformity, and start acting like rebels again. Stop collaborating with bullies and caving to them. If they have to stay silent, so be it, but at least stop publicly collaborating with the regime.

Perhaps then there'll come a time where we can stop despising artists and start respecting them again.

18
National Traitors

During a recent argument, I criticised the ABC, Australia's national broadcaster. The person I was arguing with replied that the ABC is a 'national treasure.'

This may once have been true, and fans of the ABC still believe it, but these days the ABC is more like a national traitor than a treasure. The BBC in Britain is even worse. In some respects, both the ABC and BBC are national traitors. This is a harsh accusation, but I'll explain what I mean by it.

The ABC still has many viewers who revere it. Outside of that group, a lot of people despise the ABC, including some who used to love it. And why is that? It's not the quality of their work, for there are many talented journalists and producers working at the ABC. It's not the public service they offer, such as during emergencies. It's not their sports broadcasts, or some of the high quality drama programs they produce. No, it's their politics. It's the political stance they have chosen to take for which they are disliked by some people who may once have supported them.

The reason the ABC is despised comes down to two main points: it's a national broadcaster which hates its own nation and, instead of realising this is a betrayal, they have a smug sense of moral superiority about it.

While the ABC is politically biased, it is not *bias* in itself, which is the problem. You wouldn't mind them being biased in *favour* of Australia. It is that they have chosen to be biased *against* Australia which is annoying. They're supposed to be the national broadcaster but they're anti-Australia.

The ABC did not have to take that political stance, although many ABC people think it's the morally correct one. If that's the stance they want to take, so be it, but they should stop being surprised lots of Australians don't like them.

In speaking of 'Australia,' of course, we are dealing with contested concepts of what the nation actually is. Modern Australia is the nation that was founded in 1788 by British settlers, and it is this Australia that people at the ABC seem embarrassed about - for to them, it is an illegally created nation that was stolen from the Aboriginals.

It may be true that the nation was stolen from the Aboriginals, but as I said in Chapter Six, they did have the place for 65,000 years. Anglo-Australians had it for barely 200 years before it was stolen in turn by the multiculturalists, so we should ease up on the weeping, wailing, and gnashing of teeth.

For better or worse, modern Australia was people of mainly Anglo-Celtic stock, which remained the majority population for around two hundred years. This fact irks the radicals at the ABC, who have a much 'grander' vision of Australia.

The ABC's concept of the nation involves a veneration of first, the Aboriginal people whose ancestors were here for 65,000 years, and second, the non-white immigrants who have moved here to become part of multicultural Australia. This is the nation the ABC supports.

As for Anglo-Australians, they are rather an embarrassment, and are tolerated as long as they share the ABC's veneration of Aboriginal and multicultural Australia. But the ABC will hardly ever celebrate Anglo-Australia in itself, or take its side on any issue. Whenever there is any kind of racial issue at stake, the ABC will almost always take the anti-Anglo side. The ABC was not always like this but has absorbed all the globalist ideas, including the obsession with race.

So, to be clear, when I say the ABC 'hates Australia' I mean the old Anglo-Australia. The ABC loves Global-Multiculti-Australia.

As many people still identify more with the former, they tend not to watch much ABC these days.

This comes back to the internal Anglo clash between the good-whites and bad-whites, as mentioned in Chapter Four. Good-whites accept the idea of guilt and observe all the racial pieties, and bad-whites do not. The ABC today is run by and for good-whites, as well as ethnic groups. The bad-whites, who make up a fair share of the population, no longer feel the ABC represents them.

Once again, many at the ABC see the settlement of modern Australia as a moral crime, a 'foundational wrong' as one journalist put it. We white people are *living on stolen land* you see. In that case, one might expect the ABC to also disdain non-white immigrants who are living on stolen land just as much as anyone else. But no - the ABC's disapproval is strictly reserved for Anglo-Australians.

If the ABC is so deeply concerned for the Aboriginals, perhaps that shows how much they value Indigenous rights - but what about their British counterparts at the BBC? Perhaps they too cherish the rights of the indigenous people of Britain. On the contrary, they seem to hold them in contempt and don't mind that they are being displaced.

So, are the ABC and BBC for or against the 'indigenous'? If you draw a Venn diagram around the causes they support and oppose, you'll find the common denominator is an anti-white, anti-Western stance. In other words, they are fully aligned with the values of globalism.

Some may say I shouldn't group the ABC and BBC together. They are in different countries. Then again, they have so much in common. A few decades ago, they were national treasures, valuing and loved by the nations they were set up to serve. Now they are national traitors, at war with their own people. They are no longer national broadcasters, they are globalist broadcasters. You might as well rename them GBCA and GBCB, for they are simply local franchises for the same channel, the Global Broadcasting Corporation.

Activism and Biased Content

The ABC produces lots of good non-political content. No one minds that. The problem is its politics. The ABC is meant to be neutral and balanced, yet its bias is clear.

In the Global Progressive Regime, the two main areas of conflict are race and gender. A balanced ABC would present various views on these matters. Instead, one can be confident that on almost any racial issue the ABC will take the anti-Anglo, anti-Western side, and on any gender issue, they will take the feminist, pro-women and anti-male side.

It's likely that these biases are now so deeply ingrained they're invisible to the leftists at the ABC. They see their subjective beliefs as fact, rather than any kind of bias. The BBC is the same, whether they're looking at race or gender, or any other political topic. A former BBC employee, Rod Liddle, speaking about the BBC's biased coverage of Brexit and the Trump and Obama presidencies said, 'They don't see it as a bias. They see it as decency. It is this liberal worldview. It's incredibly arrogant.'

What's more, ABC leftists all seem to have the *same* bias, and think alike on all key topics. At this point, it's inconceivable anyone at the ABC would ever take a contrarian stand on race or gender issues, or any of the other sacred cows of the Global Progressive Regime.

After the martyrdom of George Floyd and the statue smashing of 2020, was there a single ABC figure who queried the BLM movement? During the Voice to Parliament debate of 2023, did even one ABC person support voting No? Is there a solitary soul at the feminist ABC brave enough to say the empress wears no clothes and Western women aren't oppressed?

For signs of the ABC's left wing bias, observe how they cover any issue with a racial aspect. For any story about multiculturalism or Aboriginals, there will almost always be a favourable slant and rarely a critical angle unless it pertains to Anglos.

The ABC will almost never take the side of Anglos on a racial issue. They would never question Critical Race Theory or Black Lives Matter. They'll never point out the downsides for Anglos of multiculturalism and mass immigration. They'll rarely admit the good that came from colonialism and the British empire. For all their obsession with racism, they'll never call out racial hostility against whites.

In the past, the ABC was far more balanced. It gave a voice to left wing causes, as it should, but it wasn't anti-Anglo or anti-male in the way it is today. Like every other institution, the ABC has since fallen victim to the left's 'long march through the institutions' and been infiltrated by people who are biased, to say the least, if not outright activists.

In this book, I've suggested that we live in the 'Global Progressive Regime,' and that two of the main areas of conflict are race and gender. The ABC isn't neutral in the coverage of either.

Gender

Let's begin with gender. Leaving aside the recent controversy over trans issues, I'll consider only the gender issues between men and women.

First, it is not much of a stretch to suggest that everyone working at the ABC is either feminist or fem-compliant. That means they believe in the main ideas of feminism, or at least give lip service to them. It's doubtful anyone at the ABC would publicly disagree with ideas about male privilege, patriarchy, the gender pay gap, domestic violence, Me Too, and so on.

It seems odd to have such uniformity of belief. Perhaps the ABC would say the feminist view of life is correct and they are just reporting the facts and taking a moral stance on them. Perhaps they can't conceive there could be any other legitimate view.

That is why the ABC should hire some outsiders with a fresh opinion. But let's say someone like that applied for a job at the ABC - what are the chances of them being hired? Or if that person hid their views until hired, what are the chances of them keeping their job if they start speaking up?

If the ABC was a neutral organisation, it would hire someone willing to question the sacred cows, but they don't. Of course, it may be that the ABC is quite happy with its stance on gender politics, but if so, it should stop pretending it is just a news service and admit it's an activist organisation.

As mentioned in earlier chapters, the ABC made a four part documentary called 'Why Women Are Angry.' In the name of balance there should also be a four part documentary called 'Why Men Are Angry.' This would not feature the skewed opinions of feminists ascribing men's anger to misogyny, 'loss of power,' being out of touch with their emotions, or the other usual false reasons. It would be made by men's advocates allowed to make their case free of editorial interference.

The ABC could screen Cassie Jaye's documentary, *The Red Pill*, in which she describes her journey from being a feminist believer to a skeptic after speaking to Men's Rights Activists. They could show something like *The Fiamengo Files*, a series in which Janice Fiamengo, a former feminist and academic, offers detailed critiques of the feminist movement.

Of course, the ABC won't show any of this sort of material. This may be because it is staffed entirely by leftists, or because the ABC as a whole has decided to back the feminist view of reality. They have no interest in a balanced discussion of gender issues, if they are even aware such is possible. To repeat, if that is true, the ABC should give up any pretence to neutrality and admit its partisan nature.

Race

We are fighting a culture war between those who support the Global Progressive Regime and those who oppose it. The main GPR battleground is race. Race is a key issue for many reasons and here are just two of them, one relating to the past, one to the future.

A few decades ago, the Anglo nations were some of the richest, freest, and most powerful nations in the world. Since then mass immigration and multiculturalism have brought some benefits, but also racial tension, which these nations are now trying to manage. The current obsession with race is a response to the problems created by these changes.

As for the future, let's speculate that the GPR has an endgame, which includes the erasure of national borders and the creation of one world and one people. This dubious Utopia is being gifted to us in the same way we were given multiculturalism - from on high without our consent.

Equality usually levels down, and this endgame requires the humbling of the West and its people. Those privileged Westerners who enjoyed first world living are to be forced to share their countries with the rest of the world. As people have gradually realised what this entails, there's been some resistance to the idea. They've then found themselves up against a lot of regime propaganda on the topic of race.

What would be the response of a *national treasure* broadcaster to all this? Its first duty of care would be to the people of the nation. In Australia, that would have been the majority Anglo population. At some point, the national treasure might have said: Yes, *some* ethnic diversity is good for the country, but in hindsight multiculturalism was a bad idea. Too much diversity has harmed social cohesion, and if demographic trends continue, our people will turn into a despised minority in their own nation. Therefore we as the national broadcaster, in our duty of care, are going to stand up for you, call out the mistaken policies from the past, and hold our government to account for its ongoing betrayal.

On the other hand, what would be the response of a *national traitor* broadcaster? It might be something like this: Australia is a tainted nation with blood on its hands. It was stolen from the Aboriginals as part of colonialism. The shameful White Australia policy was finally replaced by multiculturalism, which is a perfect policy beyond criticism. Australia must atone for its past sins by welcoming as much diversity as possible. Anyone who complains is a xenophobic far right extremist.

It might seem like I am straw-manning the ABC here, but this is more or less what leftists believe. Knowingly or not, the increasingly left wing ABC and BBC have bought into the globalist propaganda about white guilt, the evils of empire, and the rest of the pseudo-moral spiel. This is not to say they are consciously doing it. It may be that they have absorbed five decades of propaganda and are now emitting it like radiation into the countries they're supposed to serve. In so doing, they are collaborators with globalism's conquest of our countries. They are national traitors.

Traitors?

The label 'traitor' doesn't apply to all. An Indigenous ABC employee might feel no loyalty to Anglo-Australia, and be glad to see it humbled. That's not treason, it's merely spite. An employee with immigrant roots might also bear a grudge. Neither of these types are 'traitors' as such, although if that's how they really think, why are they working for the national broadcaster?

The real traitors are the white middle class leftists who collaborate with the globalist project. Mostly working from delusions of morality, they've been persuaded to undermine their country in the belief it's the right thing to do. They may also be acting from short term self interest, or have a personal axe to grind.

Whatever the combination of these three types, the ABC as a whole is a treasonous organisation. It's supposed to be the *national* broadcaster, but serves globalism. The ABC might say the nation has drastically changed and is now ethnically diverse. The ABC now serves *that* version of the nation, so in that sense it is still the *national* broadcaster. That may be so if we accept that nations are now just franchises for Globalism Inc, but it's hard to see why Anglos should have any affection for an ABC which seems to hold them in low regard.

The nation *has* changed, but it was done without consent. This new version of Australia was never presented as a concept to the Anglo-Australia of a few decades ago for their consideration. It was imposed from on high, and by stealth, with the help of both sides of politics.

Given the problems we are now seeing in Australia and other Western nations, a national treasure ABC might have admitted this was a mistake, and done something about it. Instead, the ABC will continue to blame Anglos for not liking the changes they never agreed to. The ABC is obsessed with racism, but for them the perpetrators are always Anglo and their victims always Aboriginals or immigrants. Indeed, with the steady drip feed of stories about racism on its news site, the ABC acts as enforcer for the globalist regime. Therefore, the ABC is not a 'national treasure.' If anything, it's a globalist treasure.

The ABC is willing to attack Anglo-Australia but will rarely defend it. They will criticise the various historical 'sins' without offering any defence, for to them, they are indefensible. As for the future, if one were to bring news of future Anglo-erasure, some of the ABC radicals would probably cheer.

The BBC

Let us turn now to the BBC, once a revered British institution. Many native Britons now believe the BBC is no longer on their side, and they are right. Like the ABC in Australia, the BBC is a national broadcaster that serves global interests more than those of its own people.

For evidence of the BBC's globalist bent, one can note its coverage of Brexit, recent US presidents, and its approach to race and multiculturalism. Some of these topics were well covered in 'Heresies Episode 5: BBC Bias Exposed,' a YouTube documentary made by a group called New Culture Forum.

In the next section, I'll look at a few ways in which the BBC is a globalist ally, rather than a national broadcaster.

Brexit

Britain is made up of the countries England, Scotland, and Wales. For convenience, I'll refer to Britain as a 'nation' even if that's not strictly correct. As the Brexit debate was a matter of globalism versus nationalism, it was a question of whether Britain would be treated as an independent 'nation' or as a state within the EU.

Britain's connection to the European Union had its conveniences and if it was simply a matter of easier trade and travel, not many Brits would have a problem with it. A suspicion that Britain was being transformed from afar by globalist organisations was seen as less desirable. For this and other reasons, more than half the population wanted to leave the European Union through Brexit.

When this matter was up for debate, how might one expect the BBC to behave? As it was the *national broadcaster*, one might expect it to side with Britain itself rather than Britain as a state within the EU. But according to one insider, Robin Aitken, the BBC has a different outlook. It has 'a clearly defined and strongly held worldview - secularist, multiculturalist, and internationalist.' If so, it's no surprise the BBC was opposed to Brexit.

Still, for the sake of appearances, they might have made a show of neutrality. The BBC is supposed to represent the people of Britain, and as half the citizens wanted to leave the EU, the BBC might have offered a balanced view of the issue. As explained in the *Heresies* documentary, the BBC's coverage was heavily weighted against the Brexit case. They slanted their coverage in favour of the Remain side (to remain in the EU) and against the Leave side (to leave it). This continued after the actual vote.

> The British people voted to get out of the EU, a result the BBC found hard to bear. In the aftermath, the BBC did everything it could to bolster those who wanted to overturn the result. Every negative forecast about how awful Brexit would be was amplified, every parliamentary manoeuvre designed to frustrate Brexit was boosted. It wasn't until the general election in 2019 which brought Boris Johnson to power that the pro-EU lobby, including the BBC, grudgingly accepted the result.

As Robin Aitken said, 'the Brexit episode had exposed in a very obvious way why the BBC's claims to be impartial were self serving lies.'

It also showed the BBC's affiliation with global interests, rather than its own citizens. As with the ABC in Australia, one wouldn't mind the BBC being biased in *favour* of Britain. It is their bias *against* Britain that is tiresome. The BBC seems to have been captured by an elite political class who have little regard for traditional Britain and ordinary people. They are fully allied to the values of the Global Progressive Regime - multiculturalism, 'anti-racism,' feminism, and an anti-Western stance - and disdain anyone who doesn't share their views.

Presidents

This was also shown in the treatment the BBC gave to recent American presidents, Trump and Obama. As mentioned in the last chapter, the hysterical joy that greeted Obama's 2008 election win, right around the Western world, was in stark contrast to the outrage, panic, and paranoia after Trump's win in 2016. According to Ron Liddle, the BBC's reaction to Obama's win was excessive.

> The way they greeted his victory... the ejaculate flying round the studios, people dancing with joy. It was just absurd. And then you compare it to Trump where they were openly hostile... all the way through his presidency.

Much the same could be seen in Australia and the US - the fawning over Obama, then the antagonism to Trump, which continued for four years of one sided coverage. They even managed to up the ante in the run up to the 2020 election, when each day brought a fresh barrage of anti-Trump stories. According to Robin Aitken, at the BBC the bias was plain to see.

> Filled with contempt for the man and his policies, the BBC contrived a news agenda which was unremittingly negative towards his presidency. In the BBC's telling, Trump did nothing right, and from the outset its reporters joined in with the American media in delegitimising the Trump presidency.

Even if they didn't like Trump, a world class media group like the BBC should be professional enough to put their feelings aside, but they did not. After four years of seeing the left wing media behave like this, many people lost all respect for these organisations and would never see them the same way again. It's surprising they exposed themselves like that, but Trump had a unique ability to draw hysteria from these people.

To speculate on the extreme reactions to those two presidents, perhaps it was that Obama symbolised GPR values and Trump their rejection. As mentioned in the last chapter, the superficially charming Obama gave lip service to every leftist cause, while the problematic Trump refused to play along. He didn't bother with PC platitudes or kowtow to anyone, but that was all part of his appeal.

As Aitken said, the BBC never seemed to understand why Trump was elected in the first place. Still, their contempt for the people who voted for him and for Brexit shows how remote the BBC elites have become. Remember, these are the people who are complicit in the destruction of their own nations, which they mostly do from a position of affluence and a sense of moral superiority.

The Great Replacement

When it comes to showing its globalist colours, the BBC's treatment of race is a key indicator. As the national broadcaster, one might think the BBC would have a certain loyalty to the majority population. Strangely, it seems the BBC are not defenders of the country's people, but collaborators in the project to remove them.

The Great Replacement, a phrase coined by Renaud Camus, means the demographic replacement of a country's main ethnic group by others. Camus was writing about France, but the same thing is happening in other nations. The Great Replacement is often dismissed as a 'conspiracy theory' but that pertains to whether or not the change is intentional. There does seem to be major demographic change happening in Britain. Whether it's been deliberately done is a separate issue. For now, an intriguing question is why this is a matter of such indifference to the BBC.

The different attitudes to this in the elites compared to ordinary people has been noticed by Simon Webb of the YouTube channel, *History Debunked*. In one video he mentioned a report which said white British children would be a minority within forty years. As Webb put it:

> Ordinary people know what a terrifying thought this is, but our politicians, newspapers, intellectuals, and of course the BBC, all treat this looming catastrophe for our nation with a complete lack of urgency and no apparent realisation at all that this would even be an undesirable state of affairs. I have not spoken to or been in contact with anybody who is not horrified by this news. But then I suppose I don't mix with the right circles, the hi-faluting kind. Thank the lord I am not an intellectual is all I can say. It does seem to have rather a bad effect upon the brain.

It is odd that the BBC seems so indifferent to this Great Replacement, and is perhaps even actively helping it. Why would they do that? Let's recall that the BBC is the national broadcaster, but is 'internationalist' in outlook. For the hypothetical Great Replacement, most BBC stances help rather than hinder the process: celebrating diversity and multiculturalism, disguising racial crime statistics, hiring diverse actors for historical dramas, aligning with the globalist EU, pushing the idea of historical guilt about the British empire, and more.

As to why the BBC would collaborate in the Great Replacement, first, the non-white BBC employees probably see a transition into multicultural Britain as in their own best interests. That is a rational approach, even showing loyalty to their own ethnic group.

It is the white British employees who are of greater curiosity, for they are not just working against their own kind, they also have an air of moral superiority about doing so. Trying to understand this leads to an examination of leftist psychology. There are several reasons for their behaviour.

First, white Westerners were not trained to think in terms of their own racial interests, and while they were the demographic majority, they had no reason to do so. As their demographic shrinks, they should be revising that policy, but white leftists cling to their outdated beliefs. This is partly because thinking racially was for a long time installed as the number one taboo for white people. This is unwise, as almost every other group *does* think racially. White leftists will be the last people to figure this out, particularly the type who work for the BBC.

Such people have a naïve allegiance to abstract values - justice, equality, or tolerance, for example - not realising such values aren't universally held. Tribalism is a far more common state of mind.

Second, they have been trained to see their own society as the enemy, as embodied in the figure of the straight white male, which they've been taught to see as an oppressor who should be brought down. Many white leftists have a personal axe to grind, whether it's a feminist wanting to bring down the patriarchy, a gay person worried about homophobia, or a left wing atheist with a hatred for the Christian church. All these people may have valid reasons for their attitudes, but they tend to buy into a package deal of beliefs in a clumsy alliance against their own society.

Acting out of perceived self interest, and often out of spite, these people ally with various causes which are against their long term interests and that of society as a whole. A feminist or gay person might ally with certain ethnic groups, for example, which are not known for supporting women or gays. More to the point, they collaborate with the Great Replacement in the over-optimistic belief it will lead to something better - assuming they have thought it through in the first place. Many leftists have clearly *not* thought it through, their short term spite clouding any sense of the long term consequences.

Third, many leftists are in the grip of what Yuri Bezmenov, a former Soviet communist, called 'ideological subversion.' This is a slow process of brainwashing an enemy society by subverting sane, healthy ideas until insanity seems like normality. This process has been done to us very effectively.

This is not the place to go into detail about this, but the evidence is all around us of its spectacular success. Subversion has happened in various ways, but perhaps the most significant is that white Westerners have been trained to assist in their own cultural and demographic replacement.

Who are the main participants in this? It is educated, middle class, white leftists - the same group most convinced of its moral and intellectual superiority. At the end of the day, there is no bigger dupe than the educated, middle class, white leftist. Unfortunately, because their egos are so bound up in the idea of moral superiority, they will maintain their beliefs long after the evidence is telling them to wise up. They will cling to their beliefs to the bitter end rather than admit that the people they despised as their inferiors were right all along - and by then it will be far too late.

State Propaganda

If the BBC is, for some strange reason, collaborating in the Great Replacement, you would find it acting as a propagandist for that cause. Here are some ways it seems to do exactly that.

One - Racial Crime Reporting

As several commentators have pointed out, the BBC has acted as a subtle propagandist in its reporting of violent crime with a racial angle. When the perpetrator is white and the victim black, this is highlighted and the story promoted. When the perpetrator is black and the victim white, the BBC often disguises this. This creates a false impression, but is part of the BBC's protection of its model multicultural society.

You have the over-reporting of black deaths like Stephen Laurence and George Floyd, and the under-reporting of white deaths or the Rotherham grooming gangs.

In 2020, the BBC joined in the racial hysteria around Floyd and Black Lives Matter (BLM). As New Culture Forum's exposé on BBC bias noted:

> The BBC became obsessed by the victim narrative put forward by BLM... the corporation, metaphorically speaking, took the knee, and clearly expected the rest of us to do the same... At the height of the BLM protests the BBC seemed hell bent on convincing us all that Britain is a hotbed of the worst kind of racism... They made no effect to look deeper into the BLM movement and find out what it really was.

The subsequent protest marches led to statues being smashed or removed - a direct attack on Britain's history. In a sane world, Britain's national broadcaster would criticise this and defend Britain. I may be wrong, but if they were anything like the ABC in Australia, they probably didn't raise a murmur of protest, and instead sided with BLM. If that is true, it's a perfect example of Yuri Bezmenov's ideological subversion.

Two – Fake History Propaganda

BBC TV dramas often have a diverse cast out of proportion to real racial percentages. One might see this as an attempt to be inclusive if it wasn't so overdone. The obsession with mixed race couples is so obvious even non-political viewers have noticed.

This attempt to shape the future is off-putting enough, but more disturbing is the diverse casting in historical dramas. This is a campaign to persuade viewers that Britain was always a highly diverse nation. This attempt to erase white Britons from the past is an obvious attempt to legitimise the new multicultural Britain, and pretend this manufactured social system is natural.

Remember that this is coming from the *national broadcaster*. Astonishing!

Times change and that is reflected in the sort of TV programs that are made. But these changes are not organic so much as contrived. DEI policies have been imposed on casting to drive social change, rather than just reflect it. A BBC head of comedy recently said that the program *Monty Python*, featuring five white males, would never be made today. Of course, leftists will see that as a victory.

An extreme example of TV as propaganda is the science fiction show *Doctor Who*. Once a quintessentially British program, it has recently been parasitised by globalist ideas and values. The next chapter will discuss this interesting case study in more detail.

Three – Nationalism vs Globalism

The BBC's imaginary moral superiority comes from its allegiance to GPR causes, which it believes are good by definition. In the same way, its enemies are believed evil for not blindly accepting those same causes and ideals.

One example was a 2020 BBC interview by a prominent female journalist, with the Hungarian ambassador, Peter Szijjarto. Hungary is one of the few European countries to have resisted the EU's dictates about refugees and diversity.

The interviewer is a familiar type, one we might call The Scold. Rather than conversing with someone, they treat an interview as the chance to berate them for their perceived moral failings. Such was the case with the unfortunate Hungarian ambassador, yet Mr Szijjarto stayed remarkably cool under attack.

This interview, while not necessarily propaganda, was an example of the deep biases within the BBC, and its globalist nature.

How the ABC (and the BBC) could change

There are some other reasons both the ABC and BBC are disliked, but enough has been said for now.

I have given some details about how both the ABC in Australia and the BBC in Britain are aligned to globalist values, rather than serving the nations entrusted to their care. While they might consider this justified, it should give them some clues about why people dislike them.

It's interesting to speculate on whether they could change, or whether the left dominance of these national broadcasters is now terminal.

It's hard to see change happening anytime soon, as the bias is so engrained. Still, one can fantasise about how they *might* change, no matter how unlikely such changes actually are. In considering this, I'll return to discussing the ABC.

As mentioned, the ABC seems to dislike Anglo-Australia, and at least some Anglos are willing to return the favour. If the ABC is unloved by such people, what would it take for the ABC to regain respect? ABC types tend to see such people as deplorables, but for the sake of the exercise let's pretend the ABC cared what they thought.

When it comes to politics, at the moment the ABC is run by and for good-whites and ethnic groups. To repeat, good-whites are those who buy into all the racial pieties. If the ABC is happy to work only for those groups, so be it, but it should become a niche media organisation rather than the national broadcaster.

There is also a large section of the population who are bad-whites. What I'm suggesting is that the ABC should start working for bad-whites as well, and more than that, should become partially bad-white itself. That is a radical suggestion and is unlikely to happen - but it should.

The ABC is disliked for two main reasons. First, it has fully bought into the values of the Global Progressive Regime. This includes an anti-white, anti-Western mentality which many Anglo-Australians see as a betrayal. It also includes an uncritical acceptance of the feminist worldview, which does not endear it to non-believers in that view of life.

Second, ABC figures often seem to think that when it comes to politics, they exist on a higher moral and intellectual plane than other people. This attitude should be replaced by the basic humility of saying *I could be wrong*. Or in relation to GPR ideas, *even though I believe it, it isn't necessarily true.*

Here are some suggestions about how the ABC could address these two problems.

One - The Balance Problem

Rather than being impartial, the ABC often appears more like an activist group than a media organisation. The ABC should be more balanced, so in contentious areas like race and gender, instead of featuring only leftist ideas they should allow opposing views. They could hire intelligent dissidents who can explain controversial ideas fairly.

The ABC could also run some programs that challenge the ideas currently in vogue, and do it in a genuinely open minded way. Here are some sample topics and titles:

- The Myth of Male Privilege.
- Why Men are Angry (a companion piece to the series on why women are angry).

- Multiculturalism or Identity Politics: You Can Only Keep One.
- The Great Replacement: Far from a Conspiracy Theory.
- 1788: Reasons for Celebration, Not Guilt.
- The 2020 Race Riots: How We Were Conned.

I don't for a moment believe the ABC will actually make any of these programs – but it would be good if they did.

Two – The Arrogance Problem

Instead of being sure that their political views are automatically correct, ABC people could consider the idea that they might be wrong.

The ABC will realise that many Australians don't like them, but rather than ascribing this to moral and intellectual inferiority, they'll admit that they may have a point. *It's not you, it's me.*

They'll realise that the ABC has been under the spell of globalist values for several decades, and that *it doesn't have to be this way.* They could take the radical step of not hating their own nation, and start celebrating it. They'll realise that the Great Replacement isn't great, and that feminism jumped the shark decades ago. They'll come to see that treason isn't a virtue, but one of the lowest moral acts.

None of this will happen. Business will continue as usual with the ABC collaborating with GPR values. If that's what the ABC wants to do, so be it, but they won't be regaining any of their former admirers, many of whom did used to think the ABC was a national treasure. Just like the BBC, the ABC is now a globalist treasure. More's the pity.

19
I'm Going for the Daleks Now

Doctor Who is a science fiction TV show that began in 1963. Having lasted for so long, plots sometimes get re-used. One plot is about an alien parasite taking over a human host. What begins as a small infection slowly spreads to the rest of the body until the person is eventually changed into the alien creature. The parasite is now in full control.

In its peak era of the mid 1970s, this plot appeared in two stories, *The Ark in Space* and *The Seeds of Doom*. It has probably been in many more.

Strangely, *Doctor Who* itself has now suffered the same fate. When it resumed production in 2005 after a long break, fans hoped this classic British TV show could return to glory. For a while, these hopes seemed to have been met - but the program had itself been infected by a parasite. The signs were small at first. They gradually worsened and the disease became hard to ignore, until eventually the hostile parasite had taken over completely. By then, many of the show's former fans had switched off.

This parasite was malignant leftism. It was the system of ideas some call 'woke' and which I've called the values of the Global Progressive Regime. Of course, the producers of *Doctor Who* did not see these values as malignant, they saw them as glorious. Clearly, the parasite isn't going to hate *itself*. In this chapter, I'm going to explain why they are malignant and why those producers had no right to turn a classic TV show into an obnoxious vehicle for GPR propaganda.

These changes haven't been good for the show itself. It is now one of the most despised programs on TV. Perhaps its producers might ask themselves why many people who used to love *Doctor Who* now dislike it. I am one of them. Put it this way. The Doctor's arch enemies are that race of beings called the Daleks. Well, I'm going for the Daleks now. If they could finally achieve their goal of killing the Doctor, I would cheer.

Some readers of this book will have no interest in this British science fiction program. They can skip this chapter if they like and move on to the next section. However, I am including this chapter because it is a fine example of the Global Progressive Regime at work, not only in its parasitic takeover of *Doctor Who*, but in using it as propaganda to promote GPR values in the real world.

Background

For those who don't know it, *Doctor Who* is a TV show about an alien called the Doctor. He is a 'Time Lord' who travels through time and space in a vehicle called the Tardis, having adventures and fighting evil.

Every so often, the Doctor 'regenerates' into a new body. This allows a new actor to take on the role. Seven different actors played the Doctor during its first run from 1963-1989, before it was cancelled by the BBC. We will call this era *classic Doctor Who*.

There was a break for sixteen years until the show was resurrected in 2005, with a producer named Russell T Davies in charge. We will call this era *new Doctor Who*. Later producers were Steven Moffat, then Chris Chibnall, before Russell T Davies returned in 2021.

Davies, a gay social progressive, helped modernise the program. The format changed from half hour episodes in a linked four or six part story, to self-contained one hour episodes. The special effects were also better, and the stories a bit faster paced (some would say, rushed).

There were other changes. The program became more emotional and also sexual. There was more 'diversity' with black, gay, and female characters coming to the fore. This seemed incidental at first, but after a while you realised it was some kind of political statement. Some of the stories themselves became overtly political. At first, these changes weren't overpowering… then gradually they were. After a while, the elephant in the room began knocking over the furniture and crapping all over the carpet.

It eventually became clear *Doctor Who* was no longer just a science fiction show, it was a leftist's fantasy about what the world should look like, and also a propaganda vehicle to help bring that world about. This was a revenge fantasy in the manner of what Bruce Bawer called the *Victims' Revolution*. Regime enemy, the straight white male, was to be displaced and the world ruled by gays, blacks, and women.

Nowhere was this more obvious than in the casting of the Doctor himself. He had always been a straight white male, through his first twelve incarnations. For the leftist producers of new *Doctor Who*, this was hopelessly archaic. In hindsight, the endgame is obvious. The Doctor would become gay, black, or female - or perhaps all three. That is indeed what happened. The thirteenth Doctor was played by a woman, Jody Whittaker, and the fourteenth by a gay black man, Ncuti Gatwa.

It wasn't just the Doctor who had to change. The producers of the show seemed to want the whole world to become gay, black, or female. Straight white males would grudgingly still be allowed to exist but only in lesser, supporting roles, or as villains. In other words, the TV show *Doctor Who* was part of the wider cultural revolution, which was trying to create a social justice Utopia.

There's no doubt the show's producers believed in this revolution and wanted to use *Doctor Who* to help it along - but think what they might have done instead. They could have created a whole new program, a spin off in the manner of the show *Torchwood*, which could have been a social justice version of *Doctor Who*. They could have been as progressive as they wanted.

Yet such is the parasitic nature of leftism that instead of creating something new, it prefers to feed on what is already created -

something strong and established. It wants to take what's been built up over many years and then subvert it.

Parasites don't take over immediately. They move in a sneaky, slow creep towards their goal. Why, might we ask, didn't the Doctor immediately become a gay black woman when the show returned in 2005? Clearly, that would have been too radical. Conversion of the fans could only happen one small step at a time.

Still, if they had made that hypothetical spin off series with a gay black female Time Lord in 2005 and called it something else, it might have succeeded, as fans would not have felt the actual program had been taken over. But such a spinoff would have been too *niche*. The producers had grander ambitions of taking over *Doctor Who* itself. They wanted to be mainstream, not niche. In the same way, they wanted to transform mainstream society, not just occupy part of it. The Victims' Revolution would not be fobbed off with trifles.

Of course, the revolutionary producers of *Doctor Who* did not see anything wrong with their approach. They clearly felt they were improving not only *Doctor Who*, but the world itself. So, what is the problem?

War On the Four Olds

Complaints about the political slant of new *Doctor Who* have often been met with the reply that the show was 'always political.' This is a leftist sleight of hand which I describe later in this book as the 'You Can't Stop Change' fallacy. It involves taking a true statement and trying to equate it with a false statement. In this case, the leftist is taking the true statement that classic *Doctor Who* was political and telling you that therefore (ultra political) new *Doctor Who* is the same as ever and nothing has changed.

It *has* changed. Old *Doctor Who* was political about, say, environmental issues. New *Doctor Who* is political about identity issues. Old *Doctor Who* fought brainwashing and authoritarian regimes. New *Doctor Who* wants to brainwash you into accepting the Global Progressive Regime. Old *Doctor Who* took moral positions, but it was never explicitly anti-white, anti-male, or anti-British like it is now.

We must keep in mind that the producers of new *Doctor Who* are revolutionaries. Their enemies are anything from the old world they are trying to overthrow. In the Chinese Cultural Revolution, war was declared on the 'four olds' - old ideas, old culture, old customs, and old habits. In the cultural revolution of *Doctor Who*, the four olds are traditional Britain, straight white males, *Doctor Who* fans, and ultimately *Doctor Who* itself. I'll consider each of these in more detail.

Classic *Doctor Who* was a TV show made in a mostly white Britain. Its hero was a straight white male, as were many of its fans, but certainly not all. (One year in the 1990s, I spent a lot of time watching old episodes with a British born Sri Lankan woman who was a friend, and a big fan of the show). The producers of new *Doctor Who* are trying to create a bold new multicultural Britain, where the former 'victims' are now in charge. It will be a Britain in which women, gays, and non-whites lead the way. If that is their ideal, its opposite must be what they see as traditional Britain, which in their view is a package deal of vices - patriarchy, homophobia, and whiteness.

It's an interesting trait of leftists that they tend to group their ideas in clusters. They accept a job lot of beliefs as a package deal. Thus being straight and white and male cluster as negative traits, while their opposites, being gay and black and female cluster as positives. In the world of new *Doctor Who*, gays, blacks, and women are assumed to be in a social justice alliance.

This alliance is rather artificial, as none of these categories really have to go together. As a thought experiment, imagine a reformer who wanted a revolution for only *one* of these groups. Imagine, for example, a society that remained mostly white but went full feminist. A patriarchal society that was multicultural. A right wing society that saw gayness as a respectable choice.

These societies might be possible, but in our own world we have this notion of an allegiance between victim groups. It leads to absurdities like gays and feminists supporting the immigration of men from patriarchal, homophobic cultures simply because they are non-white. What these fake alliances show is how much leftists have been trained to hate straight white males, for opposition to them is about the only thing these groups have in common.

The producers of *Doctor Who* seem to share this attitude, and their hostility towards straight white males is clear. As another idea to file under *Things we might have done differently*, perhaps they could have cast a gay, black, or female Doctor, then written scripts which did not contain open contempt towards straight white men. Their social revolution might have been more successful.

The notion that everything will be better if we simply put women, blacks, and gays in charge is optimistic indeed, although it would be an interesting social experiment. In the name of research, we should set aside a large city and remove all the straight white men. We should make sure that only women, blacks, and gays are in charge of running this city, and let us all learn from the improvements that they make.

The Rubbing of the Nose

In modern *Doctor Who* stories, straight white males have limited roles. They're either a weak sidekick to a strong diverse character, an enthusiastic ally to one, or an evil villain. A major problem for the producers of *Doctor Who* is that a lot of the show's fan-base were straight white males too. These fans would also have to adopt one of these stances to the show itself as it was taken over by diversity. They could be a weak, passive observer of the new episodes, an enthusiastic ally, or a villain if they didn't accept the changes.

The producers wanted enthusiastic support but were worried the British public were too conservative to accept their bold new vision. They adopted much the same strategy as the British Labor party in the Tony Blair era towards the conservative (or right wing) parts of the public. It was reported that, at one point, the Labor Party decided to increase immigration into Britain to 'rub the right's nose in diversity.'

It seems the producers of *Doctor Who* had the same idea. They were going to rub the fans' noses in diversity - and then some. They would make the show as aggressively diverse as possible. Why does one rub someone's nose in something? To punish them. Apparently the fans of *Doctor Who* had to be punished - chiefly, it would appear for being straight, white, and male, not to mention British. They would have to accept the new *Doctor Who* or else, just as Labor was going to make the right accept the new multicultural Britain.

What this meant was that the final story of the twelfth Doctor, Peter Capaldi, was used to lecture the fans about sexism, and warn them they had to support the new female Doctor. Three years later, after some online backlash about the imminent black Doctor, the makers of *Doctor Who* openly attacked the fans in the press. *Doctor Who* was now at war with many of its old fans.

So far, we have three enemies for new *Doctor Who*: traditional Britain, straight white males, and unenthusiastic fans. The show's producers had contempt for all three. Then we come to the fourth enemy - the program, *Doctor Who*, itself. As this chapter will explain, it would not be long before the parasitic producers showed their contempt for that too.

In the glorious cultural revolution of new *Doctor Who*, old Britain was going to be swept aside in favour of the new Britain led by gays, blacks, and women. It's now time to examine the parasite at work and look at each of these in more detail.

The Feminist Agenda

In old *Doctor Who*, the Doctor's female travelling companions played a supporting role - but so did the male ones. The Doctor was, after all, the star. Some of the female companions were a bit weak, but others were strong. Sarah, Leela, and Romana from the Tom Baker era were all strong characters, as was Barbara from the supposedly sexist William Hartnell era.

In the new *Doctor Who* after 2005, we got to witness the feminist influence in various ways. The most obvious was that key male characters from the past began to be played by women. The Brigadier role was taken by a woman (his daughter), arch villain the Master became Missy, and finally the Doctor himself became female.

Women were cast in positions of authority, playing high ranking officials of various kinds right up to the prime minister. As with other recent science fiction, *the future is female* became a guiding policy. This is tied to the idea society will automatically improve if we simply put women in charge.

The above changes could have been made without being overtly anti-male, but the writers of *Doctor Who* saw fit to make an anti-male slant part of their female empowerment campaign. This was done in various ways. The first way was to erase men. Or rather, the specific kind of men feminists have been trained to hate, the straight white ones. Therefore all the white female companions - Rose, Donna, and Clara - were given black boyfriends. What an odd coincidence.

The only female companion to get a white boyfriend was Amy, who was given the rather weak charactered, Rory. This is the other way *Doctor Who* targeted (white) men, by making them weak and a little contemptible. They couldn't do it to the Doctor himself.

After all, he was supposed to be the hero. But by the time twelfth Doctor, Peter Capaldi, came in even that restraint was gone. Capaldi's Doctor was disrespected, and by his final story he had become a cringing apologetic man that fitted perfectly the politics of new *Doctor Who*.

Before that, we saw open misandry in the program. Masculinity was mocked and derided. To take a few examples, a female character named River Song says to the Doctor 'What's that face? Are you thinking?! Stop it, you're a man, it looks weird.' The companion, Clara, says 'The Universe is full of testosterone. Trust me, it's unbearable.' Arch villain, the Master, says 'Is the future going to be all girl?' and the Doctor replies that 'We can only hope.'

Needless to say, if such remarks were made with the genders reversed, we would never hear the end of it. In another scene, a white male Time Lord regenerates into a black female and immediately makes a snarky remark about who she has just replaced.

Now we come to the low point, which is Capaldi's regeneration story, 'Twice Upon a Time.' This was the last new episode of *Doctor Who* I ever watched, before giving up on the show. Yes - that means I've never watched a single episode of the Jodie Whittaker or Ncuti Gatwa eras.

Producer, Steven Moffat, who had overseen much of the anti-male slant of the previous three years, took on the job of writing the 2017 Christmas special, the one where Peter Capaldi changed into Jodie Whitaker, the first female Doctor. This episode, 'Twice Upon a Time,' has little purpose except to make this change.

To achieve it, feminist propaganda is laid on with a trowel. The main device is the resurrection of the first Doctor from 1965, originally played by William Hartnell, now played by a lookalike. (For convenience, I'll refer to him as Hartnell.) Hartnell's Doctor is back for one reason only - to chastise traditional *Doctor Who* fans who object to the new female lead.

First, we're told the Hartnell Doctor knows he has to regenerate to survive, but he's holding back because he's afraid. So presumably, Hartnell is at a point in his timeline soon before his own regeneration. Capaldi's Doctor urges Hartnell to submit. 'Either we change and go on... or die as we are,' he says. Capaldi is really talking about his own regeneration into Jodi Whitaker. This line is pure propaganda meant to imply that *Doctor Who* is a hopeless relic of a past age, simply for having a white male lead, and the only way the show can survive is by changing its lead actor's demographic.

Hartnell, of course, is a proxy for the traditional *Doctor Who* viewer. Writer, Steven Moffat, lectures that viewer along the lines that: *We know you're afraid, but look: the first Doctor regenerated in 1965 and life went on. That's exactly what will happen now with the first female Doctor.*

Resurrected purely as a propaganda device, Hartnell's Doctor is portrayed as a dreadful old sexist. He speaks down to Bill, the story's female companion, encouraging her to give the Tardis a good tidy-up. To do some housework, in other words. If Hartnell is the awful sexist from the 1960s, Bill is black, female, and gay, ticking three of the BBC's diversity boxes and symbolising the progressive Britain of 2017, when the episode was made.

As for Capaldi's Doctor, he too has a function. While the episode sets up a conflict between Hartnell's awful old white male and Bill's young, black, empowered lesbian, Capaldi's role is to play the cringing, emasculated, 21st century man. He winces in embarrassment at Hartnell's sexism, walking on eggshells at thoughts of the offence caused to Bill. He's cringing in mortification, and indeed fear, at Bill's possible reaction.

At one point Capaldi's Doctor turns 'white knight' on Bill, ordering her to stay in the Tardis for safety. His final words are

'I want you to... respect me.' It is now that Bill turns on Capaldi and yells at him that he's 'an arse. A stupid bloody arse.' What is Capaldi's response? Does he stand up for himself, or tell Bill off? No, he just stands there and takes it like an abuse victim, a look of guilty apology on his face.

Capaldi's Doctor, therefore, has been turned into a feeble male leftist bowing down to his progressive masters at the BBC. After one of Hartnell's sexist remarks, Capaldi begs forgiveness from Bill, saying 'we won't ever talk about this.' Bill, victor of the gender wars, lets him off with 'I hope we spend years laughing about it,' thus combining contempt and forgiveness in a magnanimous benediction.

Following Bill and Capaldi's confrontation, Hartnell steps out of the Tardis and warns Bill about her language, also threatening to give her a smacked bottom. This is pure parody. We then get dialogue suggesting that Hartnell's Doctor has never heard of a male nurse, or doesn't know what 'browser history' is, and by extension, the internet itself. Thus, any sense that Hartnell's Doctor is a time travelling alien goes out the window. His only function is to embody a sexist 1960s British male, so logic be damned. Why *not* just pretend Hartnell's Doctor never travelled any further into the future than 1960? When plot is secondary to message, who cares?

All this byplay is meant to harangue the traditional *Doctor Who* fans, who supposedly equate to Hartnell. *See?* Steven Moffat is saying. If you oppose the new female Doctor, you're an awful old sexist like Hartnell. *You need to cringe like Capaldi if you want to win the forgiveness of the new regime, embodied by Bill.* Thus, Moffat simultaneously warns and chastises the old fans.

To hammer in the message even more, the story includes a British army officer who's been picked up from World War One. He's white and upper class to contrast further with Bill, the black, working class lesbian. At one point, Hartnell makes a joke about ladies being 'made of glass' and the officer chuckles along, going so far as to say 'Good one, Doctor!' Have you absorbed your propaganda lesson yet viewers? If you make sexist jokes, you're a relic of World War One and a collaborator in the patriarchy.

All this is meant to usher in the glorious feminine takeover of *Doctor Who* and the appearance of Jodie Whitaker's new female Doctor. Let's recall the plot point that Hartnell's Doctor is 'afraid' to regenerate. I don't know if this was really a theme of 'The Tenth Planet,' Hartnell's 1965 regeneration story, but it would be no surprise if this was simply added to this new story for convenience. The traditional *Doctor Who* fan is being told: *come on, don't be afraid of the brave new world of diversity, and don't you dare object to the new female Doctor.*

I have certainly cringed through some *Doctor Who* episodes in the past due to bad acting or bad special effects. This time I cringed because one of my favourite TV shows had become a BBC propaganda vehicle for the Global Progressive Regime.

The Racial Agenda

If the feminist agenda in *Doctor Who* wasn't bad enough, the racial agenda was even worse. The producers of new *Doctor Who* had clearly accepted the GPR premise that the straight white male is a regime enemy. The problem was the Doctor was a straight white male himself. What were the producers to do? The answer was obvious. They would change the Doctor first into a woman, played by Jody Whittaker, and then into a gay black man, played by Ncuti Gatwa.

If that was the endgame of the racial agenda, there were various intermediate steps to take along the way. As mentioned, almost every white female companion - Rose, Clara, and Donna - was given a black boyfriend. The writers of *Doctor Who* felt interracial relationships was a new norm they wanted the show's viewers to absorb.

There were also non-white companions - Martha, Bill (also a lesbian), Yazz (also a lesbian), and Ryan. The Master, having already been a woman, changed back to being a man but was now Indian. Finally, the Doctor himself turned into a black man (also gay).

You might think this would be enough racial revolution for the show, but that would be to underestimate the megalomaniac producers of *Doctor Who*. Not content with turning the Doctor black in the present, they created a new origin story for him in the episode, 'The Timeless Children.' It turned out the first Doctor was not the white British actor, William Hartnell, as we'd all thought, but originally a black woman played by actor Jo Martin. I'll return to this shortly.

At this point, we might ponder an odd feature of this approach to racial reform. *Doctor Who* is just one TV program that's sought to diversify its cast. There have been various other BBC shows doing it too. We know they want to replace white actors. That's obvious - but why are most of the replacements *black* rather than, say, Asian? When we got the first non-white Doctor, why was he not played by a Chinese actor? A Japanese man or an Arab? Why not a trans woman from Thailand? How about a Mexican or Hispanic?

Perhaps there are two main reasons. First, in the ideas of racial hierarchy held by British scientists of the Victorian age, black Africans were considered the lowest, so the leftist reformers at the BBC want to elevate them as a thorough, if spiteful, rejection of that idea. Second, doing this is maximum social subversion, and when you're trying to create a cultural revolution, maximum subversion is best.

While there's a clear racial agenda in casting diverse actors in key roles, a more subtle tactic is casting diverse actors in non-speaking roles. This was most obvious in the Capaldi-era story, 'Thin Ice,' in which crowd scenes from London in 1814 were half-filled with non-white actors. The makers of *Doctor Who* wanted to suggest England historically was not the white nation we had always thought, but was in fact a diverse multicultural nation all along.

Coincidentally, that same Capaldi series featured a plot about a race of hostile aliens taking over the Earth and brainwashing people, *1984* style, with a whole fake history of Earth. For the writers of *Doctor Who* to do that straight after 'Thin Ice' shows either no self-awareness or epic chutzpah, for they were doing much the same thing in propagating the lie that Britain had always been a diverse multicultural nation. Here is what producer Steven Moffat said at around that time.

> We've kind of got to tell a lie. We'll go back into history and there will be Black people where, historically, there wouldn't have been, and we won't dwell on that. We'll say, 'to hell with it, this is the imaginary, better version of the world. By believing in it, we'll summon it forth.'

There is a further irony here when we consider that when *Doctor Who* began in 1963, one of its main purposes was to educate British children about history. The time travelling Doctor would go to various historical periods and arouse children's interest in those times. For the despicable new *Doctor Who*, the purpose was instead to *lie* to children about history so as to create an 'imaginary better world.'

Leaving aside the dubious practice of lying about history, we should stop and ask why this racial vision is so desirable in the first place. For leftists, apparently, a global multicultural society is absolutely the most ideal kind of society anyone can have. It is so desirable that we should have it not just in the present and future, but also the past, hence Moffat's false history of Regency England in 1814.

It follows that a racially homogeneous society is the worst kind. It's not simply bad, but shameful and embarrassing, as was implied in the 2024 episode 'Dot and Bubble.'

The question Moffat and other leftists should answer is what convinces them multiculturalism is the most ideal social model? Which of the multicultural nations have succeeded? Which have failed? If diverse societies are automatically the best, why is there so much ethnic tension in Western nations now? Is the mono-ethnic Japan a failed society? Was Britain more stable and cohesive in 1974 or 2024? And perhaps more to the point, why do they hate the Britain into which they were born? Tell us.

I would suggest that the idea multiculturalism is the ideal social model is simply an article of faith. Optimistic at best, delusional at worst. As the crowd scene in 'Thin Ice' shows, it is not enough for *Doctor Who* producers to depict the multiracial Britain of the present, they have to pretend Britain was also multiracial in 1814. Such is their disdain for white Britain and belief in the superiority of multiculti-Britain that these Orwellian lies seem justified.

In a similar way, the Doctor himself is to become black. Not just in the present, with the regeneration into Ncuti Gatwa, but also in the past. In the episode 'The Timeless Children' we are finally given an origin story for the mysterious character of the Doctor himself. Written by then producer, Chris Chibnall, we learn that the Doctor was not originally the straight white male played by the actor William Hartnell, but actually a black woman played by actor Jo Martin.

Chris Chibnall is not one of the better writers in the show's history, and as a producer he led the unpopular Jodie Whitaker era. Yet whatever his shortcomings, they're not as offensive as what he did to the origins of *Doctor Who*.

It was extraordinary enough that Chibnall felt entitled to create an origin story for the Doctor. That was his first piece of bad judgment. Dabbling in dim witted social justice was his second. What right did Chibnall have to impose racial politics onto the origins of *Doctor Who*? He could have confined them to the present era, which would have been merely irritating - but that wasn't enough for him. He had to inflict the racial agenda onto the origins of the character. In so doing, he showed contempt for Britain, for white British people, and for *Doctor Who* itself.

Regardless of his fictional status as an alien, the Doctor's cultural status was always that of a British white male. That should have been left alone, just as iconic characters from other cultures are left alone. Instead, we are asked to pretend that the first Doctor was actually a black woman.

Having molested the show's origins, it was now time for the ultimate racial triumph of new *Doctor Who*, which was the casting of Ncuti Gatwa as the Doctor. As mentioned, I gave up on *Doctor Who* after Capaldi's regeneration story and haven't seen any of Gatwa's episodes. However, it's worth noting his era has been neither a critical nor commercial success, and the viewer ratings are the lowest they've been in the whole history of *Doctor Who*. Treating your audience with contempt can do that.

The Gay Agenda

The gay agenda is the least obnoxious of the three diversity trends in *Doctor Who*. So there are gay characters in *Doctor Who*. So what? Still, the returning producer, Russell T Davies, couldn't stop himself overreaching. He had to make the Doctor himself gay.

This had already more or less happened with the female Doctor, implied to have been romantically attracted to the gay companion, Yaz. Now, with Ncuti Gatwa, the Doctor was completely gay.

Regardless of straight or gay, the bigger question here is why the Doctor had to become a sexual being at all. In the original series, there was no suggestion of it. He was an asexual, unromantic alien. He should have stayed that way. We don't need either a gay or a heterosexual Doctor.

Since new *Doctor Who* began in 2005, there was said to have been a 'gay agenda' behind the program. This entailed gay characters and themes becoming increasingly part of it in the effort to make gayness mainstream. While this was acceptable up to a point, the question was: *what has any of this got to do with Doctor Who?* Classic *Doctor Who* was never about people exploring their sexual identity, to put it simply, or subverting heteronormativity, to put it academically. That wasn't what the show was about.

Still, the gay elements could be accepted as long as they didn't become too intrusive. They were just part of the landscape. By the time of the Capaldi era, they were intrusive. Black lesbian, Bill Potts, was now a main character, and viewers were regularly reminded of her gayness just in case it slipped their minds for a moment.

There were also ham fisted efforts to include random gay references. In the 2017 story 'Knock, Knock,' a minor character, for no apparent reason, mentioned that his grandfather and his grandfather's boyfriend had once been arrested for trying to steal part of the Great Wall of China. You might waste the next couple of minutes of the episode trying to unravel that. Was this during the grandfather's gay youth before marriage? Or did the grandfather live his whole life as a lie before finally coming out, gaining a boyfriend, and being arrested in China? Was the grandmother in on it, perhaps secretly gay herself, or turning a blind eye while her bisexual husband went off to China with his boyfriend? Or was this all just completely irrelevant to *Doctor Who* in the first place?

The focus on gayness continued into the era of Jodie Whitaker, the first female Doctor, and her implied attraction to the lesbian companion, Yaz. This was merely a warm up, however, for a fully fledged gay Doctor, Ncuti Gatwa.

Gatwa was chosen by returning producer Russell T Davies in 2022. Since leaving the show in 2010, Davies seemed to have become more political in his writing, especially about gay themes. By the time he returned, *Doctor Who* was a chance to place gayness front and centre through the character of Gatwa's Doctor.

There is a series of essays on Substack by a writer called Millennial Woes which analyses new *Doctor Who* in great detail, far more than I have included here. He considers many aspects of the program between 2005-24, including the Ncuti Gatwa era. The series is worth reading.

Once again, the Doctor shouldn't be a sexual being at all, but if Davies had really wanted a gay Doctor, it would have been better to make him a gay, white, upper class English eccentric and been subtle about it. At least such a character would have seemed more British. Instead, Davies went all out in casting Ncuti Gatwa, a flamboyant, almost cartoonish young black man who wore a different outfit in every story, danced exuberantly, and cried almost once an episode.

I have only seen snippets of Gatwa's performance, but he doesn't seem very *Doctor-ish*, compared to past versions of the character. He seems to have been mainly cast as part of the wider cultural revolution against Old Britain. Even parasitically latching on to British cultural icons like the Beatles, as one Gatwa episode did, should not fool anyone about the program's contempt for Old Britain and the desire to transform it.

As mentioned earlier, many leftists accept a job lot of beliefs and fail to evaluate them one by one. Being a supporter of gay rights doesn't mean you have to accept all the other leftist causes too.

In this sense, there are two contrasting kinds of gays. First, there are gay conservatives - the likes of Douglas Murray, Peter Whittle, or Bruce Bawer - who realise that accepting gayness doesn't have to mean a complete revolution against your own society.

Then there are gay radicals who seem to think supporting gay rights requires the subversion of every existing social norm.

You have to turn Britain completely multicultural, be highly sycophantic to women, thumb your nose at every British tradition, and generally smash the four olds with as much fanaticism as possible.

In this spirit, the last few years of *Doctor Who* became a parody of aggressive leftism. In one story, former companion, Donna Noble, was revealed to be a white single mother with a mixed race trans child who was soon lecturing the Doctor about pronouns. Almost every straight couple seems to be mixed race. Other characters are gay or, to up the ante, trans. The plots are overtly political. British mathematical genius, sir Isaac Newton, has become Indian, and Ncuti Gatwa's Doctor travels back to England in 1813 and kisses an English lord. Women are all girl bosses, and white men are wimps or villains. Above all, let's not forget that guy's grandfather who went to China and got arrested with his boyfriend.

The End of *Doctor Who*

The original series of *Doctor Who* was already morally good, and a British cultural icon to be proud of. It was very much a British program, about the adventures of a charismatic alien who was also recognisable as a straight white man.

This wasn't good enough for the producers of the new *Doctor Who* which came back in 2005. They had a much grander vision of a diverse multicultural Britain run by women, blacks, and gays with the support of compliant white male allies. The producers believed in that world so much they decided to use *Doctor Who* as a propaganda vehicle to help bring it about.

In so doing, they allied with all the dubious causes of the Global Progressive Regime - multiculturalism, feminism, 'anti racism,' and an anti-white, anti-Western mindset. Perhaps their campaign to change Britain would have been more successful if they had not made their contempt for the past so obvious.

While they succeeded in parasitising *Doctor Who* for their own ends, they also managed to alienate many of the fans, and have probably destroyed the show for good.

I have nothing against women, gays, or non-whites per se and have always accepted them as equals in principle. Yet the fantasy of a diverse Utopia where they are celebrated as inherently good, while my own demographic is weak or evil, leaves me cold. If as a white male viewer of this program the only available roles for me are passive acceptance, enthusiastic support, or being an enemy, I'll take the enemy role. I wasn't an enemy before. They made me one.

I am not going to ally myself with the social justice fantasy believed in by the producers of *Doctor Who*. I do not support their worldview, or the program itself. Not anymore. In fact, I'm now on Team Dalek and will be cheering loudly as they try to finally succeed in killing their arch enemy, the Doctor. I hope the Daleks succeed in exterminating the Ncuti Gatwa Doctor, and then they travel back in time and exterminate the Jody Whitaker version too, as well as Peter Capaldi, and the latter day David Tennant.

Still, in a way, that is superfluous, for the Doctor is already dead. He was killed by the recent producers of *Doctor Who* itself. Therefore, they succeeded where every previous *Doctor Who* villain failed. Just think of all those villains: Davros, Sutekh, the Master, the Daleks, the Cybermen, the Sontarans, and so many more. They all tried and failed, but the *Doctor Who* producers succeeded.

They succeeded in finally killing the Doctor.

Part Five

Leftist Pathologies

20

It's a Miracle!
From Hatred to Healing

I used to be a leftist. When I was growing up a few decades ago, all that meant was supporting equal rights for women, gays, and racial minorities. This is the 'soft leftism' mentioned in an earlier chapter.

The 'hard leftism' of today is a whole other deal. It means unquestioning support for feminism, multiculturalism, and Black Lives Matter. It means accepting identity politics, and false statements like 'diversity is our strength.' It entails an anti-white, anti-Western, anti-male stance, and support for censorship and cancel culture. It means equality of outcome, inherited guilt, and other dirty tricks.

If this is leftism today, I don't want a bar of it. However, as many of the above ideas are still powerful, hard leftism is hard to escape. We can at least try to understand it, and what has gone wrong. There's a morbid fascination in seeing how insane our world has become under the influence of these ideas.

This part of the book will offer a list of 'leftist pathologies.' Pathology is the study of disease - its symptoms, causes, and effects. At times, leftism does seem like a mental illness. The next few chapters discuss sixty-three forms this disease can take. These will either be beliefs, attitudes, or ways of thinking.

It's likely such frank criticism will alienate leftists who might be reading this book - but that must surely have happened long before now. For any who are still here, perhaps they might see that the well intentioned ethical views they started with have little to do with what leftism has become.

Before starting, here are some disclaimers. First, many leftists act from good intentions. They believe they are fighting injustice and working towards noble goals.

Second, there are also plenty of 'right wing pathologies.' Other people can discuss these if they like. I'm more interested in left wing pathologies because they are trickier and often hide behind a façade of virtue.

Third, pointing out faulty thinking in others doesn't mean my own thinking is free of errors. There's no doubt I'm wrong about some things and make my own reasoning errors, perhaps even some of the same ones to be listed here.

Fourth, this part of the book is speculative. I can't claim to read minds, but I am speculating, based on observing the ways leftists behave, and the things they say and write.

Fifth, listing common leftist traits and patterns means making generalisations. That's inevitable. There are always exceptions, and not everyone is the same - but if these traits and patterns weren't fairly common, you wouldn't notice them in the first place.

Sixth, the main point of doing this is to understand these mistakes, point them out to others, deal with the frustration they cause, and perhaps undo some of the incredible damage they have done. Some of these pathologies are merely irritating, while others may be civilisation-ending.

So, let's begin to look at some of these strange states of mind. It's time to examine left wing pathologies. The format I'll use is to give each of them a name and a number: Leftist Pathology One (LP1), Leftist Pathology Two (LP2), LP3, LP4, and so on.

The following page contains a full list.

LP 1 - It's a Miracle! From Hatred to Healing

The culture war between the left and right side of politics has raged for a long time, and rarely so viciously as during the first Donald Trump presidency of 2016-20. But when Joe Biden won the 2020 US election, he declared peace. The civil war was over. After four years of leftist rage and bitter conflict during the Trump era, it was time for unity. For healing.

How about that? From hatred to healing overnight. It's a miracle!

Except it was a bit late for that. Too much had been seen and revealed. Unfortunately for Biden the Healer, people could remember how leftists had behaved in the last four years. They remembered the tantrums after Trump's win in 2016, the protest marches and impeachment attempts. They recalled the hysteria about Trump, who was apparently always on the verge of launching a white supremacist, neo-Nazi regime with women reduced to breeding slaves like in *The Handmaid's Tale*.

People remembered four years of relentless hostility from the mostly left wing media - from CNN in America, the BBC and *The Guardian* in Britain, or the ABC and *The Sydney Morning Herald* in Australia. That same press was now printing identical 'Time to Heal' headlines in unison. After those four years, people could never look at the media the same way again.

People recalled the daily denunciations from artists and celebrities, as they sucked up to the Global Progressive Regime. They also recalled the endless GPR propaganda - the anti-male, anti-Western, anti-national messaging, and dire warnings about white supremacy. They remembered the obsession with race and, more recently, three months of rioting from Antifa and Black Lives Matter leading up to the 2020 election.

Now Biden had won that election, and suddenly there was going to be peace and healing. It's a miracle!

Did leftists really think that after the way they'd carried on for four years, there was going to be any kind of peace? Did Biden himself believe it? Perhaps it was all a bluff. After all, it's normal for an election winner to call for unity. This time it was laughable.

It wasn't just the Democrat politicians trying it on. Former actress, Alyssa Milano, for example, said on Twitter she wanted to offer an olive branch to Trump supporters, so they could all move #Forward-Together. So, after four years of rabid hostility from Milano towards Trump, when an election went her way she was going to offer the olive branch.

How about no, Alyssa?

Some people who'd been the target of leftist vitriol weren't inclined to accept any peace offer, as a few tweets from the time will show:

> I don't know about you, but I don't foresee myself ever "unifying" with a bunch of hateful people who called me racist, sexist, misogynist, chump, deplorable, sell-out, Nazi, Trumptard, transphobe, and told me that white people were what's wrong with the world for four years.

*

> Yeah, nothing says peace and love like burning down buildings, beating elderly people, looting businesses while they struggle to survive during the pandemic, and exploiting someone's last moments alive for political gain. But hey the left is about peace and love, right?

*

> And just like that the rioting and looting has ceased overnight. And now the half of the country that

pummelled America like a battered wife is telling her to put on sunglasses, hide her black eye, be a good girl, and "come together as one." Her answer? "Go fuck yourself."

It's hard to believe leftists were serious in expecting any kind of unity after the way they'd behaved the last four years. If they were, you almost have to admire their gall. They'd spent the last four years creating as much chaos as possible to 'resist' Trump. Now they were blaming all that chaos on Trump himself, and declaring a new age of peace when they were back in power.

It was a similar story in Australia. When Anthony Albanese won the 2022 election, he said Australians had 'conflict fatigue.' He wanted to bring everyone together and change the way politics was done. This was the same man whose party, while in opposition, had helped create that conflict by endlessly attacking the government of the time.

It is all very well attacking your opponents, but you can't expect the rules to change once you get into power yourself. Still, that is the leftist way - relentless aggression while in opposition, then expecting full unity and cooperation while in government.

This strange attitude was shared by leftist voters. As someone observed: 'When Morrison (the previous leader) was PM, everything was his responsibility and he was to blame when anything went wrong. Since Albanese has become PM, nothing is his responsibility and he is not to blame for anything. What an amazing change occurs when the left have their man in power!'

When hate turns to love. It's a miracle!

LP 2 - Right Side of History

Perhaps the sudden call for healing was because leftists think they are on 'the right side of history.' So, with Biden's election win, history had been restored to its true course. Those four years of manic leftist 'resistance' had been history trying to regain its natural path.

Many leftists do see an endpoint, which is a world free of injustice. One of the many problems with that is leftists are too confident their pet causes will lead to it.

Take the Indigenous 'Voice to Parliament,' discussed in Chapter Eight. This will be mentioned a few times so, as a reminder, this was about creating a new part of the Australian parliament. This was solely for the Aboriginal people, but was bound to affect the rest of the country too. The 'Voice' was going to be permanent, which made it serious enough to go to a national vote in a referendum. The Yes campaign pushed hard for the Voice to go ahead, while the No campaign wasn't convinced it was a good idea.

The Voice to Parliament was very much an unknown quantity. Yet despite literally *no one* knowing how it would play out over the next few decades, many Yes voters were sure they were on the 'right side of history' in supporting it. Remarkable.

The Voice never went ahead, so we don't know what would have happened. It's possible the Voice may have improved the lives of Indigenous people. It's also possible it would have been empty symbolism and just another piece of bureaucracy with no real benefits. Or it may have created new, unforeseen problems. It may also have given power to Aboriginal activists with a bitter grievance against modern Australians, who they see as 'colonisers.'

It would have taken at least a decade to see how the Voice worked out - but our total ignorance of the short and long term consequences did not stop its leftist supporters proclaiming that they were on the right side of history.

'The right side of history' idea implies not just a belief in progress, but that progress follows a direction which - by pure coincidence - aligns with causes that leftists support. Some other ideas on the right side of history include multiculturalism, a policy which has seen Western nations become highly fragmented, and feminism which, after some good early reforms, has helped make men and women deeply antagonistic to each other.

We can only hope these causes really are on the right side of history, and the turmoil they are currently causing is just a growing pain in history's journey to its natural end state.

LP 3 - Agree or You're Divisive

A common move from the leftist playbook is to call those who disagree with them 'divisive.'

Again, the Voice to Parliament was a good example. Its main supporter, prime minister Albanese, thought the issue would unite Australia. The bitter twelve month brawl that followed proved him wrong.

Those who were skeptical about the Voice raised concerns about it. For that, they were called 'divisive.'

If you do support a new idea like the Voice, you naturally hope others will agree with you. If it turns out they don't, calling them divisive won't help. You can do your best to persuade them, but agreement needs consent.

To put it in terms leftists will understand, suppose a man tells a woman he has a vision of them together and he wants to… 'unite' with her. Sadly for him, she might not agree. If she declines the offer, the man could call her divisive - but his idea of unity is not something she wants.

It would be convenient if everyone shared our values, but clearly they don't. Some people are so sure their view of the world is correct, they take offence at anyone who disagrees. Thomas Sowell notes that leftists often have little patience for non-believers.

> The left takes its vision seriously - more seriously than it takes the rights of other people. They want to be our shepherds. But that requires us to be sheep.

Some leftists project their ideas of 'unity' onto the media. For example, they accuse the Murdoch media of being divisive, and want it shut down. While Murdoch media is certainly flawed, it does at least allow some alternative views to the steady stream of GPR viewpoints coming from the BBC, *The Guardian*, CNN, and so on. This outrages leftists, who apparently want to ban any public disagreement with their sacred GPR causes.

While it would indeed be a more unified world if our information came only from *The Guardian* or the ABC, that's not the sort of unity many people want.

When leftists don't get the agreement they want, we get to see how 'tolerant and inclusive' they really are. In other words, their true authoritarian nature comes out.

As a final point, one might remark that the whole leftist system of identity politics is about dividing people up into teams. To do that and then expect any unity is optimistic, to say the least.

LP 4 - The Fake Consensus

Of course, it *is* possible to achieve unity if you bully your opposition out of existence. During the Voice to Parliament campaign, a well known leftist on Twitter joyfully noted that every public organisation was supporting the Yes vote. Almost every corporation, sporting body, and other public group was going to vote Yes!

This man thought the 'unity' had arrived naturally in a right-side-of-history orgy of goodwill. In truth, it was gained through intimidation in the age of cancel culture. With the obsession with racism, and the 2020 Black Lives Matter protests fresh in the memory, no one was going to risk being seen as anti-Aboriginal. No public group was going to become a social pariah by supporting the No vote. That would only have invited shaming from leftist scolds.

But yeah, three cheers for your fake consensus.

In the Voice to Parliament debate, there were good reasons to vote either Yes or No, or to be undecided. In a free society, this would have been reflected by some public groups being for Yes, some for No, and some staying neutral. The fake consensus for Yes was achieved through the fear of public shaming and the inevitable loss of business, sponsors, or government funding (the government was heavily pushing the Yes vote). It was driven mainly by pragmatism, not ethics. It was certainly nothing to do with 'history' driving everyone into a joyful dance of racial harmony.

Leftists love unity and will pursue it by any means necessary - praise, shame, bullying, jailing their enemies… whatever it takes. Still, a fake consensus is only valuable if you want to pretend it's the same as a real one.

LP 5 - Always the Underdog

Leftists have a need to think they're the underdog, even when their side is in power. The Voice referendum, again, was a good example. Incredibly, some leftists on Twitter claimed that the Yes campaign was the weak outsider, with one even calling it a 'David and Goliath battle.'

One might point out that the Yes campaign was backed by the government, the national broadcaster, nearly every big company, schools and universities, all the sporting codes, and almost every artist, celebrity, and public figure. None of this would convince such leftists they weren't fighting a heroic battle against all odds. Such is the deep need of the leftist to always be the underdog, even when all evidence says otherwise.

The only big public group which supported the No side was the opposition political party, as well as some commentators on Sky News Australia. If any other public figures or groups supported

No, they kept their views to themselves. The vast majority were for Yes.

In general, leftists need to face the fact that their side is no longer the underdog. The left won the culture war many years ago. It is the Global Progressive Regime that is in power now. Let's go back to the simple test proposed in Chapter Three.

Is it more socially acceptable to praise or to criticise X?

Now apply this test to the main GPR causes: multiculturalism, 'anti racism,' feminism, diversity, or the Black Lives Matter movement. Is it is more socially acceptable to praise or criticise any of these? The answer to that shows which side is in power.

For the Voice to Parliament, lots of people were comfortable putting their *Vote Yes!* stickers on display in car windows, but I can't recall seeing a single *Vote No!* sticker.

As others have said, when your views are in line with those held by the government, media, and big corporations, you are not the resistance. You are the establishment.

Another example is censorship, which has mostly been aimed at right wing figures, especially by Big Tech since about 2018. Yet we get the occasional lefty complaining they're the victims of it, as if we're still living in the 1950s. This might refer to gay or trans books being kept out of school libraries, for instance. Even if that does occur, it is a tiny amount of censorship compared to, say, right wing figures being barred from YouTube or Facebook. These days, it's not a right wing establishment censoring leftists, but the other way around.

As to why leftists adopt this 'always-the-underdog' mindset, perhaps they need to see themselves as sympathetic figures, always in need of special attention, help, and funding. Those with a Marxist bent have been trained to see power as inherently wrong, so are unwilling to admit their side ever has it. Maybe they need to believe they are rebels, and cling to the idea long after they've become part of the establishment.

There are also some leftists who identify with a particular cause so strongly, they can't imagine reality from another perspective. Feminists, for example, still seem to think men are by definition powerful and women are being ground underfoot by the patriarchy. In reality, there's barely a politician in the Western world who would dare criticise the feminist movement or speak up for men's rights.

For several reasons, many leftists will continue to see themselves as Always the Underdog, even when they are not. In reality, they're no longer fighting the Man, they *are* the Man. Resist them if you dare.

LP 6 - Cartoon Villains and Low Hanging Fruit

If leftists want to win political arguments, they need to defeat their opponents - but that means they have to understand them. Leftists often fail to do this because they assume themselves to exist on a higher moral and intellectual plane than everyone else. As a result, they tend to think anyone who doesn't agree with them is either stupid or evil. The next two points will address this belief.

Leftists see their beliefs as unquestionably good, especially their quest for RAGE, or Racial And Gender Equality. Anyone seen as an enemy of RAGE gets classified into a stock range of villainous archetypes. For feminists, there's the conservative Christian who wants to dress women in Handmaid's Tale outfits or, more recently, the angry incel, who they depict as a thwarted low level patriarch. For race obsessives, the cartoon villains may be the redneck-hillbilly type, the KKK member, the neo-Nazi, or the football thug.

While these types do exist, the belief that all opposition to RAGE consists of these cartoon villains isn't right. There are plenty of intelligent critics of feminism, multiculturalism, or Critical Race Theory who can't be fobbed off so easily. If feminists were serious, they would answer the criticisms of people like Karen Straughan and Janice Fiamengo. If 'anti-racists' were serious, they would seek out the more intelligent right wing thinkers and assess their views.

Then again, it's much easier to pretend all your enemies are hillbillies, football thugs, or misogynists. A British right winger named Laura Towler remarked on this when returning to Twitter after a two year suspension.

> One thing I've noticed about the far left on Twitter that hasn't changed during the 2 years I was suspended is that they still think all nationalists are football thugs. It's like they got their info from the British press 15 years ago and haven't been able to move past it since.

Having conceived of one's enemies in such limited terms, leftists can find validation in seeking out some of the dumber right wing people, beating them in arguments, and assuming the battle is won. This 'low hanging fruit' is an easy victory in the culture war, though of limited worth in the long term.

Right wingers can also be guilty of this vice, in mocking some of the dumbest social justice warriors, for example, or using 'cat ladies' as a slur. Stereotypes exist on both sides. Cat ladies vs Maga Men, for instance, was a brief cartoonish symbolic battle during the 2024 US election. Stereotypes are useful up to a point, but ultimately quite limited if you want to understand how your enemies really think.

LP 7 - Bad Faith

Having a superior intellect is one thing, but it's even more important for leftists to believe in their higher morality. As Thomas Sowell has said:

> No one can really understand the political left without understanding that they are about making themselves feel superior, however much they may talk piously about what they are going to do to help others.

With the firm belief in their own moral superiority, we come to a key pathology - the 'bad faith' fallacy. This is the leftist assumption that they alone act from good intentions, and that their opponents do not. This is at best merely arrogant, at worst cultish and fanatical. In practical terms, it means they don't understand their opponents so can never defeat them, except by brute force.

A better way to see political conflict is to compare it to dramatic fiction, say, in a book or film. In a simple drama, you have a one dimensional tale of good and evil. The heroes and villains are clearly marked and there's no doubt who to cheer for. This is the sort of struggle many leftists think they're engaged in. They're fighting racists or fascists, or whatever cartoon villain they think it is.

In a more complex drama, two opposing parties act from their own ideals, pursuing their own goals. Each is entitled to consider itself the hero of the story. They understand that their opposition feels the same way.

Another analogy is a big sporting event, like a World Cup football final. Each team is trying to win the same prize and sees itself as the hero, while realising that the opposing team has its own aspirations. That doesn't make them evil.

Many leftists instead see life as a simple tale of good and evil, with themselves on the side of good. They can't seem to empathise with their opponents, or see the other side of an argument. This can lead to a warped view of the issues themselves.

In our own age of the Global Progressive Regime, this manifests in certain ways. Many leftists see GPR causes as good by definition, so pro-GPR media like the BBC or *The Guardian* must also be good. It follows that other media groups which allows criticism of GPR causes must be evil. They can't be justified in criticising good, so they can only be 'acting from bad faith.'

It might seem like I am straw-manning them here, but I had an online exchange with a leftist academic who stated his view that Murdoch media, for instance, was purely a destructive tool acting for malicious interests. He seemed to find it inconceivable anyone there might have good intentions or a valid point of view. There are plenty of other leftists who agree and have called for Murdoch media to be shut down.

This is pure fanaticism. Some of these leftists believe the media should consist only of the BBC, *The Guardian*, *Sydney Morning Herald*, CNN, and so on, and the rest should be banned. After all, the others are only spreading lies, 'misinformation,' and hate speech, aren't they?

Murdoch is still a mainstream media group. What would these leftists think of other speakers further right, for example, those who openly discuss 'the Great Replacement' or say multiculturalism has been bad for Western nations? This is a rational position to take, but many leftists would assume it could only come from 'bad faith.'

In a similar way, most feminists see their own cause as synonymous with good, so a counter movement like Men's Rights Activism, by definition, can only be coming from a place of malice. Once again, this is mere zealotry.

One step which could help free leftists from the 'bad faith' trap is to realise the following two things are not the same:

A: The ideal of racial and gender equality.

B: The particular forms these ideas have taken, some of which are: Critical Race Theory, multiculturalism, DEI principles, and feminism.

A does not equal B. B is simply one form A has taken at the moment. Critics of B do not necessarily disagree with A. They might see B as a poor attempt at achieving A.

Having said that, some people will critique A in itself, saying that the races or genders may be different but not equal.

If leftists really engaged with counter arguments, they might end up changing their views. That could be rather threatening to them. It's far simpler to revert to the default assumption that their opponents are stupid or evil.

When you believe you are the side of absolute good and your opponents are evil, it makes it easy to dismiss anything they say as a conspiracy theory, hate speech, or misinformation. After all, what else could it be?

So, do leftists themselves operate from 'bad faith?' No, and therein lies a key difference in right / left thinking. Leftists tend to think right wing people are stupid or evil. Right wing people might think leftists can be stupid, but they aren't necessarily evil. On the contrary, they realise most of them act from good intentions, as they perceive them to be.

If only leftists would return the favour.

LP 8 - Blame the Consequences

Ideas have consequences. In politics, ideas lead to policies which affect the real world. Some ideas translate well and some do not.

When ideas don't work out, leftists usually decide it's not the fault of the ideas, it's the fault of the results. Blame the consequences. Communism is one idea which has rarely worked out well - but that's never the fault of communism as an idea, just the way it was done.

There's also a stage that comes before blaming the consequences, and that is being *surprised* at the consequences.

For example, there have been reports in the last few years of young men - especially white men - becoming more right wing. These reports often contain an air of puzzlement. What an unexpected trend. Why on earth would young men be turning right wing?

Here's a bold hypothesis. Is it possible the general antagonism towards men and boys might have turned them off the feminist cause, and leftism in general? Does shaming about toxic masculinity and male privilege make men less than enthusiastic allies to women? Might the simultaneous You-Go-Girl cheerleading for all things female serve as a blindingly obvious contrast?

What about the rise of 'right wing populism' in almost all Western nations? That one really is a mystery. Here's another wild theory. Is it possible this is a response to the diversity cult, multiculturalism, and a few decades of anti-Western messaging? We need some more academic studies to get to the bottom of this puzzle.

The reasons for these trends should be obvious, but leftists seem to find them surprising. Will this give them pause for thought and self criticism? Not at all. They'll simply blame the consequences and double down.

The consequences may take a while to be noticed, but will eventually be undeniable. In the meantime, there's a lot of 'quiet quitting' going on. The MGTOW movement, for one, was about men who simply opted out of relationships with women.

Men are also quitting some other institutions. It was reported in 2023 that the US army had seen a steep decline in recruitment from straight white men, who had always been their main demographic. After years of denigrating that group, as well as the concept of America itself, here was an unforeseen consequence.

Did the Global Progressive Regime really think they could trash straight white men and the nation, and these people would just keep on showing up? Apparently they did.

Seems they were wrong.

LP 9 - Pieties and Kowtowing

For middle class left wing whites, the downside to being morally superior to other whites is you're inferior to everyone else. If you buy into the Oppression Olympics, there's a hierarchy. You almost have to feel sorry for straight white male leftists, due to their low status. They're right at the bottom.

Within the hierarchy, white leftists have to observe the pieties and kowtow to those above them. White men must defer to feminists, white women to black women, and so on up the ranks.

The performative rituals can be quite amusing. There's one Australian white male leftist who is highly aggressive towards non-leftists, often blasting them online with vile invective. Yet he becomes a pure lamb before his betters. In one post, he kowtowed extravagantly to the Indigenous, requesting they let us use the Aboriginal flag for our national flag. It was odd to see someone so arrogant become humility personified.

In another case a young white woman wrote a book, and felt obliged at one point to confess her own privilege. She went on to recite a catechism about all the marginalised groups - LGBT, refugees, the disabled, and so on in a long list. The only ones left off it were straight white males, who are thought the most privileged and thus the most low status in the bizarre leftist value system.

Sometimes a leftist gets it wrong, like those feminists who criticise trans and find themselves terfed out of the club. Or a white leftist makes a faux pas and has to issue a panicky, grovelling apology. A couple of years ago, an aggressive Australian feminist re-tweeted a joke which some people saw as racist. Suddenly she was forced into an online 'struggle session' and scrambling to apologise. This same woman, often vicious towards white men, is almost always deferential towards non-whites.

One of the great things about not being a leftist is you don't have to care about all this nonsense. You don't have to feel guilty or apologise. You don't have to live in fear of being cancelled, or kicked out of the club. You don't have to observe these social pieties, or kowtow to someone simply because they happen to be female, Indigenous, or have some other high ranking identity.

That's my sales pitch to anyone wanting to leave the left. You no longer have to apologise for your existence, or kowtow to any of these people. Not in the slightest. It is highly liberating.

LP 10 - Death at a Dinner Party

Speaking of being part of a club, an amusing account was published in *Quadrant* magazine about a middle aged conservative man who fell in love with a left wing woman from hip inner city Melbourne. They began an intense love affair which worked well in private but became a problem whenever the couple had to socialise with the woman's circle of friends.

These friends had a predictable list of beliefs on every political topic: refugees, climate change, Islam, Aboriginals, misogyny, the wickedness of conservatives, and so on. The man in this story noticed some familiar leftist traits. Everyone in the group seemed to hold exactly the same views, and assumed he did too. There was an air of smug self congratulation about them, and a casual contempt towards anyone who thought otherwise. The man noticed some other odd behaviour, similar to that mentioned in chapter fifteen about the literary festival audience. For example:

> At another party, the wag raising the toast made derisive mention of (Sky News conservative) Andrew Bolt, a gag apropos of nothing relevant to the day but which drew an immediate gale of Pavlovian howls. These people applaud on cue, I thought; they applaud to be seen applauding.

The man found himself an outsider at these dinner parties, and was obliged to hide his opinions on all political topics. Yet his leftist girlfriend knew he was really a conservative, and lived in mortal terror of this secret being exposed to her hip circle of friends.

After several nerve racking social occasions, the man eventually slipped up with a questionable comment about Islam. This escalated into an argument with the couple hosting the dinner party. That was the end of the love affair, for the man's partner found his opinions intolerable.

From this account, you can draw a few points. When you stop being a leftist, you notice in hindsight that you were more or less given an entire belief system. Once you start to question it, or reject its premises and taboos, you realise how much social pressure there was to believe in it.

This dinner party set embodies some key leftist traits. First, these people's assumption that their political beliefs are not just correct, but morally superior. Second, the astonishing level of groupthink involved. This was discussed in the chapters about feminism, artists, and the ABC. It seems to be an abiding trait of leftism to demand that everyone think as one. There may be disagreements about minor details, but when it comes to core premises, full agreement is required.

Third, and as a consequence of the first two points, leftists often seem to be deeply intolerant. It is not only incomprehensible that anyone could disagree with them, it's forbidden.

Fourth, there is an implied cowardice involved. This man's female partner was terrified of being shunned as a result of her partner's wrong-think. This suggests a deep need for social approval in such people. It used to be thought that conservatives need social approval, but it seems inner city leftists need it even more. It's hard to believe such people really do think exactly the same on every topic. Most likely, some disagree in private but are too frightened to say so.

When the expression of dissenting views can lead to 'death at a dinner party,' it's clear the notion of the tolerant inclusive left, respectful of difference, is a myth. The fact that their claimed values are so different to their actual values is one of the biggest red flags when it comes to seeing through leftism.

Perhaps this astonishing groupthink is just a phase and eventually leftists will become more open minded, and less frightened by people who don't think like them. Until then, we have this odd inversion of norms. As someone wrote in the comments below the article: 'Being a conservative today is like being a homosexual in the 1950s. I am one, but don't tell people until I know they are one too.'

21

Jesus was a Refugee

This chapter will look at some more problems with leftist thinking. Some of these are attitudes, while others are specific false beliefs leftists have adopted. The beliefs then lead on to faulty reasoning, often as an attempt to justify them.

LP 11 - Building the House on Sand

Why are there so many leftist pathologies? One reason is people believe things that aren't true. This puts them at odds with reality, which leads to various complications. They accept a false premise then build a lot of false beliefs on top of it.

An example is the premise that people are - in theory - equal, and if they currently aren't, they *should* be. Different groups of people should be equal to each other in social power, wealth, life expectancy, or whatever else. As they clearly are not, this is seen as a major problem. We're told that any kind of 'gap' urgently needs fixing. We have to 'close the gap' between indigenous people and other Australians, or the 'gender pay gap' between men and women's average wage.

Of all the many problems with the belief in equality, the most basic is that people aren't equal and never will be. Consider a family with four children. The children come from the same genetic stock and grow up in the same family environment, yet may be completely different in ability and personality. They will never be equal to each other. If you can't achieve equality in that small group, how can you expect to achieve it in society overall with thousands of families and all their differences? These days, with our diverse multicultural families, it's even more impossible.

That doesn't mean reforms shouldn't be made if there is a way to help someone. Indeed it would be a 'right wing pathology' to go from the true statement that *people will never be equal* to the false conclusion that *therefore there's no point trying to help the less advantaged*. Of course it is worth trying to help people who need it.

Leftists see inequality in terms of identity groups: male and female, black and white, or whatever the case may be. I will list just a few problems with this. First, there are vast differences between individuals even within a given group, yet leftists force group identity upon them and often speak as if all members are somehow the same. They take a given factor - like income or life expectancy - average it out for the whole group, then imply that the average applies to each member.

Second, even if you insist on thinking in terms of these averages, what reason is there to think the average for one group would be the same as for another? To compare men and women, for instance, the average wage for men is higher but the average life expectancy for women is higher. There are many reasons for both results - but why would we expect either the average wage or life expectancy to be the same for both genders in the first place?

Third, comparing groups is usually grievance based. Knowingly or not, activists are often engaging in Marxist class struggle, a process specifically meant to stir up anger. There are dubious motives at work here.

Fourth, the kind of 'gaps' mentioned are highly selective. Some are seen as more important than others. For example, the lower life expectancy for Aboriginals compared to Anglos is seen as a serious gap, but the lower life expectancy for white men compared to white women isn't serious at all. No one is trying to close that gap.

A fifth problem with the belief in equality is that leftists are generally not very honest about the actual causes of inequality.

This might be because they deny unwelcome facts, like the role of biology, believe 'victim groups' must never be criticised, or reject any other possible cause not compatible with their ideas.

These are just a few problems with the idea of equality, and there are many more. While some forms of inequality *are* unfair, the obsession with equality is misplaced. Leftists' core premise is that if we don't have 'equity' - that is, equality of outcome between groups - it's a serious problem. This false premise leads to the creation of lots of new problems.

It would be much better to admit that we just aren't equal. This might seem a simple statement, but it's better than the convolutions that come from trying to achieve the impossible goal of equity. Thomas Sowell has said:

> People who pride themselves on their "complexity" and deride others for being "simplistic" should realize that the truth is often not very complicated. What gets complex is evading the truth.

One truth we should stop evading is that equality doesn't exist within groups, and it doesn't exist between groups either.

People aren't equal. They never will be.

LP 12 - Denial of Biology

Since the discovery of genes, it has been believed that a person is shaped by two main types of influence - cultural and genetic. In recent times, the biological side has fallen out of favour with leftist academics. This tendency has been so strong it sometimes amounts to a denial biology plays any role at all.

There are many reasons for this. One goes back to the Nazis, whose belief in genetics and eugenics put biological factors in a bad odour. Marxism, on the other hand, favours social engineering. With universities now dominated by leftists, the Marxist influence remains and a lot of weight is given to social explanations of human behaviour, and not much to biological causes. Race and gender are seen as 'socially constructed.'

The field of Sociobiology was an exception as it deals with evolutionary causes of behaviour, but most other social sciences prefer to think behaviour is created by culture and social factors.

Still, it seems obvious there are differences between men and women, and between different racial groups. Why would genetic factors not play a major part? If you believe human beings evolved over many thousands of years, then surely men and women evolved differently, as did racial groups who came up in very different physical environments.

This simple premise is ignored by many academics. Leftists don't like these sort of explanations because they have a vision of a better future. They believe an equal society can be created as long as they are put in control, especially of education. Their vision requires a 'blank slate' view of human nature, which means everyone is born the same and can thus be molded as part of their ideal future society. They don't like the idea people may be very different even at birth, due to genetic factors.

Therefore, you find feminists claiming all differences between men and women are just socially constructed. Anti-racists claim the idea of race was a concept invented for political reasons by white Europeans a few centuries ago, rather than having any basis in biology.

This would be fine if biology was as unimportant as leftists want it to be. The problem is that if it actually *does* play a big role, then the denial of biology is a denial of reality. If you start from a false premise like that, a lot of your other theorising is going to be spurious.

LP 13 - The Is and the Ought

However, some leftists do want to deny reality, because reality is unacceptable. They want to create a new reality more in line with their wishes.

This is a key point in the psychology of hardcore leftists. They're not interested in discovering truth, but in creating it. This was shown in the story of a Canadian woman named Caylan Ford who fell foul of cancel culture. In reflecting on her experience, she explained it as follows:

> I struggled for a long time to understand why people are often 'cancelled' for making true statements in good faith. This didn't compute for me; there's nothing immoral about saying true things. After lots of conversations with 'cancellers,' I understood the problem.

> I consider truth to be a form of the good. It's noble to try to apprehend the order of the cosmos and the laws of nature - which are beautiful and just - and attune ourselves to them. In a disagreement, I take for granted that truth is an authority to which both parties can appeal.

> People in thrall to ideology do not believe that truth is a good. They don't think the universe is well ordered, or that the laws governing it are just. Because they perceive reality as defective and wrong, appeals to truth are meaningless. It has no moral authority.

> As I was once told by someone who participated in my own cancellation: it doesn't matter what's true. What matters is what *should* be true. In Marxian terms, "philosophers have hitherto only interpreted

the world in various ways. The point, however, is to change it."

Proponents of cancel culture believe that if they can stop the accurate observation and description of reality - e.g. by corrupting the meaning of words, delegitimizing hard sciences, and through the threat of social ostracism - they can actually change reality.

Sadly for them, and happily for the rest of us, the fundamental order of being can't be actually changed, because it lies outside man's control. In the war against reality, reality always wins.

In trying to understand this mentality, there are a few more points to be made.

First, we don't yet know all the answers about what 'reality' actually is. We don't always know if we are seeing reality, or just a mistaken idea of what we *think* it is. Second, many times in history what we have been told is reality is just someone's preferred version of it.

While both those points are true, some leftists interpret them to mean that there is no actual reality and we can just create the one we want, and that all past theories of reality have simply been created for political gain.

I take the view there are some aspects of the world that are objectively true, whether we believe in them or not. Whatever we try to create ourselves, we have to work with these basic facts as a starting point.

Some leftists refuse to accept any such limitations. Their ideology comes first and they expect reality to fall into line.

As mentioned, if your ideology means people should be equal, you need to believe both race and gender differences are purely social in origin. But if biology *does* play a major part, that is a reality you should acknowledge.

It's this sort of thing some leftists don't accept. They have almost made the idea taboo and are prepared to ban it and cancel anyone putting it forward. In that case, they are putting limits on inquiry.

We don't fully understand reality, and we should keep an open mind about it. Demanding reality conforms to your ideology is not a good idea, because if it doesn't, you are living in a fantasy world.

If leftists' ideas of gender and racial equality are objectively false, they are themselves pushing a false concept of reality for political reasons. Perhaps they think everyone does that anyway, and they're just playing the same game. It does lead to real world consequences, though, for example when they try to force diversity to match up with equality.

When you think about it, the terms 'diversity' and 'equality' actually contradict each other.

Unfortunately, the Is and the Ought do not always match up in the way leftists would like.

You can't always get what you want.

LP 14 - Constrained vs Unconstrained Vision

Thomas Sowell has been quoted several times because his insights are so good. In one of his main books, *A Conflict of Visions*, he has a theory of what he calls the constrained vision and the unconstrained vision. To summarise it very briefly, he suggests that there are two main outlooks on life. Some people hold an over optimistic view of what is possible in this world. People of this type see no limits to what may be, and believe in the perfectibility of human society. This is the 'unconstrained vision.'

The second outlook is a more pessimistic, perhaps more realistic view of life and the human condition. There are limits to what is possible, and nothing will ever be perfect. We can only find the best compromise in a flawed and complex world.

'There are no solutions, only tradeoffs,' is Sowell's succinct quote on the topic.

With their constant demands for movement towards their Utopian ideals, most leftists hold to the unconstrained vision. Their trademark anger may be from disappointment at how far short reality falls of their wishes. If they could only have more of a 'constrained' outlook, the anger would decrease and we might achieve some better compromises between perfection and reality.

LP 15 - Jesus Was a Refugee

This next pathology is to do with poor reasoning, but also disposition. Just as leftists can be too perfectionist, their approach to difficult problems is sometimes too simple and may be just an emotive, feelgood slogan.

Take the issue of refugees and what to do about them. This is a problem so complex that trying to solve it will inevitably lead to many new problems, whatever you do.

In Australia, a Christian leader hung a large sign outside his church that said 'Jesus Was a Refugee.'

What this presumably means is that just as one would not turn away the baby Jesus from the inn, Australia should not turn away the many refugees trying to enter the country. If that baby had been turned away, Jesus might not have lived and we'd never have had Christianity. If conservatives were real Christians, they'd show proper values likes charity and compassion, and let those refugees in. If they don't, that shows they're fake, and if that innkeeper in Bethlehem was like them, Jesus would have died. So basically, right wing conservative Christians are hypocrites and meanies who killed Jesus.

This sort of thinking is faulty, as well as emotionally manipulative. In response to 'Jesus was a refugee' one could simply say 'Refugees are not Jesus' and be done with it, but here are a few more points:

1. There was only one Jesus but there are thousands of refugees.
2. If you let in the first lot of refugees, thousands more will come.
3. If you let in very large numbers of refugees that leads to further consequences, many of which we can't yet predict. So it's unwise to make rash decisions without thinking them through.
4. It is also unwise to make big decisions purely on emotion, and in response to manipulative slogans like 'Jesus was a refugee.'
5. Short term virtue is easy, long term consequences are hard - so be careful.
6. While charity and compassion are fine qualities, they must work together with reason and calm judgement in making important decisions.
7. Allowing a young pregnant women to give birth in a stable is not the same as allowing thousands of refugees to settle in your country.
8. Many refugees are good people, but some are just ordinary and others not that great. So the percentage of refugees who are like Jesus is pretty small.
9. If most of the refugees are coming from Islamic countries, that may eventually lead not to peaceful coexistence, but to the decline of Christianity in your country. Is that a concern for Christians?
10. If you are going to support these causes in the abstract, you should show a personal willingness to bear the cost - like

hosting a refugee family in your home for twelve months. This will show commitment and that you are prepared to take on the practical consequences rather than just trying to display virtue and support values in the abstract.

To repeat, the problem of refugees is a complex one to which there is no simple answer. It would be wonderful if we could take in thousands of refugees without any short or long term consequences, but that would be to hold what Sowell called the 'unconstrained vision' of the world. To have a constrained vision is to once again realise that 'there are no solutions, only tradeoffs' and we have to tread carefully finding the best answer to a difficult problem.

LP 16 - Lack of Humility

Leftists often show a lack of humility, which manifests as a certainty that their political views are correct. In many cases, they are so sure their ideas are morally right they can't understand how anyone could oppose them except from evil motives. This is similar to LP7 Bad Faith, from the last chapter.

You see this in feminists, in 'anti-racists,' and in those who believe only left wing media outlets deserve to exist.

Although many of them are atheists, these people are like religious zealots. In their political views, they can't conceive that anyone could think differently to them, or that they themselves might be mistaken.

This shows a lack of humility, which can be a weakness. It's also quite obnoxious, and many leftists have a smug sense of moral superiority.

In science and philosophy, at least as they used to be practised, humility was a basic virtue. Philosophers were supposed to believe that they might be wrong about everything. Scientists were supposed to concede that no matter how much they might like a particular theory, it could be proven wrong. With leftists, not much of this is on show.

In this book, I've been very critical of leftism and the Global Progressive Regime. Still, it's possible I am quite wrong in my views, and very likely I'm wrong in at least some of them. I stand by my opinions, but with the awareness they might be proven wrong.

I also realise other people will have their own views on the topics raised in this book. Feminists will see gender issues differently, and non-whites may think differently on racial issues. I realise they may have reasons to think and feel as they do, and I make at least some effort to understand them. But it's rare to see a feminist who genuinely tries to understand men's rights activists, or an anti-racist who tries to understand a race realist like Jared Taylor.

The absolute conviction that one's views are correct can lead to fanaticism, which gives rise to support for things like censorship. If it turns out that your ideas are actually wrong, this means the truth is hidden and only a fictional view of the world will be permitted, which can eventually lead to real world consequences. A lack of humility can come back to hurt you in the end.

LP 17 - Won't Take Their Own Side in an Argument

This next trait will seem to contradict the last one. The poet Robert Frost once said 'a liberal is a man too broad minded to take his own side in a quarrel.'

On the one hand, this shows a person is open-minded enough to see another point of view, and even to have a certain empathy for their opponents. But the way this manifests in our own time is to actually be opposed to your own side, not just in an argument, but in life.

The especially applies to race. In the Global Progressive Regime, there's a distinct anti-white, anti-Western push. For white Westerners, the rational thing would be to push back against it - and many do - but white Western *leftists* don't do this. Instead, they enthusiastically join in the war against themselves. They have been coerced into not taking their own side in the argument.

There's a perverse fascination in this sort of betrayal. It is perhaps the core leftist pathology, and the one with the most real world consequences.

In this book, I have defended straight white males. One of the main reasons is because I'm a straight white male. I realise that my demographic has been declared a regime enemy and this is neither fair nor helpful. It is rational to fight back against it.

For the same reason, I defend Anglo-Australians - because that is my own tribe. While that's not a complete justification, at least it shows loyalty. Many white leftists have been conned into being anti-white. They consider this the height of virtue, rather than treasonous or self destructive.

The topic of race is the most contested battle of the culture war and a key part of the Global Progressive Regime. It's impossible to understand the GPR without discussing race.

It is here that leftist pathologies are at their worst. Many white leftists have been fooled into not just failing to take their own side in an argument, but actively taking the other side to fight against themselves.

This bizarre trend will be the focus of the next chapter.

22

Edenist Follies

This chapter will move on to the key GPR battleground of race and racism, identifying some leftist pathologies in this area.

LP 18 - The Japanese Soldier

There's a well known story of a Japanese World War Two soldier who was found living on an island nearly thirty years after the war. He was under the illusion the war was still happening, though it ended decades ago. He didn't realise the world had moved on.

There is a similar type among today's leftists. This type grew up in the heady days of the 1960s and 70s when the left were actually the rebels. These people are now part of the establishment, perhaps living in affluent suburbs and even having key roles in the media. Or they might be aging artists who were famous decades ago and have been living off it ever since.

No matter how privileged they are now, in their minds these eternal hippies are still fighting the ancient battles of their youth. When they rail against white racism today, they're reliving their youthful heroics (conducted from afar) against apartheid in South Africa. They're oblivious to the fact that modern South Africa is a shambles and it's now the white South Africans being discriminated against, or even murdered, in racial hate crimes. None of that matters, because in their minds they're still standing shoulder to shoulder with Nelson Mandela.

Living comfortably on the 'islands' of the affluent white suburbs where they reside, these aging heroes are shielded from the diversity they cheer on in their war against racism.

As for the female Japanese soldiers, they are still fighting their antique feminist battles. Even though the main victories were won decades ago, the war never ends. Why spoil the party? For some people, it's always 1972.

In other words, the ideas of these people are hopelessly out of date, but unfortunately we're still stuck with them sounding off their ancient politics for a few more years.

LP 19 - The Magnanimous Ruler

The Japanese soldier type is also a magnanimous ruler, cheering on immigration and diversity, and scolding those who fail to join in with his cheerleading.

He's magnanimous because he does see himself as a 'ruler' in the sense that he's always been part of the white racial majority. He thinks he's being noble, dispensing blessings onto those powerless minorities who need his protection.

He might watch a 'diverse' BBC drama on TV, and nod approvingly at the racial equality on display in this small context. Yet our magnanimous ruler doesn't see the bigger picture that exists outside the pleasant and sheltered area where he spends his time. He doesn't see that in the global picture, whites are the minority, especially compared to highly populated areas like China, India, and Africa. He does not see that in Europe, Britain, America, Canada, and Australia, whites are headed for ethnic minority status in countries they once dominated.

Our high minded hero is an anti-racist, happy to condemn 'white privilege' in these countries. He would never dream of condemning racial privilege among the majorities of Asia, Africa, or the Middle East. Let the Chinese dominate China, and Arabs the Middle East, but whites are not allowed to own any country. They must step aside and let themselves be displaced for the good of the post-racial Utopia.

Our magnanimous leader does not realise that while in his own noble mind he 'doesn't see race,' almost all other racial groups do. So his righteous anti-racist sentiments will not be returned, especially when whites are no longer the majority. All the anti-white propaganda he's been approving for decades will do its work in generating resentment against the former 'colonisers.'

I have called our magnanimous ruler 'he' but there are plenty of females of the type. Indeed, white middle class left wing women may be the most magnanimous of all. They often favour short term virtue over long term consequences. During the Voice to Parliament debate, one such proclaimed that white people have never suffered from racism in Australia, and never would in the future. This pronouncement was made from one of the whitest, most affluent suburbs in Sydney. Time will tell if her views are correct.

The magnanimous ruler has been cheering on anti-white sentiment for decades, nobly dispensing, in his or her own mind, social power to ethnic minorities. The magnanimous ruler will die a noble death without ever having felt the consequences of this noble generosity. If there's any cosmic justice, we can only hope he or she will be reincarnated as part of the despised white ethnic minority of the future.

LP 20 - You Can't Stop Change

A British man rang a talkback radio show to complain about mass immigration, saying people were sick of seeing the country change without their consent. The progressive radio host told him he'd have to 'suck it up' and 'you can't stop change.'

You can't stop change? This is sometimes expressed as 'you can't stop progress,' with the implication the change is always a good one.

There is a sleight of hand here. The trick is to take a true statement - change is inevitable - and then pretend that a *particular type* of change is inevitable, which is false. History could have taken any number of paths. It was not predestined to take only one.

Politicians, lobbyists, and activists are the ones who help bring about change. 'You can't stop change' say the politicians who have done everything possible to move change in a particular direction. They have also impeded, attacked, or silenced those who try to stop it.

In other words, they've made an enormous effort to stop those who are trying to stop the change that cannot be stopped!

To draw a false conclusion from a true statement is either a mistake or a deliberate scam. If you challenge the false conclusion, the leftist points to the true statement, as if the person is arguing with that rather than the conclusion. One might make the true statement that we're all going to (eventually) die and falsely conclude that there's no point eating or trying to earn a living. To say that there are some things we can't control doesn't mean there are *no* things we can control, or that all our actions are futile.

The world is changing all the time. That doesn't mean it has to change in a particular way - and not towards some alleged 'right side of history' either.

LP 21 - The Fear Monger

But what if you're one of those people who thinks not all change is for the better? You may hold reservations about some changes, even warn against them. You know what you are? You're a fear monger.

This is a term applied to any political leader who resists GPR values. Mind you, such leaders are thin on the ground, mainly because they don't want to be accused of being a fear monger. These sort of shaming tactics do work.

Does it ever occur to those who cry *fear monger* that some fears are legitimate? There are some things we *should* be afraid of, or at least cautious about, rather than rushing into with gung ho enthusiasm.

Take the situation of importing large numbers of men from non-Western countries which are openly patriarchal and anti-gay. You might think leftists would be hesitant about this, given that gay and women's rights are so important to them. But not a bit of it. If you raise any concerns, a leftist will ignore them and call you a fear monger.

Progress isn't always progress – but any conservative leader who does query 'progressive' changes should get ready to be accused of stoking fear and division.

Let's not forget that while making such accusations, the left have been busy with a little fear mongering of their own - about white supremacy, patriarchy, fascism, climate change, and so on. But their fears are apparently legit, so we must never accuse them of panic and hyperbole, let alone fear mongering.

I'm agnostic on the topic of climate change, but let's suppose it was a legitimate fear. If someone did warn that it was a serious problem, it would be silly to shout *fear monger* at them as if this was some kind of refutation. One should listen to their arguments to see if they were justified. Perhaps they are right and we should be afraid.

LP 22 - Don't Look at the Horse

A variant of the fear monger pathology is the left's insistence that we accept any new reform at face value, and not regard it with any suspicion. Indeed, we shouldn't really look at it at all. We should simply accept it in good faith.

When we are given some new policy by leftist reformers, we should never consider it might be a Trojan horse containing hidden dangers. No, it is a *gift horse*, and we should never look a gift horse in the mouth. That would be rude. All leftist reforms are gift horses and never Trojan horses.

We must always accept progressive reforms as being automatically good, with no potential for abuse. We must never be skeptical about any of the wonderful reforms offered by our GPR overlords. We should accept them gratefully and with full faith in their goodness.

With proposed 'hate speech' laws for instance, we should accept that they're just meant to 'keep us safe' and would never be a portal to heavier censorship.

For the idea of a cashless society, there's no need to examine any potential problems. We should simply accept that making all our spending public and subject to external control is a great idea.

With the Aboriginal Voice to Parliament, we should have accepted the sales pitch without question. They said it was only a tiny reform and would never affect us in the future. We should not for a moment have wondered if there were hidden dangers and future problems. We should have voted Yes without hesitation, despite the fact the Voice would have become permanent, and was therefore a marriage with no chance of divorce.

We should never treat these wonderful progressive reforms as suspicious, or as some kind of Trojan horse. *How dare you* said the Australian leftists in 2023. Don't look at the horse.

Stop being a fear monger.

LP 23 - The Edenist

In continuing with some race related pathologies, we have to realise that race poses no threat at all in the mind of white leftists. This is because they are often Japanese soldiers and magnanimous rulers, and do you realise you can't stop change? And of course, the biggest racial threat these days comes from white supremacy and the far right.

However, another reason race is a non-issue for some people is because of a mentality we can call 'the Edenist.'

In the Bible story, it's said that God created Adam and Eve, who lived in the Earthly paradise of the garden of Eden. There was no sin, sorrow, or suffering. It was Heaven on Earth. Then came the fall and the birth of sin, and Adam and Eve were cast out of Eden.

Some leftists also believe in a kind of Eden, which is the world of indigenous peoples around the world before the coming of Europeans. This Eden was a place where indigenous folks lived in harmony with nature in an idyllic state. They only hunted in tiny amounts, taking strictly what they needed. They revered Nature and were part of it. These societies were democratic and equal. Indeed they were probably matriarchal. Everyone treated each other wonderfully, and they were all happy. Then white Europeans came and it's been downhill ever since.

I'll admit my picture is a bit of a straw man and not all leftists have such a simple minded view. Still, many do have such a conception of non-Western people, to varying degrees, as morally superior to Westerners.

It is a version of Rousseau's 'noble savage,' adopted by white people who have either a Romantic disposition or an overly harsh view of their own society, such that they need to imagine something better.

As silly as this conception may be, it is still held by some young and not so young white leftists. This could remain as a harmless fantasy but it does have real world effects.

An over-critical view of Western people can lead to the foolish policies of ceding land and power to non-Western people in the mistaken belief they are kinder, wiser, and more enlightened than ourselves. For this reason, we must puncture the Edenist's illusions by pointing out the less than Eden-like behaviours that did and do exist among such people.

Just like us, non-Westerners have practised almost all the crimes known to man. These include murder, human sacrifice, inter-group warfare, rape, conquest, infanticide, slavery, tyranny, and a host of other bad behaviours. Rumour has it some of them even had toxic masculinity.

Some non-Western societies may be better or worse than our own, in particular ways, but the idea that they all existed on some higher moral plane is an illusion we should lay to rest.

LP 24 - Immigrants vs. Bogans

There has often been a snobbish element to the white leftists who embrace diversity and multiculturalism. Although the working class were once seen as the agents of a Marxist revolution, middle class leftists have long had a horror of particular kinds of working class people. In America this might be the redneck, in Britain the football thug, in Australia the 'bogan.' In each case the person is seen as crude, uncultured, or deplorable.

It need not even be those extreme types but just ordinary working class people, who are often socially conservative. They voted for Brexit, for example, or might be openly patriotic. Some white leftists look down their noses at such people, seeing them as uneducated, or as bigots. British leftists even invented a new term, 'gammon,' to insult them. So, they revel in occasional symbolic victories over this type, especially if it means a win for diversity.

As an example of this, an anecdote was published in a British newspaper about a Muslim woman wearing a niqab on a bus in Newport, Wales. She was speaking to her son in another language. A man sitting nearby got angry and told her she was in the UK and should be speaking English. Another passenger then piped up and said 'We're in Wales and she's speaking Welsh.'

This story was triumphantly posted online by a smug leftist of my acquaintance, who saw it as a fine victory over the bogans. Because look - not only was the Welsh man so ignorant he didn't even know his own native language, the Muslim was proven to be actually more Welsh than the bogan. So it's the Muslim who's the exemplary Welsh person rather than the white fellow. If only that man could reach into his bigoted heart and overcome his small-minded hate, he would realise we are all the same.

For a more sane interpretation of the story, a few points can be made. If the Muslim lady of the story had really mastered the Welsh language, well done to her, for she must have respected the host country enough to integrate to that extent. A white Welshman who *did* speak Welsh and heard her speaking it would have been impressed, not hostile. He would wish more immigrants were like her.

But does the smug leftist who posted this story online really think this is a typical Muslim immigrant? What is the actual percentage of Welsh Muslims who speak Welsh in public? It's likely this person is an anomaly. Yet our white leftist wants to present the anomalous as typical.

According to one guidebook from 2010, 99% of *all* Welsh people could speak English but just 19% could speak Welsh. Yet apparently our white leftist believes all *Muslim immigrants* to Wales speak fluent Welsh.

Still, why worry about reality when you can achieve another symbolic victory over the hated bogans and bigots of your own society, and prove your own moral superiority at the same time? This is the real reason our smug leftist posted this story online.

The story is a wonderful piece of globalist propaganda. Even if it is true, there are lies by implication: that all Muslims have assimilated to Britain enthusiastically and well, and that Muslims are just as British as the locals, indeed more so, and could serve as role models for the ignorant locals.

What's more likely is that the incident is unusual; that many immigrants to Britain have no interest in assimilating, let alone learning an obscure language like Welsh; that there are some areas in European cities that are No Go Zones and may even operate under Shariah law; and that multiculturalism does not make a harmonious, happy society, but a fragmented, distrustful one.

The role of propaganda is to shape people's perception of reality. Perhaps the propagandists have the optimistic hope these perceptions of reality will eventually turn into reality itself. The trouble is that actual reality keeps getting in the way.

LP 25 - Why Can't We Just Get Along?

White leftists like to hold up model migrants as proof that multiculturalism is a success. Welsh-speaking Muslims, Jesus as a refugee, and so on. It's true that if only all immigrants were like that, multiculturalism would succeed.

Even so, there is still the problem of social cohesion, which was greatly underestimated by those who launched the multicultural experiment in the 1970s. Some still don't see it as a problem at all. Just recently, a leftist tweeted the following:

> Social cohesion in a multicultural country is really quite straightforward. Ensure every cultural, ethnic, religious group is treated equally. Equal representation, access, treatment, same standards everywhere. Shouldn't be that hard.

So easy! In fact, the only way to achieve this sort of equality would be with a colour-blind policy, which means ignoring race altogether and treating people as individuals. But what this person means is that every 'cultural, ethnic, religious' group should be acknowledged as different, and then treated equally.

What this entails is a sort of tedious administrative nightmare in which one has to first classify a person by their identity, and then ensure that their group is treated exactly the same as the hundreds of other identity groups. 'Shouldn't be that hard.'

Here is the leftist paradox in which people demand to be *different but the same*. They make a big deal over their difference, but also want to be treated the same as everyone else.

You then throw the concept of 'equity' into the mix and it's all over. One suspects there are those of malicious intent who know that diversity plus equity is the formula for chaos. You create hundreds of identity groups and then tell them to strive for equity, which is the impossible goal of equal outcomes.

Soon, everyone is at each other's throats - and there's the answer to *why can't we just get along?* Because 'getting along' is impossible in the leftist system which obsesses over identity, and demands both diversity and equity.

A further problem is that some immigrants have no interest in getting along. There was a recent case where an immigrant taunted native Germans about their coming demographic replacement. Someone else posted online about some British cities now being minority white, to which a high profile British non-white replied 'So what?'

It is here we see the naivety of the *why can't we just get along* crowd, with their delusion the altruism they show others will be returned. We will eventually realise what a mistake this was. In the meantime, we will just have to try to all get along.

'Shouldn't be that hard.'

LP 26 - The Cure is Worse than the Disease

Did you know Australia might become a republic? What an achievement, throwing off our old British imperial masters. The only drawback is we've replaced the Brits with a new set of rulers, the globalist overlords who've allowed us to start a franchise in their multicultural world order. One that'll be almost identical to all the other franchises, but never mind. We're a republic.

At least we're not as badly off as Ireland. They spent all that time gaining independence from the British, only to find their country too is turning into a non-Irish multicultural outpost of Globalism Inc.

Leftists are sometimes so focused on their temporary hatreds they solve problems in a hurry and end up creating even bigger problems.

Take the feminists who, through their vindictive hatred of white men, chose to spite them by supporting the import of masses of non-white men, from far more patriarchal cultures than our own. It might one day lead to future generations living under Shariah law, but at least feminists will have enjoyed a spiteful victory over white men in the meantime.

Er… hooray!

Or as Peter Hitchens admitted, one reason his generation of radicals supported immigration was to spite British conservatives. The resulting transformation of Britain was a minor side effect of this splendid victory. It was yet another triumph for leftism. When they diagnose a social sickness, they sure know how to cure it, even if the cure is sometimes worse than the disease.

LP 27 - The Guilt Flip Trick

One of the main ways to manipulate people is through their emotions. Especially potent are emotions like pride and shame. Both have value, but on the whole pride is a far healthier emotion. This applies for individuals, groups, or whole nations.

In a sane world, white people would be proud of their countries, and Westerners proud of being a part of Western civilisation. Yet we have been the victims of a sustained con job meant to induce a sense of shame, rather than pride. In founding the Anglo nations, we have supposedly sinned against the rest of the world.

Most leftists have fallen victim to this conquest of the mind. Some of them believe the founding of America and Australia were crimes, and the British Empire was one of the worst developments in world history.

There are plenty of reasons not to accept this whole belief system, but some leftists have decided, or been duped into deciding, that a state of permanent guilt is the right one to adopt.

A very different response is possible. One could say: *The drive to expand and flourish is simply human nature and the way of the world. These sins that you imply are the sole preserve of the West have been part of all other major civilisations, and are therefore nothing unusual. While the empire was a mix of good and bad, on balance, the spread of Western civilisation was a good thing, not a cause for regret. Besides, it is our civilisation, and we should stay loyal to it for better or worse. What's more, your attempt to persuade us otherwise seems to have dubious motives and even worse consequences.*

That would be a valid approach. Leftists, however, obsess over our supposed guilty past. Why do they do this?

At this point, we might recall Thomas Sowell's belief that the political left 'are about making themselves feel superior.' Morally superior, that is. But a heightened sense of morality also makes them vulnerable to ideas about guilt. As leftists like to feel superior, the idea they are somehow guilty of wicked historical sins must be a major blow to morale.

To resolve this, the white leftist embraces the guilt fully in order to transform it. He replaces a feel-bad emotion, guilt, with a feel-good emotion, virtue, about feeling guilty. This is not just a relief, it's intoxicating. The leftist has become a good-white.

Then he notices not everyone is following his example. Some other white people reject the concept of guilt and all that goes with it. This makes them bad-whites.

The good-white sees this and is enraged. He may feel a little foolish. He may be resentful that others aren't getting with the program. He may also feel some of that intoxicating moral superiority as he condemns the bad-white. The good-white feels *even more virtue* for chastising and berating the bad-white for not agreeing to feel guilt. The good-white has made himself superior once again.

All this was on display for the tedious twelve months the Voice to Parliament was up for debate in Australia. Never before did so many good-whites get the chance to chastise their bad-white brethren. Never before did the good-whites get so long to show how much they cared about the wickedness done to Aboriginals.

As mentioned, guilt has some value. The point of guilt is to recognise when you have done something wrong, and then stop doing it. In that case, guilt has functioned as it should, as a corrective measure.

However, guilt can easily become pathological when it leads to self harm, or if it allows you to be manipulated.

As a simple example of guilt rightly and wrongly applied, let's take the leftist's lament about empire and colonisation. For the sake of argument, we'll accept the premise that colonising other countries is wrong. Or that while there may have been reason to do it hundreds of years ago, it is no longer justified.

If we accept that idea, then we could use guilt as a corrective measure in guiding our current actions. Guilt, correctly applied, means that we no longer colonise other countries. Guilt, pathologically applied, means that we let others colonise us. This is supposedly a form of apology, or even reparations. It is also insane. But never mind. At least white leftists have made themselves feel morally superior again, and that's what really counts.

23

Acting Dumb…
Or Not Really Acting

The next chapter contains yet more classics of leftist thought and behaviour. We'll start with a big one.

LP 28 - The DIE LIE

DIE stands for the holy trinity of Diversity, Inclusion, and Equity. Realising that this acronym is not the best, our masters changed it to the less punchy DEI. It's more honest to call it DIE as the main aim is to kill off regime enemy the straight white man, and society as it used to be.

DIE is a good example of destructive values hiding beside a façade of morality. For surely each of the three terms refers to something good, one might suppose. Let's consider them one by one.

Diversity is meant to refer to all the different racial, gender, and sexuality types. In its most benign form, the principle is that we're supposed to accept all of these types of people as they are. If that was all it entailed it would be no big deal. On closer inspection, there are several problems.

For a start, the idea of diversity is closely tied to identity politics, which encourages people to be obsessed with their race, gender, and sexual nature. Ideally, these characteristics should be of minor interest, and people should get on with their lives without obsessing over them.

Second, diversity has been set up as a great virtue in the Global Progressive Regime. In this concept system, its opposite is the category of the straight white male, which then takes on a negative meaning.

This might be a mere technicality if the practical effects weren't so obvious. That is, that the straight white male is the target of envy, enmity, and general negativity. It can lead to actual discrimination in hiring. If you're trying to achieve a more diverse organisation, the one type you'll try to exclude is the straight white male. One might ask for identity-blind hiring on the basis of merit, but the alleged virtue of diversity rules that out. Diversity, in itself, is seen as of higher value than merit.

In Western nations, straight white men were generally the most productive group. To attack them is to weaken your most productive group, as well as causing resentment. That doesn't seem to make sense - but if destabilising society is the real goal, then it *does* make sense.

Third, when you put a lot of diverse people and groups together, it automatically makes it harder to unite them, as by definition they'll have less in common. That includes their beliefs and values. At the time of writing this chapter, for example, a Muslim-led local council has just banned some books on same-sex parenting from their library. So, the magical principle of diversity does not always work out as it's supposed to.

The obsession with diversity would not have been needed if the multicultural society hadn't been set up in the first place. Having now created a fragmented, incoherent society, the globalists act as if the ritual praising of diversity is going to make it all work. Not everyone is convinced. To once again quote Thomas Sowell:

> Can you cite one speck of hard evidence of the benefits of "diversity" that we have heard gushed about for years? Evidence of its harm can be seen - written in blood - from Iraq to India, from Serbia to Sudan, from Fiji to the Philippines. It is scary how

easily so many people can be brainwashed by sheer repetition of a word.

Diversity is more likely to create conflict than harmony. The more obvious this becomes, the more leftists try to force everyone together in some kind of contrived unity.

This is difficult, to say the least, and leads to authoritarian measures. A major problem of diversity is that it's only skin deep, for one thing the regime does not permit is diversity of thought. Instead, they demand adherence to a limited set of values. They try to force unity of thought onto the mess of diversity they have contrived.

This leads on to the second part of the DIE LIE - inclusion. It's obvious you will only be 'included' in the new world if you conform to GPR values. The whole point of cancel culture is to enforce unity of thought.

Take a look at universities or the arts world and see how 'inclusive' they are of those who don't toe the party line on GPR values. Left wing people generally do not tolerate those with different political views, as mentioned in LP 10 Death at a Dinner Party. As Stefan Molyneux commented:

> Leftists cannot imagine integrating with conservatives of the same race, language, culture, country and history. Yet somehow they believe people from the Third World will integrate just fine. Show us how it's done Leftists: integrate with conservatives, and maybe they'll believe you.

What white leftists will also discover is that many of the diverse people they welcome are actually more right wing than the conservatives already living here.

As for the third member of the trinity, equity, this means pursing the impossible goal that is equality of outcome. First, you splinter society into a lot of identity groups, tell them all that if there's any kind of 'gap' between them and other groups they're being ripped off, then pursue the impossible goal of equity by discriminating against the stronger ones. This is the foolish path down which we've been led.

Therefore the real meaning of diversity, inclusion, and equity is conformity, exclusion, and discrimination.

LP 29 - The Package Deal

Here's a pathology that applies to people on both sides of politics - the tendency to accept a 'package deal' of beliefs, rather than evaluating ideas one by one.

Beliefs tend to cluster in groups. Leftists often have the same views on a range of topics, and rightists (or conservatives) another lot of same views. This will involve generalising, but let's take some stereotypical views often held by right and left wing people.

Imagine some hypothetical recruitment agency which was signing people up to become either left or right wing. The recruiter might say: 'If you want to be left wing you have to believe in feminism, gay rights, climate change, and Black Lives Matter. You also have to be pro abortion and support the new 'anti-misinformation' bill. But if you want to be right wing you have to be a Christian, like guns, want lower immigration, support free speech, oppose DEI, and oppose same sex marriage.

The person being recruited might ask if there's a third option, only to be told no, they have to accept one deal or the other.

This would be rather absurd. A person might be a feminist and believe in climate change, but also want lower immigration and free speech. Another person might be a Christian who supports DEI. Or they might be a right wing atheist or Buddhist who also supports gay marriage and Black Lives Matter.

To accept a job lot of beliefs is a bad habit on both sides. Just because you believe in one idea assumed to be left or right wing doesn't mean it has to come with a whole package deal of beliefs. Surely we can be a little more individual than that and assess ideas one at a time.

LP 30 - Denial of the Culture War While Waging the Culture War

A couple of years ago, there was a new tactic from the left, a form of 'gaslighting' in which they denied there was a culture war. To clarify, it was not a denial that the war existed, but a denial of their participation in it. They claimed the culture war was purely an activity of the right.

This came from a couple of regime comedians, media figures, and some politicians lamenting 'the importation of American style culture wars.' The Australian PM, Albanese, got in on the act claiming that opposition to his pet project, the Voice to Parliament, was an act of culture war.

Of course, all these people are fully immersed in the culture war on a daily basis, but the tactic was to try to pretend the whole left wing project is simply normality. So, all the usual controversial issues were just normal life and anyone questioning them was making a fuss over nothing.

Essentially, the culture war is a battle between the left-dominated world we live in - the Global Progressive Regime - and those who query and critique it. The fact that there is such a battle proves the GPR is not yet established as a full regime. If it was, there would be no culture war. We would simply see the complete domination of GPR values.

So, yes, there is a culture war. It is being waged by those who want the GPR to have full control against those see it as a false and tyrannical movement, and want to resist it.

I've used the term the Global Progressive Regime in this book. Another, better known term for the whole left wing project is 'Cultural Marxism.' Briefly, what this means is the attempt to achieve communism by stealth in the Western world. The original plan for a worldwide communist revolution by the working class failed. Plan B was to achieve revolution by attacking the social institutions - family, education, media, and so on. The idea was to infiltrate these to gain influence. Once that was achieved, further attacks could take place on history, symbols, and general morale.

It's been highly successful so far. Cultural Marxism is about destroying society as it was and replacing it with something new and allegedly better. The culture war is about Cultural Marxism's assault on traditional values, and the resistance to that same assault.

It's rather obvious that the culture war is real. The attempt to deny this is a typical sneaky leftist strategy. They have some chutzpah even attempting it. Thankfully, some can see through it. For example, one comment on a YouTube video makes a fair summation.

> Leftists still claim Cultural Marxism is a right-wing conspiracy even after statue toppling, political correctness, cancel culture, subverted American institutions, and BLM's founders admitting they're 'trained Marxists.'

> Destabilisation. Ultra-feminism. The erasure of gender. The destruction of the family. The loss of a cohesive moral structure - previously from Christianity. The idea of toxic masculinity used to attack gender roles. The self hatred of nation. The destruction of institutions. The rewriting of history. False ideas of white privilege used to ferment race war leading to BLM riots. All called the Long March

through the Institutions set out by the Frankfurt School decades ago - coming to fruition.

Imagine leftists living through all that and then pretending nothing of significance had happened. This leftist pathology should really be moved to the next chapter, 'Dirty Tricks.'

LP 31 - Double Think and the Refusal to Make Connections

If you're a leftist, the 'far right' are your enemies. This is because leftists believe the far right repress women and gays, have conservative values, and follow an authoritarian religion. However, one group leftists have to *support* are Muslims, because Muslims are part of a diverse non-white minority. But wait - isn't Islam 'far right' too? Are some Muslims not *also* reputed to repress women and gays, have conservative values, and follow an authoritarian religion?

If leftists had consistent belief systems, opposing the far right would mean opposing Islam too. But Muslims are an ally group. What is the leftist to do with such a contradiction? The way to solve the problem is with what Orwell called double think. That is, holding two contradictory beliefs at the same time. You can oppose the white far right, but ignore the Muslim far right.

To help make this easier, you can defer to whatever is the stronger programming. In this case, the anti-white / anti-racism programming is stronger than the anti-far right programming. After all, criticising Islam would make you xenophobic, Islamophobic, and a racist. So, best to just ignore their far right traits. Problem solved, as long as you use a little double think.

In a similar way, white feminists in Australia protest violence against women when it's done by white men, but rarely mention the violent men who live in Indigenous communities. Leftists must never criticise Aboriginals and should always defer to their moral superiority.

Still, reports of male on female violence among Aboriginals do pose a problem if one's normal stance is to condemn that behaviour in your own kind. One way out of this bind is to say Indigenous violence is a legacy of colonialism, so it can be blamed on the British. That does resolve the problem.

That's what one Australian leftist did when she piously posted a graphic online suggesting that Aboriginal women were thirty times more likely than other women to be hospitalised due to 'family violence.' She was trying to make a point about white privilege or something, but accidentally made one about Indigenous violence instead. Realising too late her blunder, she then tried to blame it all on colonialism. No doubt she believes in the Edenist concept of Aboriginal life before 1788.

It's hard to form a consistent worldview when reality doesn't do what your beliefs say it should do, especially if those beliefs contradict each other. The best option is to give up the need for a consistent worldview altogether. Failing that, leftists can fake a semi-coherent worldview by ignoring some facts, rationalising others, and practising plenty of helpful doublethink.

LP 32 - Double Think and Conspiracy Theories

As well as double think, leftists have another special talent, which is the refusal to see patterns.

Take the 'conspiracy theory' called the Great Replacement which is that white populations are gradually being replaced in their own countries. On occasion, high profile Democrats like Bill Clinton or Joe Biden have each said we're heading for a time when America is no longer majority-white, and this is good news. So, the Great Replacement is essentially true and it's a good thing. On the other hand, if some right wing figure mentions the idea of the Great Replacement like it's a bad thing, leftists dismiss the idea as an absurd conspiracy theory.

One might point out a few facts to leftists: a heavy influx of immigrants - legal and illegal - to Britain, America, and Australia; these countries' governments doing nothing to stop it; anti-white messaging in media and education; the constant scolding about racism, and praise for multiculturalism; diverse casting and the rewriting of history by our national broadcasters, and much more. One might suggest that all such trends are in keeping with the idea of a Great Replacement. But leftists will never see any connection between any of these facts.

Is the Great Replacement true or not? Perhaps we could look to the UK and contact some of their leaders for clarification. In early 2024, for instance, we could have asked the Indian descended prime ministers of England and Ireland, the Pakistan descended first minister of Scotland, and not forgetting the Muslim Lord Mayor of London. It's likely these high profile Britons would have confirmed that the Great Replacement is just a conspiracy theory after all. What a relief.

What aren't conspiracy theories for leftists, but rather facts, are things like patriarchy and white supremacy. This is rather odd. Feminism is so part of the establishment that almost all Western male politicians kowtow to it. Women, on the whole, are praised and celebrated, while men, as a class, are criticised or treated with indifference. If there's an all powerful patriarchy crushing women underfoot, it's not doing much of a job of it.

As for 'white supremacy,' former white nations are now diverse, and their universities teach courses on the problems of whiteness. Whites are the only people not allowed to celebrate their identity, and the only ones that can be criticised. Yet leftists somehow believe they are in mortal danger from white supremacy, a force so powerful it has abolished itself.

Some conspiracy theories are a lot more plausible than others. Which ones, should be obvious to anyone not blinded by ideology.

LP 33 - Ideologgles and Bubble Blindness

There's no such thing as a purely objective thinker. We are all biased - but we can at least try to get outside our biases, perhaps by reading books or listening to talks by people we don't agree with.

Yet some people are so deeply locked into an ideology that they've lost touch with any kind of objectivity, so used are they to perceiving the world through ideological goggles. We might call them 'ideologgles.'

There are probably hundreds of things people believe that are obviously wrong, but seem true to those wearing ideologgles. I'll take just one example, which concerns New Zealand's former prime minister, Jacinda Ardern. When she resigned, some people said she'd been the victim of misogyny and more harshly treated by the press than male world leaders.

This was pretty far-fetched. First, Ardern had been the most fawned-over world leader since Barack Obama. This was partly *because* she was a woman. Whatever her strengths and successes, these were seen as even more laudable due to her being a woman. Sections of the Australian press gushed over her to the point of embarrassment. If 'philogyny' is the opposite of misogyny, then that is a better term for how Ardern was treated.

Second, for those people who did dislike Ardern, it was largely for her left wing values and air of moral superiority, not her gender. Those people would have hated Canadian PM, Justin Trudeau, just as much. No gender discrimination was involved.

Third, when a right wing woman, Giorgia Meloni, became Italy's PM she did not draw the same kinds of criticism as Ardern.

Thus criticism of Ardern must have been due to her policies and persona, not her gender.

Fourth, and most conspicuously, male politicians like Trump or Australia's Scott Morrison drew ten times as much press criticism as Ardern, and none of the fawning praise. Trump in particular, was subjected to four years of vitriol the likes of which had never been seen before - *part* of which was because he was a white male.

So, for people to claim Jacinda Ardern was the victim of unusual levels of gender discrimination is clearly untrue. To believe it, you would have to be completely blinded by ideology. At the time, I did ask a Twitter leftist if she thought Ardern was worse treated by the press than Trump, and it turns out she did think that, and that Trump had 'a cushy ride.' Extraordinary!

Someone else opined that Jacinda haters were also haters of Meghan Markle, Greta Thunberg, and other high profile women, due to misogyny. But if these women *were* disliked, it would be for quite different reasons. Ardern was the Uber-Karen, Markle an apparent social climber who disrespected the monarchy, and Thunberg a climate warrior turned full Marxist. Their gender was not the defining feature for any of these women.

Imagine a hypothetical female leader who emerged and called out the GPR for what it really is - a tyrannical movement with delusions of virtue trying to conquer the West by stealth. Does anyone really think right wingers would say: *No, we don't want her. She's a woman! We want one of those spineless compliant male leaders?*

Of course not. National leaders of both the left and right are loved or hated for their politics, not their gender.

A related pathology here is what we might call 'bubble blindness.' To live in a bubble is to surround yourself only with people who think like you. This can be insular and lead to the delusion that everyone shares your values and beliefs.

One example was when an ABC journalist quoted with horror the views of conservative politician, Tony Abbott. Abbot had said that if the Voice to Parliament debate was won by the No side, it should also mean scaling back other 'separatist measures… like flying the Aboriginal flag co-equally with the national one (as if Australia is a country of two nations) and the routine acknowledgement of country by all speakers at official events.'

The ABC journalist seemed to think Abbott's views were shocking - and they probably were to those in her inner city left wing bubble. Still, what to some is shocking and cause for cancellation, to others outside the bubble is the voice of sweet reason and common sense. Or, if we could be more broadminded in general, we could see it as just another opinion, not necessarily better or worse than our own.

It would be as well for leftists to realise that some people they consider 'far right' are really just mainstream. A few years ago their views would have been seen as normal and reasonable, and some would even have been classified as left wing in the 1970s. It's all relative.

To repeat, we are all biased. To a greater or lesser extent, we all wear ideologgles and live in a bubble. That's inevitable - but we should try not to let it become pathological.

LP 34 - Panic and Hyperbole

Continuing on the theme of outrage in the eye of the beholder, leftists do seem prone to hyperbole. In recent times, accusations that so and so is a 'Nazi' have been tossed around at the slightest provocation. US border detention centres become 'concentration camps,' and 'micro-aggressions' are treated as if they're giant sized.

One example of hyperbole came when Tucker Carlson was fired from Fox News in America. According to one leftist, Carlson had been allowed 'to spew racism and bigotry' for many years.

To describe someone as 'spewing racism and bigotry' conjures an image of someone wild eyed, frothing at the mouth, ranting and raving like a lunatic. That image better describes leftists on

Twitter during the Trump presidency, including the person who made the comment. As for Tucker Carlson, he usually comes across as mild mannered and reasonable.

You might not agree with Tucker Carlson's views, but there's no need for hyperbole. If you describe someone mild mannered and reasonable as 'spewing racism and bigotry,' it does tend to cast doubt on your grasp of reality - and if it's as shaky as that on one topic, you might not have much grip on reality in other areas either.

LP 35 - The Source and the Info

Tucker Carlson worked for Fox News, part of the Rupert Murdoch media group which many leftists see as an evil force working against their own media like *The Guardian* or the ABC.

As much as leftists might like to see Murdoch as an all powerful right wing enemy, Murdoch media hasn't done much to stop the decline of Western nations and their capitulation to the GPR. If Murdoch really was a powerful right wing force, these mass social and population changes wouldn't have happened. So, a mighty force for conservatism? Not really.

Having said that, the Murdoch media does at least allow some alternative opinions to be aired - opinions that would never be allowed on the ABC, or in *The Sydney Morning Herald*. So, some people on Murdoch are allowed to question the value of diversity, criticise 'wokeness,' or even occasionally raise a couple of MRA talking points.

Many leftists are outraged at even these small concessions to conservatism. There really seems to be a sort of fanaticism here. It's as if these people believe the ABC or *The Guardian* are waging a holy war for truth, and Murdoch is the devil. It sounds like I'm straw manning them, but some really believe the sole purpose of Murdoch media is, as one leftist told me, to 'spread hate, division, misogyny, racism, lies and propaganda.' On that basis, some have called for Murdoch media to be shut down.

These people seem unable to conceive there could be anything wrong with their pet causes, so any criticism of them can *only* be evil and maliciously meant. This is a far too narrow approach to knowledge. Even your enemies are right sometimes. At the very least, you might try to understand why they hold the opinions they do, and get past your default assumption it's because they're stupid or evil.

One problem with dividing the world into good and evil is it keeps you trapped in your echo chamber and shuts off alternative views. As a commentator named Will Kingston said:

> The most fascinating thing about the anti-Murdoch cult is just how intellectually lazy it is. Cult members are encouraged to avoid any consideration of alternative viewpoints because "Murdoch is the Devil." Sensible people look at the words on the page, not just the masthead.

For another example, I had an online argument with a leftist about whether the ABC and BBC were politically biased. I linked to the documentary 'BBC Bias Exposed' produced by New Culture Forum, a conservative British group.

This documentary made a detailed case about the deep political bias within the BBC. The leftist I was arguing with declined to watch it. Instead, he said New Culture Forum were white supremacists. As evidence, he linked to the 'Our Aims' section on their website. This made no mention of race at all, but stated the group's intention to critique left groupthink and the liberal establishment, and defend traditional Western values and culture. For the leftist, this made them white supremacist and was sufficient for him to dismiss the documentary unwatched.

This is the usual arrogance, and further evidence that leftists are estranged from basic intellectual values. Among those values are humility - *I could be wrong* - and curiosity - *why would someone hold beliefs about reality so different to my own?* That these traits are so common suggests leftist thinking is far more a political than an intellectual pursuit.

In fact, the truth of a statement is irrelevant to who is making it, and whether or not they are on 'your team.' Someone you consider an enemy is capable of speaking the truth or being right, just as an ally is capable of lying or being wrong.

A hidden motive for dismissing information that comes from an 'enemy' source as that most people resist changing their minds when it comes to politics. It can be deeply disturbing to listen to an enemy and find yourself agreeing with them. This can threaten your self-image or your whole worldview. Not many people are willing to put themselves through such an experience. It's far easier to dismiss someone out of hand. Once again, Thomas Sowell is familiar with this common trait of ignoring information because you don't like the source.

> It is amazing how many people think that they can answer an argument by attributing bad motives to those who disagree with them. Using this kind of reasoning, you can believe or not believe anything about anything, without having to bother to deal with facts or logic.

LP 36 – Acting Dumb... or Not Really Acting.

Some people lose arguments by being stupid. However, some people *win* arguments by being stupid - or at least pretending to be. Pretending to be stupid is a great way of refusing to admit you're wrong, and as an added bonus, you can then declare victory and pretend to believe it.

Let's take three examples. First, one might observe that knife crime has gotten worse in London since the increase in mass immigration to Britain. Instead of accepting this simple fact, the leftist counters by saying 'there's always been crime in Britain.' This is of course true. Having made a true statement, the leftist then declares victory, even though the true statement doesn't refute the first one about knife crime getting worse in London. It doesn't matter to the leftist. In their mind, they've won the argument. They're either acting dumb... or not really acting.

False equivalences are useful here. For a second example, take the recent trend of Drag Queen Story Hour, that is, drag queens visiting schools and libraries and reading stories to young children. This has upset some conservatives, which again triggers the Pavlov's Dog defence reaction from leftists.

An ABC presenter posted a photo online of himself wearing a dress while hosting a children's TV show thirty years ago. The idea was to imply Drag Queen Story Hour was nothing new, as this sort of thing has been going on for decades.

I remember the cross dressing of a few decades ago and it was usually done for a laugh because gender roles were stricter then. It was more surprising to see a man dressed as a woman. Whatever one thinks of that, there was little of the overt sexuality of today's drag queens, as should be obvious to anyone, including the ABC presenter. He still had to pretend that his wearing of an innocuous dress in the 1990s is the same as a highly sexualised drag queen in the 2020s. He was implying that neither society nor the ABC have changed. The man in question was too intelligent to really believe this, but had to feign stupidity in order to 'win an argument' that Drag Queen Story Hour is perfectly normal.

For the third example, we can revisit the Uluru Statement, upon which the Indigenous 'Voice to Parliament' idea was based. As mentioned earlier, the Uluru Statement was said to be a one page document of just 443 words. At one stage in the campaign, the counter claim was made by critics that it was really a twenty-six page document, with some of the real agenda revealed there.

This was an embarrassment to the government and others pushing the Voice to Parliament, who then staged the charade of pretending the other twenty-five pages were nothing to do with the first page.

At best, they could claim that the real Uluru Statement was just the first page, and the rest was mere 'background material' (even though key activists had been earlier filmed admitting the longer version was the full Uluru Statement.) The government then had the chutzpah to carry on as if the other twenty-five pages were nothing to do with the first page, and anyone suggesting they were was a conspiracy theorist. The cause was not helped by the prime minister's admission of never having read those extra pages.

If someone was completely literal minded, rather thick, or simply dishonest, they could indeed say the Uluru statement was only one page. Yet to imply the other twenty-five pages were irrelevant was to be wilfully obtuse in order to win an argument.

Still, that's how leftists roll. If they have to win an argument by pretending to be stupid, so be it. They'll do whatever it takes to win. Acting dumb… or not really acting.

LP 37 - Cultural vs Historical Relativism

In our diverse multicultural society, there are some ethnic practices which would be thought strange, archaic, or morally wrong if they were done by white people. We don't judge them because they are part of another culture and they do things differently.

When it comes to our own historical past, no such latitude is given. Here, we deal in moral absolutes and the harshest condemnation - despite the famous quote that the past too is 'a foreign country: they do things differently there.'

In the present, by the rules of 'cultural relativism,' no culture is better or worse than another. Each can only be judged on its own terms, rather than by our own Western standards.

A commonsense approach to the past would admit that historical relativism should also apply. You should only judge a past society by the norms and moral standards of its own time. But no. Instead we judge the past by the moral values of today, and condemn it completely if it falls short of the alleged perfection of our own time. Statues will be torn down in righteous rage to show our disgust.

Some people have been taught that slavery, for example, is a uniquely Western sin. One might point out that slavery was practised for most of human history until it was abolished (by the British, incidentally) - but it would never do to consider historical context. In cultural relativism, all cultures are equal. In history, all our past eras must be compared to the flawless morality of the present day.

As it happens, the other cultures we must never criticise today also committed historical sins like slavery, but the leftist is oblivious to that. It is only white Western culture, past and present, that must be singled out for special condemnation.

LP 38 – The Over-Reaction

A very extreme form of thinking would be the idea that every negative thing that happens to a person is their own fault. This sort of thinking might have a religious origin, be part of a self help cult, or believed in by a fanatical right wing society.

In our own time, we've gone too far the other way to think every negative thing that happens to a person is *never* the fault of that person. So, for example, African-Americans are never responsible for any problem they may have. It's always down to external factors - slavery in the past, systemic racism in the present, or whatever else. If such a person has a low paying job, for instance, we can blame it on the poor schooling of which he was the systemic victim, but never his behaviour within that system.

We must never suggest that the victim of any crime or misfortune was in any way responsible for it, for that would be 'victim blaming.'

Somewhere between these two extremes is the truth. The events of a life are caused by a mix of internal and external factors. Some events are completely outside a person's control, some are fully within their control, and most are somewhere on the spectrum in between.

Some leftists act as if anything bad that happens is never the fault of the person suffering it. This is for various reasons - a heightened sense of injustice, or the wish to be compassionate, for example. It may be an overreaction to people who think victims are to blame for their own misfortunes, or to past eras when such a belief was widespread.

Still, while it's silly to think unhappy events are *always* the fault of their victims, it's just as silly to think they are *never* the fault of their victims, or that it's not a combination of the two.

To always put the blame on external factors isn't helpful. Sometimes accepting blame is just about being accountable. Some people *are* the victims of others, but some are the victims of their own mistakes or their own stupidity.

LP 39 - Cult of the Victim

Still, in the strange and eccentric world of leftism, being a victim does have a certain currency. Leftists are obsessed with power - its abuse by the wicked and the suffering of their victims.

Combine this with class thinking and it means that members of an approved victim group - women or the Indigenous, for example - possess an assumed moral innocence simply from belonging to those groups. In the same way, whites or men have guilt by default without having to do anything to earn it.

Victimhood can be automatic in this way, or can be heightened by actual events. It can bestow a certain aura on people, such that they are now assumed to be in possession of a special insight. For some, the victimhood acts as a sort of shield, making them immune to criticism. One must never criticise a 'survivor' or make them feel uncomfortable.

If you belong to an oppressed class, the victimhood can act as an excuse, perhaps even a free pass. Never mind if your own life is a mess or you've got umpteen personal shortcomings. You get to proclaim your moral goodness thanks to the systems that are oppressing you, or events that happened hundreds of years ago to someone else.

See? That's leftism for you. Always turning a negative into a positive.

24

Dirty Tricks

The political left presents itself as the moral side of politics. If that were true, you'd expect them to act honourably when dealing with their opponents. Yet it often seems that leftists will do almost anything, honourable or not, to gain power. This chapter will look at some of the dirty tricks leftists get up to in pursuit of their goals.

LP 40 - Ad Hominem

This Latin phrase literally means to attack the man, rather than the argument. Politics should be about the worth of an idea or policy, not the person who holds it. The only time the person should be relevant is if their own behaviour contradicts the idea, which would make them a hypocrite.

It's possible some may level the same charge at me, for am I not attacking leftists? I am certainly criticising them - but there are key differences. First, I am not saying they are evil people, driven by terrible motives. I'm saying they're often fanatics who'll do almost anything to achieve what they are believe are noble goals. Second, I'm not trying to censor them. On the contrary, they should be free to express their views. Third, I'm not trying to destroy them and remove them from public life. But when they make their *ad hominem* attacks, this is usually what leftists try to do to their enemies: claim they're evil and therefore should be silenced by being removed from public life.

Also, in this whole Leftist Pathologies part of the book, I'm not attacking specific individuals, but a type of person, a state of mind, or a flawed way of thinking.

Why do leftists so often engage in ad hominem attacks?

The three main reasons are that they're a sign of moral fanaticism, they help force people to support your agenda, and they're a way of removing enemies without having to beat them in a debate.

Moral fanaticism is a trait associated with religion. These days, a person's morality is defined by their adherence to correct political views. Every public figure must have an impeccable record in relation to GPR values. A serious offence against race or gender taboos can be fatal.

The second and more effective point of ad hominem attacks is to intimidate people into supporting your agenda. The mere threat of being attacked is enough to make most people obey you. This is why, for example, most male politicians are too afraid to call out the lies or half truths pushed by the feminist lobby. They know they would be personally attacked for doing so, and their careers would be over.

Third, ad hominem attacks are about destroying enemies. Leftists have a vision, and to achieve it, they need power. There will always be people in the way of this vision, so the leftist has to defeat them. That might be done by arguing against their ideas, but as this can be a long and tedious process, it's easier to just get rid of them. In crude dictatorships, this can be done by murdering or jailing your opponents. In our own culture, you just have to destroy their character enough that they can no longer participate in public life.

It is hard to win arguments. You have to understand your own position, the opposing position, and persuade others than your own is better. It's far simpler to remove the opposing position altogether.

Argument is unnecessary for leftists, anyway. Because they're sure they have the moral high ground, they assume anyone opposing it must be evil so they're entitled to destroy them.

If put under scrutiny, leftist arguments might crumble. It's possible they realise this, hence the importance they place on censorship. If some so called far-right arguments were heard, people might realise they are correct. That would never do. Thomas Sowell notes that this trend goes back a long way.

> Anyone who studies the history of ideas should notice how much more often people on the political left, more so than others, denigrate and demonize those who disagree with them - instead of answering their arguments.

Leftists may be mistaken in their vision, but if so, they don't want to know about it. Anyone voicing criticisms is a threat, and the better the criticism, the greater the threat. Don't attack the arguments. Attack the man.

One reason the left was driven so insane by Donald Trump was that the usual method of destroying enemies didn't work against him. In the decade since he first ran for president, Trump was called every name under the sun, and faced endless denunciation. Somehow, it all seemed to bounce off him. This was utterly confounding to leftists. When Trump won the 2024 election, many were at a complete loss how this was even possible.

LP 41 – Guilt By Association

This LP follows on from the last one. It's not enough for someone to have merely said or done the wrong thing him or herself. If they've ever had dealings with *someone else* who has, that might be grounds enough to destroy them. Thus if someone has ever attended a meeting or gone to a party with a suspect person, or even liked a non-approved social media post, that will do.

These tactics are reminiscent of high school with their use of gossip, reputational damage, and social exclusion. Worse, they suggest the fanaticism of a Middle Ages witch hunt, or a modern day socialist purge.

This sort of manoeuvre is an attempt to control people through peer pressure. It's the carrot of social acceptance and the stick of social exclusion. So much for 'inclusion.'

For social climbers it's not what you know, it's who you know. In the Global Progressive Regime, who you know can also be a ticket to social death.

LP 42 - Weaponised Pearl Clutching

Pearl clutching is the act of being excessively shocked. It suggests a 'church lady' seeing something far outside her normal polite existence, then grabbing her own pearls as she swoons on the fainting couch.

Pearl clutching is a deliberate act in these days of outrage culture. If you say something to offend against one of the sacred cows of race or gender, you're fair game.

'Weaponised pearl clutching' is when leftists take exaggerated offense in order to get someone cancelled. It involves real or feigned outrage, social shaming, then the sinister appeal to authority to get someone banned.

It's just one of the weapons leftists use to push their agenda of pure love and tolerance.

LP 43 – Shaming

Pearl clutching belongs to a 'family' of dirty tricks. Another family member is the tactic of trying to control people through shaming them.

Shaming has long been a part of human life as a way of enforcing social norms. It often had a practical purpose. For example, pre-marital sex was for a long time frowned on, so as to prevent children being born out of wedlock. Today in the age of contraception, the risk of children born out of wedlock is far less. Some conservatives might still shame those who have pre-marital sex to make them conform to their preferred moral values.

Shaming isn't always a bad thing, but can become a dirty trick if used for manipulation. For example, a woman might try to get her boyfriend to do something by saying that a 'real man' would do it. Shamed for his lack of masculinity, he is then supposed to obey her.

On a far larger scale, shaming a country over alleged historical crimes can be a way to manipulate that country's present policies.

For leftists, shaming is a tactic to make people conform to their preferred values and agenda. Or it's meant to make people think or act a certain way.

In the Brexit debate, a respectable way of persuading Britons to remain in the EU was to persuade them of the benefits of doing so. The other method was to shame them, for example, by calling them small minded, old fashioned, scared, or 'little Englanders.' This is not about winning someone to your point of view, but manipulating them into doing what you want.

It's a tactic beloved of leftists. In the Voice to Parliament debate, prime minister Albanese told us 'the world is watching,' with the implication anything less than a Yes vote would be to our global shame.

Another media figure wrote about how proud we would be if the Voice got up. The implication was how ashamed we'd be if it didn't. Another accused us of being a 'scared little backwater' if we voted No.

It's like the old childhood taunts about being a 'chicken.' *Do what we say or you're a coward.* For today's leftists it's, *accept the globalist agenda or you're a chicken.* The same playbook is used time and time again. 'White fragility,' 'male fragility,' 'little England,' 'scared little backwater,' or whatever the insult may be.

It's a dirty trick. Don't fall for it.

LP 44 - Ignoring Context

There are many different types of lies. 'Lies of omission' for example. A lie of omission is when something is presented as true, but crucial details are left out to deliberately give a false impression. One way to do this is by ignoring the context in which something happens.

The so called 'insurrection' by Trump supporters on January 6th, 2021 is one example. A group of Trump supporters entered the Capital building in Washington to protest what they saw as election fraud in the 2020 election. The protest was presented by the Democrat party as a threat to 'Our Democracy,' a catchphrase that was repeated *ad nauseum* from that point on. Of course, and whether they were right or wrong, the protesters' belief that democracy had been harmed was why they were there in the first place.

More to the point, the context in which the event happened was ignored. The Democrat party framed this 'insurrection' as an isolated event, with no connection to any other recent events, apart from the 2020 US election. The context was that the US had just seen more than three months of protests by Antifa, Black Lives Matter, and other left wing groups. These protests were often violent, involving rioting, looting, and destruction of property. The idea of protest had become normalised. It was in the context of three months of violent protests by left wing groups that the so called 'insurrection' occurred. The Democrats ignored this context as they swooned on their fainting couches.

For further context, Trump's 2016 election win had also been met with protests - not just in Washington, but in several other major cities. After that, the Democrats resisted Trump's presidency throughout his entire term, with several impeachment attempts. Such was their reverence for 'Our Democracy' at the time. All this was the larger context to the January 6th 'insurrection.'

Still, these lies of omission were nothing new from the Democrats. A YouTuber named Red Pill Germany discussed their attacks on Trump before the 2020 election, which was also the year of Covid lockdowns.

> When it comes to the pandemic and jobs and the economy, it is very clear - and the Democrats play this game all the time - they act as if you could have both. You can shut down the entire economy *and* you can have a booming economy at the same time. Absolutely insane, and all these attacks on the Trump administration are completely bogus because they must say what they would have done differently instead, and they never say that.
>
> So you cannot say 'you caused 200, 000 deaths *and* you crashed the economy, as if these were completely independent things in this year 2020.

Context matters - but leftists mention it only when convenient. At other times, they ignore it completely.

LP 45 - Removing the Goalposts

Long ago, racism was established as the cardinal sin in the Global Progressive Regime. This was used to help create the diverse multicultural world in which we live. The threat of an accusation of racism had real power.

Let's suppose racism really is the cardinal sin leftists say it is. Racism as defined by negative or hostile attitudes from people of one race to another. This was easy to see in terms of whites against non-whites. A problem for leftists was there was also plenty of hostility coming from non-whites to whites - 'reverse racism' as it used to be called.

This was a problem because apart from showing the difficulty of creating diverse nations it upset the perpetrator-victim hierarchy. If non-whites could be racist, their moral innocence was gone and whites could become the victims. This was unacceptable.

The leftist solution was simply to change the definition of racism to 'racial hostility plus social power.' As whites were still in the majority, they were said to have social power, and non-whites did not. That meant white hostility to non-whites was racism, but not the other way round. It was, by definition, impossible for non-whites to be racist.

When whites become the racial minority, leftists might have to change the definition again - but by then they will no longer have to pretend to care.

This is the dirty trick leftists played when called out on hypocrisy. Rather than admit that non-whites could also be guilty of their cardinal sin, racism, they simply changed how that sin was defined.

This meant that they weren't just 'moving the goalposts' for their own convenience. They were removing one set of goalposts from the playing field so that, in the game of racism, only one team could score.

This dirty trick is testimony to the hypocrisy leftists allow themselves when it suits them. Their claim to be guided by some universal moral principle - in this case, anti-racism - is exposed as a sham, for what they really want is a license to be as racist as they please, with zero consequences.

You have to admire the epic chutzpah on display in this classic dirty trick.

LP 46 – The Roman Neck

Angered by some crowd dissent at a public event, the emperor Caligula once exclaimed, 'Would that the Roman people had a single neck!' Presumably so he could cut it off.

In a similar way, leftists try to put their enemies into classes, all the better to try to cut off their collective neck. Having assigned some group enemy status, they then treat every individual member of this group as part of a collective.

This is most commonly done by feminists in regard to men. Feminists often accuse men-as-a-class of various sins against them. This might be in terms of male privilege, the gender pay gap, or even murder.

The fact is there will always be some exceedingly rich men at the top of the wealth charts, and some exceedingly evil men at the bottom of the moral charts.

What feminists do is attribute both wealth and evil to men as an overall class. So the wealth owned by the top 10% richest men is somehow seen to benefit the other 90% of men, and the rapes and murders committed by the worst ten percent morally is somehow also the responsibility of the other 90% of men, who must share in the guilt.

Feminists then smear 100% of men for these crimes, irrationally berate them for it, and demand they stop doing it.

It seems that for feminists, men really are part of a gestalt organism with a single neck. They'd cut it off if they could, but then there'd be no one to blame. Women would then also have to create and maintain an all-female society. Whether that would turn out to be Heaven or Hell will never be known.

LP 47 - Impossible or Absurd Demands

But wait, there's more. Not only are men-as-a-class guilty of these murders, women-as-a-class are victims of it. So, even an upper middle class woman in a nice suburb, perhaps never having known violence herself, is a victim of the dreadful crimes against women in poor and violent neighbourhoods far away. Thus, the victimhood is shared by women as a gestalt entity, and the guilt is shared by men as a gestalt entity.

One can almost imagine such a woman slapping her mild mannered husband in the face and exclaiming *how dare you*, as if he has any control over the behaviour of violent men he's never met. It would probably not be an actual slap, but a cold and haughty silence to punish him for the crimes he's never committed.

With this kind of gestalt thinking, we get absurd demands urging men to *Stop murdering women*, as if millions of individual men are somehow telepathically aware of what each other are doing. So, presumably if a man in Perth, Western Australia, is about to assault a woman, another man 3000km away in Melbourne is going to magically know it and send a telepathic message: *Whoa, hold on buddy, that ain't cool. Respect women.*

One can only hope female activists don't really think 'men' are a collective entity whose individual members can control what each other are doing, as that would be insane. It would be a welcome change if a male politician called this out for the foolishness that it is, but the weak men who get into office are all too eager to join in the shaming of men as a collective. These obsequious fellows get into power through going along with this, so nothing will change once they get there.

This class or gestalt thinking also applies racially, of course, as has been discussed elsewhere in the book. One racial group and its members are thought to be responsible for what happens to another racial group and its members. This applies not just in present time, but seemingly from one historical era to another. The rort of reparations for slavery is a prime example. If followed through, this would mean people who never *owned* slaves paying reparations to people who never *were* slaves.

There is no end to the absurdities if you allow leftists' class thinking to continue unchecked. It only ends when people call it out for the scam it is.

LP 48 - Just Trying to Live Our Lives

This pathology is about the slow creep of leftism. It starts with modest requests - women's right to work, respect for the Indigenous, the loosening of gender norms, accepting gay marriage, or whatever else. 'We're just trying to live our lives,' they say. This is fine, and you don't mind at all. *Of course. You are part of society the same as anyone else. Live your life.*

Some indeterminate time later, the requests have turned into demands. You have to be a male ally, use the pronouns, take the knee, listen to Welcome to Country, wear a gay pride ribbon, renounce your privilege, or whatever the latest thing is.

Even leftists sometimes get tired of this. One older lesbian said that if she'd known the gay rights campaign of the 1970s was going to turn into the endless hoopla over pride displays of the 2020s, she wouldn't have bothered. Or, as one YouTuber remarked, 'the love that once didn't dare speak its name now won't shut up about it.'

Please, live your lives. No one is stopping you.

A variation of this is when someone says they just want to be accepted for who they are so don't make a big deal about it, and then they make a big deal about it.

The first blacks and female actors to star as the Doctor in *Doctor Who*, for example, would have been more successful if the program hadn't made such a big deal about them being black and female. But that's the problem with obsessing over identity. What should be fairly unimportant - one's race or gender - gets blown out of all proportion.

Just trying to live your lives? Please do. No one is stopping you - but there's no need for a brass band and a ticker tape parade.

LP 49 - Rewriting History and Lying to Children

There are plenty more dirty tricks practiced by leftists, which could fill a whole book if covered in detail. But let's finish this chapter with one of the dirtiest tricks of the lot, the rewriting of history to brainwash children.

It's been said that leftists care little for truth and only for power. This doesn't apply to all, but there are plenty willing to lie shamelessly for the sake of their goals.

There seems to have been a concerted effort, by some people at the BBC for instance, to convince people that Britain has always been a diverse multicultural country. This is the propaganda arm of the Great Replacement. The practical side has been the importation of millions of non-whites into Britain, such that the country's demographics have changed. The propaganda side wants to persuade people there's nothing odd or unnatural about this major transformation of the country, because Britain was always like that anyway.

The BBC has done this by the simple method of inserting 'diverse' actors into its historical TV shows. It was first done in fiction. An early example was an episode of *Doctor Who* in which a crowd scene from 1814 was half composed of diverse actors. When this was pointed out, the response was that *Doctor Who* is only a fictional fantasy show, so why take it seriously?

Then, step by step, the propagandists go further. You get incidental black actors in historical dramas. Then you get *Bridgerton*, a black Ann Boleyn, and they keep on upping the ante.

There's also the propaganda specifically aimed at children, like the BBC's *Horrible Histories* program, and the song 'Been Here From the Start.'

Anyone over the age of fifty knows that Britain was always a majority white nation. Observing almost any old photos or film footage of Britain in the past will confirm that - but younger people, and especially the children of today, do *not* know.

The propagandists are doing their best to imply that Britain, rather than being a majority white nation, was always diverse and multicultural. While this is a lie, what these people realise is that once the older generation dies off - those who were young in the 1960s, 70s, and 80s - that fact will no longer be widely known. The whites who 'inherit' a newly diverse Britain will never know that they are the indigenous people of that land and were robbed of it. They will believe that Britain was always multicultural.

To recall an earlier pathology, 'The Is and the Ought,' leftists care little for facts, and are willing to rewrite them to fit their idea of how reality should be. They know Britain was never diverse but, in their wisdom, they believe it should have been, so they pretend it was. Stephen Moffat, one of the producers of *Doctor Who*, cast diverse actors in episodes set in the past as a *noble lie*. He thought he was portraying an 'imaginary, better version of the world' which would help bring it about in reality.

It would be interesting to ask Moffat, a white British man, why he thinks the new multicultural Britain is a 'better version of the world.' In its classic era, *Doctor Who* stories were often about resisting alien invasions. Now, apparently they want to assist them.

It's one thing to invade a country physically, but at least be honest about it. Don't pretend it's something other than it is.

Imagine if such a situation played out in Australia. The British did invade this country in 1788, gradually taking it from the Aboriginals as they built the new colony over a number of years. I have criticised today's white Australians for excessive kowtowing, but to give them some credit, at least they do acknowledge the Aboriginals' prior occupation of the land.

Suppose, however, white Australians made it a mission to pretend whites had always been living here, prior to 1788. Imagine they invented a fake history and made TV dramas about whites living in Australia thousands of years ago, then made Aboriginal kids believe it was true.

That really would be a dirty trick. Yet this is the kind of despicable manoeuvre GPR propagandists are using on the children of Britain.

You dirty bastards.

25

The Way of the Coward

LP 50 - Leftist Debating Methods

When I was at school, debating contests were held between two teams, with three speakers on each team. The problem with debating is that the other team might be right about a topic and also better arguers, so you could lose. Never mind. There's a method that guarantees a 100% success rate. You don't even need debating skills. Here it is:

1. When the other team's first speaker gets up, turn off their microphone so no one can hear them. If they start talking louder, duct tape their mouth shut.
2. When their second member rises to speak, organise a protest, storm the stage, yell abuse and slogans, and shout them down.
3. When the third speaker stands up, declare that what they're saying is hate speech and misinformation, then have them arrested and thrown in jail.

And there you go - your side has won the debate and you hardly had to open your mouth.

Yes, this is censorship - the way of the coward. In the heady days of the 1960s, leftist rebels used to complain about censorship from the establishment. These days, it's the leftist establishment and their supporters doing it themselves.

The chief targets are, to put it simply, anyone who criticises the Global Progressive Regime. It has been done by various methods: demonising, banning, cutting off finance, or denial of access to media and social media.

Why do leftists support censorship, when it is clearly dishonourable? Here are five reasons:

1. It's an expression of pure power. Leftists have made the GPR their goal and any resistance will simply be swept aside. There are also some powerful people who know the GPR is a sham, and a front for something else. They care little for ethics, but only for power. Censorship is a cynical way to maintain it.
2. It's fanaticism. For those who do believe in the coming left wing Utopia, anyone who opposes it is by definition evil. It is their moral duty to erase them.
3. Censorship is much easier than debating. Why argue with your opponents when you can just erase them? It's so much simpler - especially when you're wrong.
4. Because their vision of the world is largely false, leftists are at war with reality. Under that pressure, they don't need the added difficulty of people pointing it out!
5. Leftists and globalists have made a terrible hash of the Western world, and censorship means they don't have to hear criticism of their mistakes. With the mess that's been made of Britain, for example, the people responsible don't want their abject folly pointed out, or the crimes of which they and their forerunners are guilty.

But censorship doesn't always operate openly. It sometimes happens by other methods, often while pretending to be something else, something 'moral.' Here are a few ways it can manifest.

LP 51 - Taboos

One way to make censorship self-powering is by making certain topics taboo. The taboos stop people speaking about those topics, or even thinking about them.

Taboos act as invisible mental chains, which confine thought to acceptable areas. In order to write this book, for example, I had to break some taboos in the areas of race and gender. The GPR is built upon such taboos, and if they were fully functional, it would be virtually immune to criticism.

Such taboos are immensely powerful. Taboos about racial thought among whites have taken us closer to extinction. The fear of being thought racist has prompted white people to meekly stand by as we were gradually replaced. It is not polite to notice 'the Great Replacement,' especially among educated people.

It was also racial taboos which stopped educated leftists seeing through George Floyd and BLM in 2020, and the Voice to Parliament in 2023. Gender taboos stop them criticising feminism.

Educated leftists are appalled at the rise of the so called 'far right,' and one of its key traits is the rejection of the taboos in which leftists believe.

LP 52 - Cancel Culture

In much the same way, cancel culture is about controlling what people think and say.

Leftists, in their wisdom, have come up with the correct set of values by which we are to live. These are both the vague ideas of racial and gender equality, and the specific GPR movements by which these are to be achieved.

If you conform to those values, you'll be accepted. If you have awkward questions or say anything to offend, you may be cancelled and won't be included in the inclusive society leftists are building. So, you had better conform - or else.

A gay woman who often criticises feminism online made the following comment:

Coming out as an anti-feminist was a lot more risky than coming out as gay. I can't think of anyone in my life who would've rejected me if I was lesbian, but I've lost some friends due to dismissing the idea I'm oppressed because I'm a woman.

Still, losing a few friends is one thing. Losing a job and social status are worse. The higher people go in public life, the more they have to lose if they say the wrong thing.

Cancel culture has been discussed elsewhere in this book. In short, both taboos and cancel culture are a way of forcing people to conform to GPR values, and to make censorship an internal habit.

LP 53 - Regime Comedians

This next category is not a form of censorship in itself, but a consequence of it.

Almost all comedians these days are leftists. While some of them believe they're anti-establishment or 'speaking truth to power,' the truth is they almost always only joke about safe targets, and wouldn't dare joke about the groups protected by the current leftist establishment.

They are 'regime comedians.' That means they only joke about regime enemies: men, white people, conservatives, Christians, 'deplorables,' or whoever else is considered an unfit person.

On the other hand, they rarely joke about regime allies or causes: women or feminism, BLM, DEI, Islam, or whatever else is a protected category. Nor do they ever stand up for men or white people, or call out the hostility against them.

It's true that in the past, a lot of humour was pretty offensive - racist, sexist, or homophobic in a crude way. Some of the 1970s British comedy has dated poorly.

Having said that, a lot of comedy today is timid and unfunny. Comedians and satirists have long had the role of joking about powerful people. If that was still the case, they'd be joking about the powerful left wing establishment. But leftists take themselves very seriously and are easily offended so, in the climate of cancel culture, most comedians only joke about a narrow range of topics. That is understandable, but they should stop pretending they're anti-establishment. They are regime comedians.

Humour is often about violating social norms, even taboos, but that is the one thing regime comedians are afraid to do. Perhaps this ties in to the familiar accusation that 'the left can't meme.' Online memes have been popular in the last decade. With an image and a few words, the meme tries to make a point that is funny and succinct. A few years ago, someone commented on the difference between right and left wing memes.

> Alt-Right Meme: Subversive humour that makes you laugh because it's shocking and you feel kind of bad for laughing afterward. Alt-Left Meme: Safe-as-fuck humour where the setup has nothing to do with the punch line. The punch line is usually a basic regurgitated statement of their opinion or a statistic they take as scripture. You don't feel bad for laughing because you never laughed in the first place.

A whole chapter could be written about the psychology behind this, but that will have to wait until another time.

LP 54 – A Threat Narrative Justifies Authoritarian Measures

Censorship is something tyrants do. It's a way to stop criticism through brute force. As leftists are the main censors these days, this gives them an image problem - for are not leftists supposed to be champions of liberty, fighting The Man?

To mask their true authoritarian nature, leftists have to invent or exaggerate a threat narrative to justify their harsh measures. So, feminists claim they are at risk of attack by incels or MRAs, governments demonise the 'far right,' and so on.

In protesting against the GPR, I support peaceful action only - debate, discussion, and other non-violent measures. This is one reason free speech is important, so these peaceful steps can be taken.

Violence is repugnant in itself, but also plays into the hands of your enemies. Leftists will always seize on any violent act as an excuse for censorship. To act violently is to justify their threat narrative and allow them to do so.

One terrible event was the Christchurch massacre in 2019, in which a right wing man went into a mosque and shot forty-two Muslims. This violence should be condemned, of course. However, it then gave leftists around the world the chance to demand censorship of allegedly right wing websites and individuals, even though the vast majority of these would never condone such an act.

The murderer's actions were blamed on these websites, as if there was no other cause. Such websites tend to be intellectual by nature - analysis rather than action. Then you have this violent fanatic acting alone, which is something quite different.

This terrorist attack, as awful as it may be, was a misguided response to the disastrous policies of Western politicians. That doesn't justify it, of course, but rather than admit any part in creating the mess, these politicians could now simply blame the 'far right' and the internet. A dishonest but predictable response.

Just as predictable is the next step in their playbook, which is to ramp up censorship and try to erase criticism of their terrible policies.

Unfortunately, this increases the chance of more violence down the track. Denying people the right to express their views leads to frustration, which can eventually turn to violence.

Presumably, the GPR tyrants will then double down even more on the whole mess they originally helped create.

LP 55 - The Karen

Regimes don't just repress from the top. There are also lots of mini-tyrants lower down the hierarchy. In our own regime, one of these is the Karen.

The 'Karen' meme came to popularity during the 2020 Covid lockdowns. A 'Karen' is an officious, bossy, rule enforcer who will call you out - or more likely, report you to the authorities - if you transgress against the rules, no matter how petty.

The Karen is a woman, although there might be male equivalents. Karen is also white. There may be non-white equivalents, but the archetypal Karen is a middle class white woman. She has led a fairly sheltered life, away from life's harsher realities. Karen has an office job or is some kind of middle manager. The men in her life are nice, polite fellows who never argue with her. They wouldn't dare.

Although Karen thinks of herself as a social reformer, she defers to authority. That may be the authority of official laws, or whatever is seen as the correct morality at the moment.

Karen believes life should be nice, polite, and rule based, and that we can all live in peace as long as everyone else behaves in the nice, polite, rule based way she does. Karen thinks no one should ever be made to feel offended or uncomfortable.

Karen is very concerned about online misogyny and the threat of the far-right. She's worried her teenage sons might be exposed to hateful online content that turns them towards misogyny and xenophobia. For the good of her sons, Karen is going to petition the government to shut down those websites pushing hateful ideas.

Better yet, Karen might run for office instead, and who knows, she might one day be the Minister for Online Safety herself.

Karen believes that no human is illegal, Black Lives Matter, women are oppressed, and hate speech isn't free speech. Anyone who disagrees with Karen on these points is a hater pushing misinformation.

So shut up. Karen knows best.

LP 56 - Tyranny of the Midwit

The term 'midwit' has recently come into use. It refers to a person of average intelligence, who may well be in a position of some authority. They might be a school teacher, a manager, a media personality, or a politician, for example.

The trouble with midwits is they're intelligent enough to understand a basic concept, up to a point. They might understand that racism is wrong, for example, but not look into the deeper and less obvious dimensions of that concept.

A midwit will know that, until recently, women didn't have the right to vote - but they probably won't know that most men didn't have it either. They'll know that there were black slaves but may not know there were also white ones. If this midwit is a teacher, their midwit understanding of things will be passed on to their students.

Most midwits have an understanding of issues that is partial at best. Midwits often don't realise this, and may overestimate both their own competence and their morality. Therefore they may believe they're entitled to influence or even rule over others.

In that sense, the Karen is a midwit - but there are also plenty of male midwits, some of whom have risen to very high positions, even to becoming heads of country. Indeed, one gets the feeling some men have been installed as the pretend leaders of their countries precisely because they are midwits. Their dim understanding allows all sorts of bad policies to slip through.

Many midwits never really face the consequences of their actions. Midwit politicians retire to collect ill-deserved pensions, having done huge amounts of unintentional damage to the countries they are allowed to ruin through their midwittery. The less fortunate citizens under their care, and future generations, will be the main victims of their disastrously midwitted actions.

LP 57 - Orwellian Words and Slogans

George Orwell's novel *1984* was a classic portrayal of a totalitarian state. So much so that the word 'Orwellian' entered the language to describe a government so powerful it could openly lie. The government in *1984* had the Ministry of Truth and Ministry of Love, which meant the opposite of what those ministries really were.

There are plenty of Orwellian phrases in our own time. That is, statements which are dubious at best, completely false, or mean something different than they pretend to. 'Diversity is our greatest strength' is an obviously false statement which national leaders have intoned as if it were holy writ.

'Build back better' was another globalist slogan, popular around the time of the Covid lockdowns. This vague statement did not inspire confidence. Better how? Better for whom? What made it worse was that leftist leaders around the world were all parroting the phrase like robots, as if they were reading from a script. Why were all these leaders using the same exact words?

'Misinformation' is the latest Orwellian word. In theory, it means false information. In practice, it just seems to mean any opinion the government doesn't like.

During the Voice to Parliament debate in 2023, Australian leftists showed their true authoritarian nature. They presented their simple view of the Voice, then got angry when skeptics didn't take their feelgood vision at face value. Skeptical opinions about the Voice were called 'misinformation.'

This came from the highest level of government. The prime minister, Albanese, was heavily pushing the Voice. He referred to conspiracy theories and misinformation, which in this case was often just any different opinion than the one pushed by the government and the pro-Voice camp.

Critics could well claim it was the government itself who was pushing misinformation. For one thing, we weren't given much *information* about how the Voice would work, but were just assured that it *would* work and was the best way to solve Aboriginal problems. We were told it was a major step for Australia, but also that it wouldn't really affect us. We heard that the Voice proposal was a 'generous invitation' but there were also rumours about treaty and truth telling. We were told the Uluru Statement was a single page, and the other twenty-five pages weren't part of it and not worth reading.

Labelling something as misinformation is a precursor to censorship. After all, you wouldn't want false information getting out there, would you? That wouldn't help 'keep people safe.' Truth is what counts and, as Jacinta Ardern's New Zealand government said during Covid, 'we are your single source of truth.'

This sort of authoritarianism is a growing trend. There have been moves by Western governments towards censorship, especially through the passing of 'hate speech' laws. Often the so called hate speech is valid criticism of the terrible mess those governments have made of the countries entrusted to their care.

After the so called insurrection by Trump supporters on January 6th, 2021, another Orwellian phrase came into vogue: 'Our Democracy.' Never mind that the Trump people thought they were protesting election meddling, or that leftists had themselves protested Trump's win in 2016 and spent the next four years resisting him. Suddenly the leftists were passionate about defending the sacred flame of democracy. As if they gave a damn about what the citizens wanted, or had not spent at least the last couple of years clamping down on free speech.

Democracy, at best, would be about the free flow of information and opinions, free speech, and letting people make up their own minds. You really have to admire the chutzpah shown by the hideous authoritarians of the Global Progressive Regime for claiming to care about any of that, and cynically adopting 'Our Democracy' as their catchphrase. Indeed 'protecting Our Democracy' was their cynically false excuse for clamping down on free speech from that point on.

When it comes to an award for most Orwellian phrase of recent times, 'Our Democracy' is a strong challenger to 'diversity is our strength.'

LP 58 – This Will Only Hurt Our Enemies

Many ordinary leftists went along with all this, compliantly parroting the Orwellian words used by the regime: 'misinformation,' 'conspiracy theories', ' Our Democracy,' and so on.

One government midwit, for example, posted the following on social media after some kind of street march: 'There is simply no place for racism, white supremacy, or hate speech. Everyone deserves to be safe.'

That is simply a whole lot of NPC-speak. That is, the mindless repeating of words and phrases, as done by Non Player Characters in a computer game. There's no doubt the same midwit would have expressed concern about the threat to Our Democracy posed by misinformation and conspiracies.

This is all about censorship - controlling what people are allowed to write, say, and even think. But what these leftists should realise is the authoritarian measures they endorse now will eventually come back to bite them - or their descendants. They have the attitude that *this will only hurt our enemies*. In due course, the same censorship laws can easily be used against them too.

The balance of power can change very quickly. To put it in terms they'll understand, suppose that in 2022 US president Biden had made harsh new laws to censor conservative Americans. Short sighted leftists might have seen this as a victory. But in 2022, hardly anyone seriously thought Donald Trump would become president again in 2024. In theory, what's to stop Trump using the same censorship laws against the leftists who applauded them in 2022?

So, this will only hurt our enemies? No. Censorship will hurt you too, sooner or later. It's only a matter of time.

26
Fifty Shades of Treason

In the last chapter of this section, we now turn to the main leftist pathology, which I call Noble Treason.

Let us consider two things to which leftists ally themselves. The first is the broad group of causes in the Global Progressive Regime - equity, feminism, 'anti-racism,' and so on. We could imagine these as planks bound together forming a raft floating downstream to a vaguely socialist better future. Critics might say the planks are rotten, the construction loose, and the destination doubtful - but it's understandable why people believe in it and think it's the right way to go.

The second thing leftists ally themselves with is more specific. It is the racial suicide of Anglo nations through the slow motion coup of multiculturalism. This is 'the Great Replacement,' in which the main ethnic group of a country is gradually replaced by others.

It has happened through history that civilisations have come to an end, or an ethnic group has declined or gone extinct. This may have happened through conquest, for example. It's less common that an ethnic group has committed suicide. In some ways, that's what is happening to the Anglo and European countries.

Under the policies of immigration and multiculturalism, whites are heading for minority status. It's not that white people will go extinct. We will survive, but become just another minority group, in the countries we once dominated. Some people are happy about that - perhaps the immigrants are - but it's hard to see how it's good for whites themselves, especially given the hostility aimed at us.

What has happened is only clear in hindsight. As a thought experiment, suppose that in the Britain or Australia of 1970 it was possible to instantly replace 50% of the Anglo population with new ethnic groups, as well as drastically changing the culture. Imagine if it was done over, say, six days. You would see it for what it was - an invasion. But if they do it over six decades - the slow motion coup - the end result is the same but they can get away with it. It happens so slowly you don't notice.

The great genius of this slow motion coup has been to persuade Anglos to collaborate in their own demise. They have managed to get Anglos not just to tolerate it, but to actively support it and fight those who resist. So, you have the noble good-whites fighting against the racist bad-whites.

This magnificent psy-op has been wildly successful. It's not just that white leftists have been persuaded to allow the erasure of their own ethnic group, they've agreed to help. Instead of seeing this as treasonous and foolish, they've been convinced it is noble and wise. Truly superb!

The last chapter in this series will address the topic of treason - but treason is not a simple concept. There are many types and shades of treason. Also, what seems treasonous to one person seems noble to another.

The paradox is that many white progressives are highly moral people. They want to be virtuous, and believe that they are. Yet from other perspectives, they are traitors, and treason is one of the lowest moral acts. However, they think they're being honourable. 'Noble Treason' will be the final leftist pathology discussed in this book.

I will build up to this topic by first discussing some related pathologies.

LP59 Leftism as Basically Destructive

Somebody posted on Twitter the following question:

> Have you ever heard anyone say 'we deconstructed
> this and discovered it was really good and we should
> leave it the way we found it'?

This is the basic difference between conservatives and progressives. Conservatives believe some things are fine as they are. They're not broken and don't need fixing. Progressives believe almost everything is broken and does need fixing.

This mentality found full expression in Mao's revolutionary China. Everything old had to go. During the Cultural Revolution, Mao declared war on the 'four olds' - old ideas, old culture, old customs, and old habits.

When our own leftist revolutionaries try to dismantle society as it is, their thinking has a magical flavour. It's assumed that destroying the status quo will guarantee the emergence of something better. Often, that isn't the case. Destroying what exists is easy. Replacing it with something better is much harder.

Now, keeping in mind the theory that leftism is basically destructive, consider the next three pathologies.

LP60 The Flag is a Hate Symbol

The Global Progressive Regime has also tried to replace what is old, not by the crude method of smashing it, but through a slower process of erosion. It has for instance tried to erode the idea of gender or racial identity. It favours 'blended' forms.

In preparing for the Great Replacement, the GPR has tried to erode national identity. A key part of this is hostility to the idea of the nation in itself. This makes sense if the goal is to create some kind of global system.

To achieve this, the first world had to be broken down and the Anglo nations humbled. Their identities were to be weakened through multiculturalism, although in Orwellian style this was described as them being *enriched* by it.

On the propaganda side, the idea of white historical guilt was pushed. At the same time, educated middle class whites were sold the notion that multiculturalism was worldly and sophisticated. In Australia, we were told Anglo-Australia was boring and had to go.

In these and other ways, the idea of the nation was attacked. Nationalism itself became almost immoral. Recently, we've reached the stage of people saying *the flag is a hate symbol*. This idea is held by the highest and the lowest. So, you get a few garden variety leftists posting like this on Twitter:

> Ever since the Cronulla riots our national flag has become a symbol of extreme right wing prejudice and racism. Has this happened in other countries? I've become embarrassed and ashamed of the flag, as well as Australia Day.

And

> It's funny how all the racist cookers have an Aussie flag on their profiles. The flag represents hate now.

'Cooker' by the way, is a left wing slur for people they see as low IQ right wing conspiracy theorists.

In the minds of these leftists, the Australian flag now represents the far-right. But if you're ashamed of the national flag, then the brainwashing has worked.

Still, we should not suppose this mental illness only afflicts the peasant folk. Some years ago, a high profile Democrat was photographed holding an American flag and grimacing. Someone said it was like seeing a vampire being made to hold a cross. Then there's that time Angela Merkel was handed a German flag and couldn't put it down fast enough, a look of distaste on her face. As for our own Anthony Albanese, he likes to give the Aboriginal flag centre stage while our national flag is shunted off to the side.

All these high profile 'leaders' are displaying the anti-national message. It is really an anti-white, anti-Western message. As one of the authors of the book *Anglophobia* remarked:

> When was the last time an Australian politician said a nice thing about White Australians, collectively, as they do with other 'diverse' groups in Australia? Most often, the only time we are collectivised in the eyes of politicians and the media is for the purpose of slander.

He's right that it's hard to recall any recent public praise for Anglo-Australians. All mainstream politicians have internalised the taboo against doing that. The programming has worked 100%.

It goes without saying that patriotism is out of favour. In fact a dumb anti-Western mindset is in fashion among those who think themselves sophisticated. For instance, a smug leftist of my acquaintance posted a meme which said, 'Say something nice about the British' along with the answer that 'You guys created the largest number of independence days around the world.'

Another answer might have been to mention the umpteen British inventions that make our lives easier, and which more or less invented the modern world - but all white leftists can do is make snarky remarks about colonialism.

There is no limit to the foolishness of these people, complacent in their false sense of superiority. This is also true in America. As Thomas Sowell has remarked:

> There are too many people, especially among the intelligentsia, who will never appreciate the things that have made this country great until after those

things have been destroyed - with their help. Then, of course, it will be too late.

LP61 Rub Their Nose in Diversity

On this topic, we now come to a pathology from the elite left. It was revealed in 2009 that the British Labour government at one point had a strategy to 'rub the Right's nose in diversity.' This was to punish their political rivals and the conservative parts of the public who weren't happy with their reforms. Labour was going to teach them a lesson by increasing immigration numbers and forcing Britain to become fully multicultural.

We can only hope this spiteful short term victory was satisfying, because the long term consequences would be much harder to live with.

LP62 I Hate my Father and Want to Destroy his World

Leftist revolt is sometimes a reaction to having conservative parents. In some cases, this is confined to personal behaviour. In others, it can lead to a desire to smash the world in which the parents believe. This is of course a spiteful overreaction.

Spite does play a part in the leftist mindset, and Labour's nose-rubbing strategy in Britain should come as no surprise. Some of Labour's ministers were young in the 1960s and absorbed the radical ideas of those times. While there was some positive intent in those ideas, there was also an urge to destroy the old order. Part of this may have been a personal revolt against authoritarian parents. Or else they projected the 'parent' outward onto the larger society. Either way, the urge to destroy played some role in their progressive values.

This was shown in comments made by now-conservative Peter Hitchens in 2013, in which he admitted he and his generation were partly driven by spite in their 1960s radical politics. In an article called 'How I am Partly to Blame for Mass Immigration' he wrote:

> When I was a Revolutionary Marxist, we were all in favour of as much immigration as possible. It wasn't because we liked immigrants, but because we didn't like Britain. We saw immigrants - from anywhere - as allies against the staid, settled, conservative society that our country still was at the end of the Sixties. Also, we liked to feel oh so superior to the bewildered people - usually in the poorest parts of Britain - who found their neighbourhoods suddenly transformed into supposedly "vibrant communities." If they dared to express the mildest objections, we called them bigots...

> When we graduated and began to earn serious money, we generally headed for expensive London enclaves and became extremely choosy about where our children went to school, a choice we happily denied the urban poor, the ones we sneered at as "racists." What did we know, or care, of the great silent revolution which even then was beginning to transform the lives of the British poor?

> To us, it meant patriotism and tradition could always be derided as "racist." And it also meant cheap servants for the rich new middle-class, for the first time since 1939, as well as cheap restaurants and - later on - cheap builders and plumbers working off the books. It wasn't our wages that were depressed, or our work that was priced out of the market. Immigrants didn't do the sort of jobs we did.

They were no threat to us. The only threat might have come from the aggrieved British people, but we could always stifle their protests by suggesting that they were modern-day fascists. I have learned since what a spiteful, self-righteous, snobbish and arrogant person I was (and most of my revolutionary comrades were, too).

While Australia does not have the same class system as Britain, the keenest supporters of multiculturalism here are educated white leftists. One can easily see parallels with Hitchens' story. Many of Australia's 1970s radicals saw multiculturalism as a way to rebel against Anglo-Australia. Some of those people are now old and wealthy, and preach their love of 'New Australia' from some of the whitest suburbs in Sydney and Melbourne.

LP63 Noble Treason

After the preamble of those three destructive LPs, we now come to the final leftist pathology: Noble Treason.

We can surmise that the Global Progressive Regime is an attempted coup against the Western world. A key part of that is the racial takeover whereby the former Anglo nations are turned multicultural with an Anglo minority. This is the Great Replacement. It may be part of a push towards some form of global communism. That is speculative, but I'll treat it as a useful hypothesis.

Communism always wears a noble mask and in the West, it operates by stealth. Most people don't see it for what it is. But if the GPR is a coup against the Anglo nations, then those who assist it are effectively traitors. Often the treason is unwitting, as people don't realise what they are supporting, or the long term consequences. Many white leftists have been duped into this 'unconscious treason' in the belief that they are being noble.

A leftist may have good reasons for supporting DEI, multiculturalism, or Critical Race Theory - but when they do so, they are also supporting the Great Replacement. When they buy into notions of white historical guilt, or accept feminism's claim that the family is oppressive, they are also assisting it. Indeed, it's hard to think of a single leftist cause that works *against* the Great Replacement.

Before discussing the psychology of leftists in the grip of 'noble treason' I will consider various levels and types operating in this coup against the West. This taxonomy of traitors will help us to see there are many shades of treason, some more obvious than others. We can begin with the most powerful people and move down the hierarchy.

(i) Globalists / Hostile Elites

This category is speculative only.

Is there a secret group of powerful elites trying to destroy the West? There have been conspiracy theories around this idea for a long time, but there is no decisive proof. Still, we can infer the possible existence of such a group from observable results.

Put it this way. It's possible there is no actual conspiracy to conquer the West and bring down white people. But as others have remarked, if there *was* such a conspiracy, how would it look any different to what is happening now?

These hypothetical enemies are not 'traitors,' as such, but hostile externals. They have no allegiance towards Western nations. They may live outside those nations, or they may live in them but see themselves as so far above ordinary people they are really separate to the rest of us.

These theorised types are not of any one ethnicity in particular. They are super elites who see us as little more than cattle.

(ii) Reckless Experimenters

It's possible there is no actual hostile enemy of the West. Instead, we may have been destroyed by our own leaders. The 'reckless experimenters' are the people with enough influence to do some real harm. Thomas Sowell calls them 'the anointed.' They believe their superior wisdom is a gift they are obliged to share with the rest of us. As Sowell has said:

> There is usually only a limited amount of damage that can be done by dull or stupid people. For creating a truly monumental disaster, you need people with high IQs.

The 'anointed' may include academics, politicians, or others in the position to direct public policy. Their most conspicuous success was the social experiment of multiculturalism. This was supposed to fix the problem of racism. Instead, it made racism a permanent part of our lives. Perhaps if we're still here in five hundred years this experiment will finally succeed. In the meantime, we have to live with the gift these geniuses have bestowed upon us.

(iii) Quislings

These are actual traitors - sociopathic leaders who go along with the globalist regime for their own personal gain. They care little for their country's past or future, or the people presently under their rule. They'll sell out their own country if it suits them. These callous opportunists have no real allegiance to their countries or a set of values, but only their own personal power.

(iv) Useful Idiots

There are many kinds of 'useful idiots' but the most useful of all are those who rise to the level of state or national leader.

These people aren't cold hearted sociopaths like the quislings, but midwits with good intentions, which is why they've been allowed to rise to positions of power.

These people may actually believe in some of the leftist principles which more intelligent people can see through. They take concepts like 'equity' or 'anti-racism' at face value, not understanding what they really are, or the consequences of such ideas. They'll support 'gender equality' but never look deeply into the concept, and will let feminist ideologues tell them what it means.

They aren't evil, and may even mean well. They usually aren't complete idiots, but rather the midwits mentioned in the last chapter. They're smart enough to grasp basic concepts but don't follow those ideas through to a fuller understanding. They're 'useful' because once they gain power, they can be used by other people for their own ends.

A second type of useful idiot, more obnoxious, is the narcissistic useful idiot. This is the type who likes moral grandstanding in front of an audience. He is your classic virtue signaller, using media or social media to show off his progressive views.

This is an effective strategy for him (or her) as it brings social approval and financial rewards if he can advance, for example, in the left-dominated media or arts worlds. As such, there's a phenomenon we might call the *Useful Idiot Feedback Loop*. The person pushes progressive views and gains money and plaudits in return. He mistakenly thinks this is just reward for his superior morality, rather than for collaborating in the globalist coup and the Great Replacement. Such rewards in turn allow him to live a comfortable, affluent life sheltered from any ill effects of the policies he supports. You will rarely find him living in Sydney's most multicultural suburbs, for example. Thus he can keep cheerleading for diversity while living as far away from it as possible. Such is the happy lot of the narcissistic useful idiot.

(v) Regime Collaborators

These people are like the quislings but lower down the hierarchy. There is also overlap with the previous category, the useful idiot, in that collaborating with the regime brings rewards.

Regime collaborators may work in government, the corporate world, or education. As long as they're in positions of influence, they can help push regime values for personal gain.

They can even work in the arts, and the authors of the book *Anglophobia* gave an example of an artist whose work pushed the globalist idea that Australia has no main ethnicity, and certainly not a core Anglo identity. It was observed that:

> People… who attempt to undermine this notion of an Anglo core Australian nation, do so knowing they will receive the highest praise, prestigious awards, and financial benefits. These are bestowed by the hostile cosmopolitan elites who have taken control of our institutions such as the ABC, *The Sydney Morning Herald*, and art galleries and foundations around the country.

On the flipside, as given in the two chapters on the arts, those who fail to get in line with regime values are shut out of the arts world.

(vi) Spiteful Revolutionaries

These are the 'I hate my father' types from earlier, including some of those referenced in the Hitchens quote.

Other examples are radical feminists who equate smashing the patriarchy with overthrowing the whole society, or the gay activists from the *Doctor Who* chapter who think gay liberation requires the complete transformation of Britain.

The trouble with spiteful revolutionaries is they fail to discriminate between what needs changing and what should be left alone. Not everything is broke or needs fixing - but they are going to burn it all to the ground.

(vii) Polite Revolutionaries

These are your white middle class leftists who are in tune with the worldview offered by the ABC or BBC. They largely accept the values offered by those globalist broadcasters, and believe they are the 'goodies.'

In accepting globalist values, they tacitly support the Great Replacement, but through a sort of polite, middle class mindset. For example, they will see black actors shoehorned into British historical dramas, but are too polite to comment on it, if they even notice it at all. They have been trained to dislike Christianity, but to respect other religions.

They have far too much faith in the alleged virtues of diversity, inclusion, and equity, and are too trusting that other people are as well meaning as themselves.

They are good-whites, and no matter how polite they may be, their good nature has been used against them, ultimately to our cost.

(viii) Fanatical Revolutionaries

These are your freshly minted student radicals. The social justice warriors. Mao's Red Guards. Their youthful energy and idealism has been hijacked by Marxist university professors.

They are aggressively conformist within their own circle, forcing each other to hold the same basic views. Outsiders who reject their social justice doctrines are seen as almost subhuman.

Cultish.

(ix) NPCs

The term NPC refers to Non Player Characters from computer games. NPCs in these games have no independent thought. They simply act and react in predictable, pre-programmed ways.

NPC has become an online slur referring to people who are purely reactive and follow whatever political trend is being engineered at the moment. One week it is BLM, the next it may be Ukraine, and then something else again.

These people always follow the crowd, take the most predictable view of any topic, and seem to be barely thinking - even though they can simulate emotion if it's called for. It's all part of the programming.

(x) Normies

Normies is a pejorative term for people who either aren't interested in politics at all, or who passively go along with mainstream ideas without being very engaged in them. They'll notice something like the George Floyd protests of 2020, and perhaps find it strange, but without much personal involvement.

They tend to drift along and accept things as they are, and will remain apolitical unless some event directly affects them. If the event is upsetting enough, the normie may become politicised. For example, a man might experience a divorce and all the upheaval it brings, then come into contact with anti-feminist views, which might lead on to other political topics. Until such an event happens, they aren't involved. Therefore they're not actually 'traitors,' just bystanders.

Normies avoid politics if they can, but it isn't always possible. As Patrick Buchanan once said, 'You may not be interested in the culture war, but the culture war is very interested in you.'

(xi) Opportunists - Internal

These are the people within society who find leftist reforms work to their personal advantage and accept them for that reason, without considering the bigger picture.

They could be white women who benefit from gynocentric policies, for example. They may be aware of an anti-male climate of thought but won't care as it doesn't affect them personally. They are unconcerned with wider implications as long as they personally benefit.

Another example might be landlords who benefit from a high rate of immigration, which keeps housing demand high, or business owners who can hire cheap labour. Whether this might be good for other people or the country at large doesn't bother them, as long as they can profit from it.

(xii) Opportunists – External

These are people who come into society from outside, the immigrants themselves. They take advantage of multiculturalism. They aren't traitors, of course, just opportunists and you can't blame them for that. They are simply using those conditions which have been set up by others.

How they behave after arrival is another matter. Those who love and respect their adopted country are showing loyalty. Those who seek to undermine the country, perhaps lobbying to change it to suit themselves are not showing much loyalty to what they were given. However, as it is human nature to behave like that, you can largely blame the host country for being naïve enough to enable it.

Who are the Traitors?

The treason in question is collaboration with the GPR's attempted coup against the Western world, and especially the Great Replacement.

Not all of the twelve types listed are traitors. The global elites are hostile outsiders so loyalty isn't a factor. The external opportunists are just trying their luck. As for the NPCs and normies, they have no real idea what's going on.

Most of the other types are treasonous to varying degrees. If we were to take the idea literally, you could only really call someone a traitor if they were doing it deliberately. While that applies to the quislings, regime collaborators, and spiteful revolutionaries, it doesn't apply to the useful idiots, who are fairly clueless about what they are doing. Therefore it amounts to a sort of 'unconscious treason.'

In this sense, we could see 'treason' as part of the consequences, but not the intentions. White middle class leftists do collaborate in the betrayal of their own ethnic group, but without realising it, and usually without meaning to.

In fact, many white leftists are oblivious to the Great Replacement. Yet when they ally themselves to mass immigration or diversity, they are collaborating in it. When the good-whites rail against the wicked bad-whites, they are fighting for the Great Replacement. Again, this 'treason' is largely unconscious.

One man who leftists would assume is a very-bad-white is an American named Jared Taylor. An educated and well spoken man, Taylor has spent decades warning people about white dispossession. He has also made a serious effort to understand the psychology of left wing whites. In one article, he argues that most white leftists are highly moral people, driven by a genuine desire to be virtuous. While this is a noble trait, it can also be used against them.

I agree with Taylor that most white leftists have high moral ideals. Yet in collaborating with the Great Replacement, they are effectively traitors, and treason is one of the lowest moral acts. This odd paradox can be explained if you realise most white leftists simply aren't aware of the consequences of their beliefs and, more to the point, they've been duped into collaborating in their own extinction through one of the greatest episodes of brainwashing in the history of our planet.

Pointing this out doesn't make me superior, because I too was fooled, having gone through the same indoctrination process as everyone else. At least I woke up, and other people should too.

Jared Taylor is right that white leftists' main motivations are honourable. Still, white leftists need to realise that what they've been told is virtue is, from another perspective, treason, and therefore not moral at all.

To begin, we should make some excuses for white leftists, because in terms of this treason, they 'know not what they do.' So, here are a few reasons why they might be excused.

First, many people live in the present moment and do not think of what life may be like in fifty or a hundred years. They rarely think about biological evolution, or cultural evolution either, and how much things can change. They are often complacent in assuming life will continue as it is now.

Second, because the multicultural coup happened in slow motion, it was never obvious what was being done. As mentioned, if the demographic changes had happened all at once, we would have noticed. As it happened over six decades, they got away with it.

Third, as discussed in the BBC chapter, whites were never trained to think racially. In fact, it was a taboo. While Western societies were majority-white, there was no need to think in those terms. Now that these societies are diverse with a good deal of animosity aimed at a shrinking Anglo population, they should be revising that stance.

Related to this, many leftists have a dimly conceived notion race doesn't matter, and that because we're all human beings we are somehow interchangeable. If so, a hypothetical future Australia that was, for example, 20% Anglo wouldn't bother them, because 'we're all just people.' This is the sort of naivety about race that's been exploited by others. Any connection between such a future and the Anglo-Australia of, say, 1970 would be almost non-existent. Unfortunately, in the mid 2020s whites need to start thinking in terms of race - not because they want to, but because they have to.

Fourth, in their approach to racial issues, white leftists think they're being noble. They think they're fighting against racism, rather than collaborating in their own ethnic extinction. They may actually be doing both at the same time.

Fifth, white leftists have been subjected to decades of propaganda about race and morality, much of which has been harmful to the long term future of their own kind.

Sixth, they have been largely surrounded by other leftists, all of whom reinforce each others' beliefs, and authority figures who reward their compliance with the 'correct' doctrines.

Seventh, they've been denied exposure to alternative viewpoints which might change their minds.

There are other factors too, but all of those listed have played a major part in the current situation. And to repeat, I went through the same indoctrination as everyone else so it's not as if I'm any better in terms of my susceptibility to the whole program. Even as I write this chapter, dealing with racial taboos, there is still some sense of 'guilt' which is the result of the brainwashing we were all given. Yet my sense of amazement at what's been done to the Anglo countries is now stronger than that original programming.

Why the Racial Suicide will Probably Continue

When it comes to the Great Replacement, people often fail to realise the magnitude of this event. Fifty years ago, Britain, America, Australia, Germany and France, were majority white nations. Fifty years hence, they may be majority non-white. This major demographic change also means cultural change, such that these countries will be barely recognisable from what they once were.

Anyone who is really thinking, unrestrained by taboos, should realise the significance of this. However, white leftists seem oblivious. They are either unaware of the Great Replacement, see it as a conspiracy theory or, if they admit it may be true, think it unimportant or even desirable. Furthermore, they think those who care about the issue are bad-whites, their moral inferiors. That alone allows them to dismiss it.

Even if someone were trying to convinces leftists that the Great Replacement is real and that, by their own attitudes they are collaborating in it, it's doubtful many of them would change their minds. They would simply continue on their merry way.

It is strange that an ethnic group would participate in its own racial extinction. It is highly eccentric for an ethnic majority to voluntarily concede demographic and cultural power to outsiders. As Jared Taylor has remarked, it may almost be unique in history.

So, what should we do at this point?

Unfortunately, Anglos have gone a very long way down this road. Still, even if it's not possible to go back to where we were, we can at least not continue any further. Let's suppose we accept things as they are now with Western nations diverse and multicultural, but call a halt to any further demographic decline. We could suspend any further immigration for a time, and also reject the whole anti-Western mindset, the white guilt propaganda, and the other factors that have harmed us.

Yet this is not going to happen, and a key reason is that white leftists will continue to collaborate in all of the factors that have brought us here, and hold to their beliefs.

In trying to understand why they do this, I have just given a list of excuses for white leftists, and admitted that they are often highly moral people driven by noble ideals. It's time now for a much more critical look at them, focusing on their negative mental traits and how they help the Great Replacement.

In looking through the list of sixty-three leftist pathologies mentioned in this book, there are some core traits uniting many of them. Three of the main ones are arrogance, naivety, and fanaticism.

Arrogance

I have come to surmise that the defining trait of leftists is arrogance.

As mentioned, leftists think of themselves as morally and intellectually superior. It follows that they think of non-leftists as stupid or evil, or combinations of the two. They often seem barely able to conceive that there are alternate views to their own.

This was shown, for example, during the 2023 Voice to Parliament debate in Australia. As a conservative named Will Kingston commented on Twitter:

> I remain staggered by the inability of almost every Yes voter to see the other side of the argument... I understand the Yes case. I just disagree with it. I am yet to hear ONE Yes voter say something similar. I can't work out whether it's hatred, arrogance or stupidity.

It's arrogance. The Yes voters were so sure they had the high moral ground, understanding the No case was beneath their notice. You see this time and again in leftists. Now, whereas in science or philosophy, it has long been considered a virtue to realise you may be wrong in your beliefs, in politics there is this misplaced sense of certainty.

In the Voice debate, it showed a lack of humility, as well as a failure of the imagination. Let's not even mention the naivety. Well, not yet.

We can recall Thomas Sowell's observation that 'No one can really understand the political left without understanding that they are about making feel themselves superior, however much they may talk piously about what they are going to do to help others.'

In terms of the racial Great Replacement, it is the leftist's need to be morally superior which is the biggest block to any change of approach. Race is the central battlefield of our time, yet on every racial issue white leftists have been persuaded that the morally superior stance is the one which - what a coincidence - is directly or indirectly opposed to Anglo interests. At the heart of this is that 'racism' has been the cardinal sin and 'anti-racism' the great virtue. As such, white leftists have taken immense pride in opposing the bad-whites who have failed to match their own elevated stance.

Now that the Great Replacement is becoming harder to ignore, it will be to the great chagrin of white leftists to find out that the people they despised the most may have been right all along. With a deep belief in their own moral and intellectual superiority, it must be truly galling for leftists to learn that the people they looked down upon were correct, and were indeed braver than themselves in speaking out about it.

Unfortunately, the deep psychological need of leftists to be morally superior will make them deny this as long as possible, perhaps to their dying day. That such people, the elite media types for instance, tend to be well off and sheltered will make this easier to achieve. It would be an act of humility for them to admit they were wrong, but there is rarely any humility on display with such people. They will deny they were wrong to the bitter end.

Naivety

Leftists generally think they are more intelligent than other people. Many of them *are* intelligent and well educated, but have this blind spot when it comes to race.

One leftist wrote an article in a leading newspaper ascribing all objections to mass immigration in Australia to xenophobia. He saw the swing to the right in Europe and America as coming from the same cause - a xenophobic 'fear of the other.'

How about that? Never mind the loss of social cohesion, the existence of no go zones and grooming gangs, ethnic quota squabbles, cultural friction, or the demographic replacement of the majority ethnic group. It's all down to xenophobia. If only all the bigots could just be as big hearted as the author of this article.

No one is denying there are many good immigrants who have contributed a lot to their adopted countries. It's also true some benefits come from diversity and multiculturalism. That doesn't mean Anglos aren't entitled to query what's been done to their countries. Anglos were never asked if they wanted them to be completely transformed, and they are right to be concerned about their future prospects.

White leftists can be intelligent on many issues, but when it comes to race, there is this odd naivety. You saw this in the gung ho enthusiasm with which they supported the Voice, to empower Aboriginals, a group known to harbour resentment against Anglos. These white leftists seemed to assume their act of generosity would be reciprocated by future Aboriginals. It never occurred to them there is any risk in empowering people who have cause to resent you. Or perhaps they assumed any negative consequences would only be aimed at the bad-whites, never at themselves, the noble, big hearted good-whites. (In his book

Whiteness: the Original Sin, Jim Goad called this delusional state of mind 'Passover Syndrome.')

On the whole, white majorities treat ethnic minorities fairly well. It is unlikely the reverse will apply once whites become a minority. White leftists assume that because they themselves hold idealistic views about racial equality, other people do too. They seem to assume non-whites will automatically like them because they're currently allies in the fight against racism.

This is chronic leftist naivety. As has been remarked by others, white people are not very tribal. They tend to be individualists, and are often driven by abstract ideals like justice and equality. Many non-whites are far more tribal, openly favouring their own ethnic groups, and showing little concern for outsiders or for the abstract ideals that concern whites.

One way this may manifest in a highly diverse society is that tribalism will play an increased role. It is unlikely non-white ethnic groups will have any great regard for a future Anglo minority. They will more likely view us with contempt for being weak and foolish enough to hand over power. This is the future the noble good-whites of today are creating for us.

These noble whites fail to grasp that many non-whites do not like us. Here's Sowell again, speaking a few years ago:

> Europe is belatedly discovering how unbelievably stupid it was to import millions of people from cultures that despise Western values and which often promote hatred toward the people who have let them in.

It is another peculiar effect of the mass brainwashing of recent decades that middle class white leftists are very critical of white societies at the same time as they absurdly over-idealise non-whites. These are the people who seem to think war and slavery were invented by Europeans. In a recent diatribe on Twitter, a good-white Karen was dressing down some bad-whites, and claimed that Australia is 'one of the most racist countries in the world.'

Really? Compared to what? Australia has been described by some as 'the most successful multicultural country in the world,' although of course 'success' is relative. More to the point, has this woman ever been outside Australia? A trip to a few non-Western nations might help her shed any illusions.

For all their pretentions about moral and intellectual superiority, naivety is a common trait among white leftists. They are too trusting, too sure their own goodwill will be returned, and far too reckless about what the future may hold. Many of today's white leftists won't live long enough to face the consequences of their poor judgment. That misfortune will fall to their descendants and others born into the future they are helping to create.

Fanaticism

We now come to the third negative trait in the unholy trinity of leftist pathologies. After arrogance and naivety, the third one is fanaticism.

Leftists are dangerously Utopian. As remarked, they don't follow the principle of *if it ain't broke don't fix it*. Instead, they work from the principle that *everything is broke and we can fix it*. And looking around the world of the mid 2020s, they sure have... 'fixed' a lot of things.

It's bad enough that leftists think they can fix society. Worse, they want to fix reality itself if it doesn't behave according to their superior ideals. Everyone not equal? They can fix that. People having 'wrong opinions.' They can fix that too. If only leftists can be put in charge of every aspect of society, they'll be able to fix everything.

To that end - gaining power so they can 'fix things' - leftists will do almost anything. They will lie, censor, and even destroy their opponents, all in their pursuit of a better world.

Let's not forget that one of the greatest things leftists tried to fix was the problem of racism. This was to be achieved by the brilliant two step plan of creating a multicultural society and then being tolerant.

The problem of racism has now been solved to the extent that you can't go a single day without hearing about it.

Moving on from Leftist Pathologies

Enough has been said in this section of the book. Listing these sixty-three pathologies will perhaps make a dent in the idea many of us were brought up with - that leftist thinking is automatically superior. Just imagine if people - people of all types - were to become aware of these pathologies and then overcome them, how much better we all would be.

I was raised as a leftist myself and know this sort of thinking is based on good intentions. But the arrogance, the naivety, and the fanaticism has all become very tiresome.

I have hesitated to write this book because it may upset people, and might also bring conflict. Still, I have chosen to express the truth as I see it and try to solve problems that come from wrong ideas and faulty thinking.

As mentioned earlier, some of these leftist pathologies are merely irritating, but others may be civilisation-ending. This is especially so for LP63 Noble Treason, in which white leftists have been fooled into collaborating in the Great Replacement. To think we have been duped not just into collaborating, but feeling morally superior about it, is quite remarkable.

Apart from that rather large issue, we are surrounded daily by conflict in the areas of race and gender, and also notions of 'equality.' Much of this conflict is based on mistaken ideas. It's time we freed ourselves of these ideas, and it may come as a surprise how much better off we are if we can do it. That leads on to a short final chapter to conclude this book.

27

The Surprising Liberation

There are few things more ridiculous these days than when a national leader calls for unity.

Almost all the Anglo nations have been victims of a globalist coup, turned multicultural without consent ever being asked or given. Our countries have been divided up among many ethnicities, several of them hostile to each other and some hostile to us.

This new order has been bestowed upon us by various hidden elites, with the collaboration of our own quisling leaders and the 'national' broadcasters. When one realises that our leaders sold us all out to multiculturalism, it's hard to fathom disloyalty on that scale of magnitude.

Meanwhile, the remaining Anglo population is divided into good-whites and bad-whites, who exist in a state of mutual contempt. To compound the mess, feminism's phony war has led us to the point where a significant number of men and women can no longer stand each other.

Much of this is thanks to the ideas of the Global Progressive Regime. If the GPR's goal was to make our nations the least unified they could possibly be, it has been a wonderful success.

When observing the clown world in which we live, it's tempting to see it as a joke and wash your hands of it. This response is a form of freedom. The regime is too absurd to take seriously. Still, the black pill approach to liberation is rather nihilistic, so in this final chapter, I'll try to put a more positive spin on it.

What is the surprising liberation?

Essentially, it is to see the Global Progressive Regime for what it is - an enormous psy-op that's been inflicted on us. One that we must see through and move beyond.

It's a surprise to realise that much of what we were taught was wrong. We were given a set of ideas which we were told were both moral and true. Eventually, we see that they were neither.

So, what is one to do? Stop being a leftist, for a start. Or rather, stop being a hard leftist. We must make that distinction between the soft leftism and hard leftism mentioned in Chapter Sixteen.

Soft leftism consists of some simple values: respect for all races, support for equal rights for women and gays, and free speech. Accepting those basic values does not mean you have to accept the hard leftism of today, which is a whole other set of ideas. These include identity politics and DIE principles, uncritical support for feminism and multiculturalism, censorship and cancel culture, Marxism, whether stated or implied, and more basically, an anti-white, anti-male, anti-Western stance.

I support soft leftism but reject hard leftism - and so should you.

The Surprising Liberation is a title I've used before, in the last chapter of my book on feminism. It was a suggestion that ideas like 'male privilege' are wrong, and that giving up the false belief Western women are oppressed would free feminists from an imaginary prison. The chapter also noted that as most feminists are deeply committed to the idea of their oppression, such a liberation was highly unlikely.

I have re-used the title for this book, because the concept applies more widely to the political left as a whole. There are many concepts from which leftists should liberate themselves, especially the harmful ideas of hard leftism. In so doing, there are a few surprises in store.

The first surprise is to realise that many of the ideas we were taught, are not true. The second surprise is to realise leftism is not automatically a morally superior way to think. The third surprise is that life feels better once you exit the leftist cult.

There will be other forms of freedom for those who leave hard leftism behind. They can free themselves from guilt for a start, whether it is historical guilt or the related pathology of class guilt pertaining to race or gender.

Another liberation is they will no longer have to kowtow to leftist bullies. They can stop bowing and scraping to those who rank higher in the leftist caste system. They can stop cowering before the threat of cancel culture. They can stop being told what to say, and even what to think.

Leftists trying to leave the cult should take the following liberating steps and see how it feels.

Next time a Western woman says she's oppressed by the patriarchy, yawn. If an Indigenous activist says you're living on stolen land, shrug. When some leftist scold says you've got straight white able bodied privilege and what are you going to do about it, laugh in her face.

Stop kowtowing to these thugs. They only have power over you if you accept their beliefs. As their belief system is a house of cards, be like Alice and laugh as it tumbles to the floor. *You're nothing but a pack of cards.*

The liberation is in rejecting this false belief system, the brainwashing, and those who try to make you believe in it.

Reject identity politics. Reject an anti-white, anti-Western stance. Reject censorship and the group think of cancel culture.

Stop trying to square the circle by pretending diversity and equality are compatible. Instead of believing white guilt is noble, see it for what it is - foolish and self destructive. Stop pretending Western women are worse off than men. The idea is not empowering. More to the point, it's not true.

Stop collaborating with the Global Progressive Regime, and reject the weak 'leaders' who do collaborate with it.

Most importantly, stop collaborating with the Great Replacement. It might cost you some worldly power, but at least when the time comes to face your own death, you'll die without the stench of treason muddying your aura.

Still, what are we to do with something like multiculturalism? That's a work in progress. To some extent, we have to live with the consequences of the betrayal inflicted on us a few decades ago. But at least we can drop all the anti-Western propaganda that has gone along with it.

To the middle class white leftists, the good-whites - you were fooled, but so was I. We all were. But it's time to move on from the absurdity of the GPR and its false beliefs. It might be late, but better late than never.

Perhaps we can move on from feminism's phony war, into a world where men and women no longer hate each other. Maybe we can make some form of multiculturalism which is at least free of anti-white antagonism.

As for where we'll end up, that remains to be seen - but at least it will be better than where we are now. That is our hope and aspiration as we move on from the clever illusion that was the Global Progressive Regime.

Afterword

If you liked this book, help spread the word. Tell a friend... or five friends. Your support is important to help make this book better known.

Website - www.vortexwinder.com

Contact - Alfadex Books can be contacted by email at matthew.alfadex@gmail.com.

Notes

This lists the source for most of the quoted material, although with exceptions of two types. First, where I have lost the source, and second, where the source may prefer not to be identified.

For books, the full publication details are given in the next section. For all Thomas Sowell quotes, I have attributed them to a list of his collected quotes, rather than specific books https://www.azquotes.com/author/13901-Thomas_Sowell.

If source is listed as TX, it originally appeared on the Twitter website now known as X.

Chapter Three
Theory of elites. James, A. *New Brittania: The Rise and Decline of Anglo Australia*, p. 195-6.

Chapter Four
Anti-white ads. '43 Anti white commercials,' https://www.youtube.com/watch?v=hvNNtBmA3SQ&t=2s

Chapter Five
Quote on ending racism. Speech by prime minister, John Gorton, at Australian Alumni dinner in Singapore. January 18th, 1971.

Immigration agreement by major parties. Sanderson, P. 'Over-Immigration putting pressure on all of our sectors.' *Daily Telegraph*, March 22, 2023.

Deception to achieve diversity. Jackson, T. 'What Happened to White Australia?' American Renaissance, March 1, 2013.

Starry idealism and hard headed ethnic activism. Source lost.

Chapter Six
Wry amusement. Hamilton, C. 'Wake up Lefties and Reject Wokeness.' Sydney Morning Herald, July 7, 2023.

Norman Conquest of England. Blainey, G. 'Before Voice Vote, Let's Get the Facts in Order. The Australian, July 1st, 2023.

Chapter Seven
Craven, R. Teacher Guidelines. 'Teaching the Teachers: Indigenous Australian Studies for Primary Pre-Service Teacher Education.' School of Teacher Education, University of New South Wales, *1996*.

Goonyandi people displaced. Powell, L. 'Truth Telling and Tribal Warfare.' Quadrant, July 2022.

Methodist lay preacher. Powell, L. As above.

Tribal battle. Buckley, W. *The Life and Adventures of William Buckley*, p.91.

Chapter Eight
Uluru Statement. Blainey, G. 'Before Voice Vote, Let's Get the Facts in Order. The Australian, July 1st, 2023.

Salter, F. *The Voice Referendum*, p. 38-39.

Price remarks given during Jacinta's Price speech to the National Press Club, September 15th, 2023.

Crocodile Tear. Blainey, G. As above.

Most disadvantaged people the least colonised. Peter Sutton, quoted by John Anderson, 'The Voice: Four Myths,' YouTube, 2024 https://youtu.be/Be8E9aagdls.

Chapter Ten
Kriegman article. Rufo, C. 'The Price of Dissent,' City Journal, January 5, 2022.

Critical Race Theory. Pluckrose, H and Lindsay, J. *Cynical Theories*. P.128, 132.

Chapter Eleven
Girl Power. Blonde in the Belly of the Beast, 'Female Entitlement Part 1,' https://www.youtube.com/watch?v=JkOPfneKvGQ&t=26s.

On power. Tim Goldich, source unknown.

On bullying. Anon, source video unknown.

Various from Eccentric Hat, TX.

Chapter Twelve
Perpetrators. Flood, M. From TX, an abridged version of the original from, Flood and Dembele, 'Putting Perpetrators in the Picture.' Briefing paper series, May 2021.

Fiamengo comments from The Fiamengo Files YouTube series, Episode 17, 'The Myth of Sexual Harassment.'

Devine, M. 'Six Reasons Why Voters Dumped the Liberals.' *Daily Telegraph*. May 22nd, 2022.

All Daphne Patai quotes are from Patai, D. *Heterophobia*. Rowman and Littlefield, USA. 1998. Quotes in order, from the following pages of *Heterophobia*: 29, 37, 59, 41, 50-51, 40, 61, 86, 112, 35, xii. This includes the first quote, on p.143 of my book.

Chapter Thirteen
Used to believe women should run the world. Patai, D. *Heterophobia*, p.140.

Parental alienation. Phil Mitchell, TX.

Women are human beings. Shear, M. *New Directions for Women*, May / June, 1986.

Chapter Fourteen
Buffet quote. Jericho Green. Source video unknown.

Fiamengo, J. TX, 2023.

Society's message to men. Honey Badger Radio, TX 22nd March 2025.

Men have crippled themselves. Paglia, C. Camille Paglia Quotes.

What kind of mentality? Steve Brule, TX.

Why they believe in the patriarchy. Judith, TX.

Blame society's problems on men. Eccentric Hat, TX.

Chapter Fifteen
Beliefs about history. Hannah Wallen, TX.

Interview with Nancy. 'Feminist House Bunny,' TX.

Girls' compensation. Quoted in Arndt, B. 'No One Cares About Boys Doing Badly.' Substack, February, 2022.

Narcissistic women. Fiamengo, J. TX.

Chapter Sixteen
Langdon, T. 'Heroines of the Hive Mind.' The Occidental Observer. June 8, 2022.

Chapter Eighteen
All quotes from *Heresies Episode 5: BBC Bias Exposed*. New Culture Forum. 2022.

White British children a minority. Simon Webb, History Debunked, You Tube.

Chapter Nineteen
We've got to tell a lie. Moffat, S quoted in, 'Dr Who: Role was offered to black actor.' BBC News. June 3, 2016.

Chapter Twenty
Post-election tweets. Tim Young, Michael Glass, TX.

On the far-left. Laura Towler, TX.

Dinner party anecdote. Wyndham, Bill. 'Waleed Aly Broke my Heart.' Quadrant, 2016.

Chapter Twenty-One
Cancelled for true statements. Caylan Ford, TX, August 12, 2022.

Chapter Twenty-Three
Leftists and conservatives. Stefan Molyneux, TX.

Cultural Marxism. Source video lost.

Anti-Murdoch cult. Will Kingston, TX, 2023

Chapter Twenty-Four
Jobs and the pandemic. Red Pill Germany, YouTube, 2020.

Chapter Twenty-Five
Coming out as an anti-feminist. Greta Aurora, TX.

Alt-right memes. Source lost.

Chapter Twenty-Six
Deconstructed. Odysseus 20, TX.

Flag a hate symbol. Misc quotes from TX.

Politicians and white Australians. British Australian Community. TX, 2024.

Mass Immigration. Hitchens, P. 'How I am Partly to Blame for Mass Immigration,' Daily Mail, March 31, 2013.

No core Anglo identity. 'A Critique of the 'Aussie' Poster Series.' British Australian Community, 2024.

On Yes voters. Will Kingston, TX, 2023.

Selected References

Bawer, B. *The Victims' Revolution*. Harper Collins. USA. 2012.

Blainey, G. *The Story of Australia's People*. Viking, Penguin Random House, Australia. 2015.

Buckley, W. *The Life and Adventures of William Buckley*. Text Publishing, Melbourne, Australia. 2002.

Camus, R. *Enemy of the Disaster*. Vauban Books. 2023.

Craven, R. 'Teaching the Teachers: Indigenous Australian Studies for Primary Pre-Service Teacher Education.' School of Teacher Education, University of New South Wales, 1996.

Dikotter, F. *The Tragedy of Liberation*. Bloomsbury, Great Britain, 2013.

Farrell, W. *The Myth of Male Power*. Simon & Schuster, USA, 1993.

Fiamengo, J. *The Fiamengo Files* video series. YouTube.

Fiamengo, J. *Sons of Feminism*. Little Nightingale Press, Ottawa, Canada. 2018.

Flynn-Paul, J. *Not Stolen. The Truth about European Colonialism in the New World*. Post Hill Press, New York, USA. 2023.

Goad, J. *Whiteness: the Original Sin*. Obnoxious Books, Stone Mountain, GA. 2018.

James, A. *New Britania, The Rise and Decline of Anglo Australia.* Renewal Publications, University of Melbourne, Australia. 2013.

Johns, G. *The Burden of Culture.* Quadrant Books, Sydney. 2022.
Lindsay, J. *The Marxification of Education.* New Discourses, Orlando, Florida. 2022.

Lopez, M. *The Origins of Multiculturalism in Australian Politics 1945-75.* Melbourne University Press, Australia. 2000.

Paglia, C. *Free Women, Free Men.* Canongate, UK. 2018.

Patai, D. *Heterophobia.* Rowman and Littlefield, USA. 1998.

Pluckrose, H and Lindsay, J. *Cynical Theories.* Pitchstone Publishing, USA. 2020.

Reynold, C. *What a Capital Idea: Australia 1770-1901.* RLPT, Australia. 2023.

Richardson, H and Salter, F. *Anglophobia: the Unrecognised Hatred.* Social Technologies, Sydney, Australia. 2022.

Salter, F. *The Voice Referendum.* Social Technologies, Sydney. 2023.

Sowell, T. *A Conflict of Visions.* Basic Books, USA. 2007.

Sowell, T. *The Vision of the Anointed.* Basic Books, USA. 1995.

Sowell, T. A-Z Quotes.

Webb, S. *The Forgotten Slave Trade.* Pen and Sword Books. Great Britain. 2020.

Also Available

Books By Duncan Smith

Conquest By Concept

Cultown

The Tightarse Tuesday Book Club

The Vast and the Spurious

The Vortex Winder

The Maelstrom Ascendant

Albums By Lighthouse XIII

Waves Upon Waves

Vortex Winder

The Maelstrom Ascendant

Cultown

Contact

Books and albums can be ordered from www.vortexwinder.com, or on Amazon and other online sellers.

Alfadex Books can be contacted on matthew.alfadex@gmail.com.

Also Available by this Author

Fiction Books:

Conquest By Concept

A novel about the culture war.

John Gilbert loves Angie, his far-left Antifa girlfriend. Then he meets Edward Hall, a charismatic right wing figure. Hall makes John question Angie's political beliefs. Soon, John can no longer tell which side is good or evil.

John begins a journey through the culture war. Along the way, he has to navigate a 'whiteness' workshop, a Me-Too allegation, and the PC school system in his job as a trainee teacher. Caught in a political 'love triangle' between the far-left and right, John has to make a choice. Will he stay true to Angie's passionate progressive values, or can the seductive Edward Hall turn him to the dark side.

Wars are fought in the mind, not just on the battlefield. It's conquest by concept - but which side is telling the truth?

Reviews

"Smith goes where more timid writers fear to tread... serious themes brought to life through brilliant characters and dialogue. Edward Hall is one of the best anti-heroes of our time." PW

"I'm halfway through *Conquest by Concept* and I can hardly put it down. It's brill! A breath of fresh air ramped up to a gale force wind." MG

The Vortex Winder

When fading rocker, Jimmy Brandt, saves the life of an insect, his own life is forever changed. The insect turns out to be an advanced being who gives him the 'Vortex Winder,' a device which grants a different special power each week. Each power leads to unexpected results.

Jimmy makes a comeback to rock music and records his album. Yet his comeback is a quest within a quest. Driven by the Vortex Winder, Jimmy makes an amazing journey. From a simple job interview, to a love affair in Germany, or a harrowing stint in a foreign prison, the adventures of Jimmy Brandt are always a surprise. Trailed by his mentor, Iolango, and his tormentor, Elijinx, Jimmy follows the events of his life to a stunning conclusion.

The Maelstrom Ascendant

Sequel to *The Vortex Winder*.

Rocker Jimmy Brandt has given up on his dreams. He's settled down in the suburbs with his girlfriend and cat... until strange forces tempt him back to his former life. Soon he faces a choice between good and evil - and life is so rewarding when you turn to the dark side.

Flying high again, Jimmy battles divas, despots, and most of all, himself. Yet the higher you fly, the further you can fall. Only an old, forgotten friend can save him. But does he want to be saved?

Cultown

Thomas Swan forms the Milinish, a cult with an odd mix of scientific and religious beliefs.

From humble beginnings in Sydney, the Milinish moves overseas to become the fastest growing cult in America. Yet Swan's mad reign spirals out of control. Finally, on the brink of disaster, he decides to tell all.

Here, in the ultimate inside story, Thomas Swan reveals the secrets and scandals inside the Milinish, the greatest cult of the 21st century.

'Exposes not just the cultishness of religion, but of science too. This is the best novel yet written on the trouble between science and religion.'
J. Williams, Fuse.

The Tightarse Tuesday Book Club

This new set of stories has some of Duncan Smith's best work. 'Hook Up Hell' is a comical Tinder farce, 'Badminton Boy' a superhero send-up, and 'Ghost Squad' a wry look at celebrities who pretend to write books. But it is 'Marla Okadigbo,' that is the most timely for its look at the hot topic of racism in modern America.

This is the story of a literary scam that takes America by storm. White male author, Winkler Jones, pens an online review of *The Handmaid's Tale*, Margaret Atwood's book about a world where women have no rights and exist only to serve men. Jones calls it a work of 'oppression porn' and says it's only a matter of time before a black American writes a novel where slavery is restored.

Jones' crooked agent tells him to delete the review and write the slavery book himself. Jones does so, publishing it under the pen name, 'Marla Okadigbo,' supposedly a black American woman. The book is a hit until the author's true identity is revealed. It then becomes a scandal, and perception of the book changes from a story of the struggle for black liberation to one of oppression by white supremacists.

Meanwhile, Jones is haunted by the spirit of the real Marla, a black slave from the early 1800s, and feuds with his girlfriend, Sonia, a white English teacher struggling to help school students in the poor neighbourhood where she works.

Non-Fiction:

The Vast and the Spurious : 25 Problems For Feminism

We live in the age of the gender wars, and there is probably more anger between men and women than ever before. Is there any hope for a harmonious future, or will these wars rage until doomsday? A clear and incisive look at some of the main gender war issues of our time, with some surprising solutions.

"Whether for the uninitiated, the curious, or the indoctrinated, this book offers a witty rebuttal to popular claims and exaggerations. Grounded in common sense and empathy, it makes the rational case, too rarely heard, for harmony between the sexes and respect for men's contributions."

Janice Fiamengo, Professor of English, University of Ottawa, Canada, and editor of *Sons of Feminism: Men Have Their Say.*

Lighthouse XIII Albums

Waves Upon Waves

Songs: Mountain Gods, SMS: Save My Sanity, Between the Stairway and the Highway, Reaper Bones, Leuchtturm, LHXIII, Temporary Kingdom, Retro Stereo, Waves Upon Waves, New World Alchemy.

Vortex Winder

Vortex Winder, Road Rage, Trade Winds, Black Art, Life Line, Spark, Z Club, Epitaph, Elijinx, Oceanus.

The Maelstrom Ascendant

Black Phoenix, High and Mighty, The Price of Dominion, Moonlight Tiger, I for an Eye, Haunted, Death Bed Regrets, Extinction.Net, Quitter, The Maelstrom Ascendant, The Ephemeral and the Eternal.

Cultown

Amnesia, Skeptic Eclectic, Evil But Not Vile, In Nihilum, Cultown, Helix Eternal, Doom Pipers, Fallen to a Higher Place, The Scythe and the Scalpel, Triangle of Fire, Transcendence, The Cultimate Culminates.

www.ingramcontent.com/pod-product-compliance
Lightning Source LLC
Chambersburg PA
CBHW021844020426
42334CB00013B/174